CW00405918

Human Resource Management in Project-Based Organizations

Human Resource Management in Project-Based Organizations

The HR Quadriad Framework

Karin Bredin

and

Jonas Söderlund

© Karin Bredin and Jonas Söderlund 2011

All rights reserved. No reproduction, copy or transmission of this publication may be made without written permission.

No portion of this publication may be reproduced, copied or transmitted save with written permission or in accordance with the provisions of the Copyright, Designs and Patents Act 1988, or under the terms of any licence permitting limited copying issued by the Copyright Licensing Agency, Saffron House, 6-10 Kirby Street, London EC1N 8TS.

Any person who does any unauthorized act in relation to this publication may be liable to criminal prosecution and civil claims for damages.

The authors have asserted their rights to be identified as the authors of this work in accordance with the Copyright, Designs and Patents Act 1988.

First published 2011 by
PALGRAVE MACMILLAN

Palgrave Macmillan in the UK is an imprint of Macmillan Publishers Limited, registered in England, company number 785998, of Houndmills, Basingstoke, Hampshire RG21 6XS.

Palgrave Macmillan in the US is a division of St Martin's Press LLC, 175 Fifth Avenue, New York, NY 10010.

Palgrave Macmillan is the global academic imprint of the above companies and has companies and representatives throughout the world.

Palgrave® and Macmillan® are registered trademarks in the United States, the United Kingdom, Europe and other countries.

ISBN: 978–0–230–23190–0 hardback

This book is printed on paper suitable for recycling and made from fully managed and sustained forest sources. Logging, pulping and manufacturing processes are expected to conform to the environmental regulations of the country of origin.

A catalogue record for this book is available from the British Library.

Library of Congress Cataloging-in-Publication Data

Bredin, Karin.
    Human resource management in project-based organizations / Karin Bredin, Jonas Söderlund.
        p. cm.
    Includes index.
    ISBN 978–0–230–23190–0 (hardback)
    1. Personnel management. 2. Project management. I. Söderlund, Jonas.
    II. Title.
HF5549.B793 2011
658.3—dc22   2011001634

Printed and bound in Great Britain by
CPI Antony Rowe, Chippenham and Eastbourne

Contents

List of Illustrations

Figures

Tables

Acknowledgments

The research reported here has been made possible through generous grants from VINNOVA (The Swedish Governmental Agency for Innovation Systems), FAS (Swedish Council for Working Life and Social Research), and Riksbankens Jubileumsfond (RJ). We are also grateful for the support from our employers, Linköping University, Sweden, and BI Norwegian School of Management.

Preface

The journey documented in this book began many years ago and has involved numerous encounters with interesting observations in practice and insights from theory. The first steps were taken when Jonas was involved in a multiyear study of project management in large Swedish engineering-intensive enterprises. The focus then was primarily on making sense of project management as an increasingly important management task to develop organizational capabilities for the integration of knowledge and technologies. HRM was not a prime focus of our research back then, but it slowly began to attract more of our attention. Some of the collaborating firms reported growing concern about stress and burnout in their projects and wanted us to explore opportunities for improvement. Volvo Car Corporation invited us to take part in a development program to explore the work situation among their project-oriented engineers. This later led to a research proposal developed and submitted in collaboration with Professor Torbjörn Stjernberg at Göteborg University, Sweden. We were happy to receive funding for our proposal from the Swedish Council for Working Life and Social Research (FAS), which gave us the opportunity to explore these issues on a broader scale. This led to a highly stimulating collaboration with Torbjörn and several other colleagues at Göteborg University for which we are very grateful. Karin entered the process initially as a master's candidate doing her graduate work within this research project, then as a research assistant, and finally as a doctoral student. Karin's thesis and her research work, focusing entirely on the HRM dimension of project-based organizations, were critical for the research to move forward. The first phase comprised a multiple case study involving AstraZeneca, Posten, Saab, and Volvo Car Corporation, which led to the book *Perspectives on HRM* (published in Swedish in 2005), which was reported on in a number of conference papers and journal articles. We then decided to explore the line-manager role in further depth. This was the focus in a study of Tetra Pak and their work with competence coaches as an alternative to the conventional line-manager model. To contrast these observations, we conducted a comparative case study in which Saab Aerosystems was a participant. These organizations generally showed great interest in our work and the questions we explored, so much so that we were energized to continue with further research.

During the entire process, we interviewed a large number of managers and coworkers within these companies – interviews that provided us not only with detailed descriptions of work, working life, and Human Resource Management, but also with fascinating examples of problems and opportunities related to the improvement of both the efficiency of project-based organizations and the management of human resources.

As the research process advanced we gradually broadened our investigation from studying HR departments and the work of HR directors to also involve other players in the HR organization. This prompted us to make a distinction between HR departments and HR organizations and to investigate further the other roles of significance in the HR organization, particularly the role of the line manager, and also the roles of the project manager and the project workers themselves. This was our initial approach to studying the HR quadriad framework that stands at the fore in the present book. However, given our interest in creating an improved contextual analysis of HRM, the concentration on project-based organizations set the focus on organizational structure and problem-solving contexts. This not only led us to a general discussion and analysis of the nature of HRM in project-based organizations, but also to elicit the variations across different types of project-based organizations. In particular, we believed that the debate on strategic HRM seemed to miss out on a few important observations documented in the initial phases of our research, namely, the importance of the operational work setting. In particular, we noticed the explanatory power of types of project-based work not only to discern dissimilarities but also to compare project-based organizations and their specific HRM challenges. In parallel, we were also involved in a number of workshops with several companies to discuss and share our experiences concerning the design of the HR department. What struck us during these workshops was the flawed analysis of the role of the HR department. Typically, the design was elaborated in isolation from the rest of the organization without explicit analysis of the work situation of employees, the needs of line managers, and so on. Given the heated debate about the value of HR departments in academic and practitioner literatures, and the many strategic decisions taken by firms during this period, we were convinced that a more sophisticated analysis of HRM and HR organizations could contribute to both practice and theory. The primary driver was the need to understand what had to be improved.

Besides the funding from the Swedish Council for Working Life and Social Research and the research project on Working Life in Swedish Projects, we also worked in several research projects together with colleagues at Linköping University. In the first stage, our collaboration with the EPOK group was absolutely critical. The EPOK members shared our interest in investigating the nature and evolution of project-based organizations. Professor Lars Lindkvist and Professor Fredrik Tell have been part of this journey, including in publications and research that provided a multifaceted analysis of project-based organizations in terms of capabilities, evolution, design, and governance. We thank Lars and Fredrik for their support, and also thank the other EPOK members and the faculty members at the Business Administration division at Linköping University, especially those who participated in our research and teaching on Human Resource Management. During the past five years, we have been fortunate enough to be part of the development of a number of new courses and a master's program on Human Resource Development and Management in collaboration with the Department of Behavioral Sciences and Learning. We are especially grateful for the opportunity to collaborate with Dr Hans Andersson, Dr Marie Bengtsson, Dr Cecilia Enberg, Dr Jörgen Ljung, Dr Åsa-Karin Engstrand, Doctoral Candidate Elisabeth Borg, Visiting Professor David Goss, Dr Eva Ellström, Dr Henrik Kock, Professor Elisabeth Sundin and Professor Per-Erik Ellström. Their teaching and ideas gave us energy to continue our research in the field of HRM, try out new ideas, and discuss articles with many talented students.

We have also conducted studies outside Linköping University; for example, in 2003, Jonas had the opportunity to spend almost a year at CRG, l'Ecole Polytechnique, which not only provided the opportunity for focused analysis of our studies but also to learn more about research on the projectification of work within project-based organizations, a topic also covered by French scholars. Professor Christophe Midler and his group were willing to share their insights into many of the changes then underway in companies such as Renault, which also informed the research agenda we pursued in the following years. In addition, we have from time to time had the chance to visit Brighton and spend time with colleagues at SPRU, University of Sussex, and CENTRIM, Brighton University. This was made possible through an institutional grant from STINT. Through this grant we were able to develop further the contacts with such inspiring researchers as Dr Tim Brady, Dr Andrew Davies, Principal Research Fellow Steve Flowers, Professor Mike Hobday, Dr Paul Nightingale, and Dr Jonathan Sapsed. These visits have been extremely important for us to push the writing process forward. They have also given us a better understanding of the challenges of technology integration and management of the project-based organization.

A substantial part of our work during the past few years has taken place within a larger research program called KITE (Knowledge Integration and Innovation in Transnational Enterprise), a collaboration between the EPOK group and faculty members from the Division of Industrial Management at Linköping University. One key theme in KITE is to explore projects, project-based organizations, and knowledge integration. The funding from Riksbankens Jubileumsfond (RJ) was a significant support for us, which made it possible to allocate the time needed to write this book. One of our major studies was funded by VINNOVA, which also led to a number of close collaborations with companies in the pharmaceutical industry, the automotive industry, and the aerospace industry. To say the least, the financial support from Riksbanken and VINNOVA was really helpful to making this research project possible. VINNOVA has also supported us in establishing a network of industry partners, which has been important to our fieldwork and our access to innovative companies throughout Sweden and elsewhere.

The atmosphere in KITE has been extraordinary, with so many talented young researchers and supportive, experienced professors. Professor Christian Berggren, the director of KITE, has shown it is possible for strong individualists to work together in a constructive manner. This is a unique opportunity, and we are very grateful to be part of it. Our wish is of course that our research into the management of human resources in project-based organizations will lead to more such research projects in this field. At Linköping University, we took part in a variety of executive education programs. These programs not only made it possible for us to discuss our research and findings with some of the most talented managers in Swedish-based multinationals, but also helped develop contacts with key personnel who facilitated access to their organizations and opened doors to their experience and ongoing work. It was through these executive programs that we met people from Saab Aerospace (now Saab Aerosystems) – an organization we have studied in several different research projects. A senior manager at this company, Stefan Andersson, has always shown keen interest in, and support for, our work, sharing his ideas and experience regarding challenges in designing HR organizations in project-based organizations. There are, of course, many more organizations and people we would like to mention and thank; however, since we promised them anonymity, we hope they recognize themselves in the book and understand how important their support has been for our research.

Research is a truly global activity, and over the years we have presented our research at conferences in diverse fields, not only Human Resource

Management but also R&D management, innovation management, and project management. We thank the participants at the IRNOP conferences, the EURAM conferences, and the Academy of Management meetings for feedback and constructive comments. Some of the conference papers have been developed further, revised, and submitted to journals. The feedback and support we have received from the editors and reviewers of journals have been astonishing. The work this book builds on has appeared in journals such as *Human Resource Management, International Journal of Human Resource Management, Personnel Review,* and *International Journal of Human Resources Development and Management,* which gave us instructive comments on how to position our research within the HRM community. We have also published some of the findings in journals focusing on innovation and project-based organizations, such as *International Journal of Innovation Management, R&D Management, International Journal of Project Management,* and *International Journal of Project Organization and Management.* We would like to thank everyone involved, the anonymous reviewers and the helpful editors who spent valuable time commenting on drafts of our papers.

In the final stages of our research, we recruited a new doctoral candidate, Elisabeth Borg, who has been very helpful with empirical studies and writings. She has also coauthored some of the papers that form part of the database for the present book. We are grateful for her insights and assistance. Around the same time, Jonas decided to move to Norway to assume a professorship at BI Norwegian School of Management. The support from colleagues and friends at BI within the areas of project management, project-based organization and HRM is gratefully acknowledged. In the later stages we also had the chance to work with Professor Henrik Holt Larsen at Copenhagen Business School, who provided us with a number of valuable comments. In collaboration with Professor Rodney Turner, Dr Martina Huemann, Professor Jaap Paauwe, and Henrik, we also arranged a symposium at the Academy of Management meeting, which further developed our perspectives on HRM in project-based organizations. During this symposium, Professor Pernille Eskerod gave us several thoughtful comments that improved our analysis. We thank these collaborators for constructive feedback and also other participants at the symposium who commented on our research.

Although we are grateful to many people, the book as such is our joint product, and any errors or omissions are the sole responsibility of the authors. The past several years have been rewarding, not only because of the opportunity to develop our knowledge on a topic we believe is extremely important and interesting, but also because the journey of doing the research presented here has been so enjoyable. As mentioned before, this has much to do with all the interesting people we have met, who have generously contributed to our work and been a source of inspiration along the way.

KARIN BREDIN
JONAS SÖDERLUND

1
Projectification on the Way

Exploring Human Resource Management

People today live in a highly organized economy where a variety of organizations – including firms, governments, and associations – constitute significant societal backbones. In many organizations, people have roles as employees; in these roles, they carry out work that is important to their well-being, identity construction, personal development, and, of course, their income. Human Resource Management (HRM) has a critical role in handling the interplay between employer and employee. HRM is particularly important in ensuring that individuals find opportunities to develop themselves and that people are satisfied with their working situations.

From the company's point of view, it is essential to have the right human resources with the required skills. Also, these resources and requirements must be matched to develop individual talent and organizational capabilities. The company's desire is to build a successful, profitable organization with talented people who have the opportunity to fulfill their professional dreams while taking part in challenging, exciting work for which they are appreciated and rewarded. As many studies and much experience have shown, however, this is a difficult equation involving trade-offs, tough decisions, and considerable complexities.

This book is an investigation into and a depiction of HRM in a particular kind of modern firm. It is an investigation into the current hot topic of management and organization studies: the area that centers on the relationship between the individual and the organization. Today, this is perhaps more important than ever since human resource management is undergoing a fundamental shift in a number of industries and sectors. This so-called human resources (HR) transformation is part of a larger restructuring of companies, industries, and sectors. New concepts have been launched, and new challenges have been identified that call for a rethinking and a further elaboration of novel ideas and approaches. Through this flow of ideas, HRM has been an area for continuous innovation and a test-bed for new management thought.

Scholars and practitioners alike speak about HR transformation in terms of employment modes, contracting, and individual skills, with the idea that people need to stay current and employable. This has also spurred developments within the area of HRM, which, to a greater extent, is considered to be an area of importance to a number of people within the organization, not only to the HR department. This brings to light the fact that HRM, to a considerable degree, involves more managers and specialists. The changes in HRM also shed light on its ever-growing complexity. In many ways, HRM encompasses a fascinating and inspiring plethora of concepts and problems – involving challenges to both practitioners and theorists. Hence, an examination of the field of HRM reveals it to be, unquestionably, an exciting and vibrant area of study (Paauwe, 2009) – the scope is growing, the innovativeness is ongoing, and its importance is increasing. That it is, equally, an exciting, vibrant area of management is evidenced by the growth of consulting firms targeting the market for HRM services, including recruitment consultants, information technology (IT) systems vendors, and training providers.

HRM has often been considered to have the possibility to generate, or at least in significant ways contribute to, competitive advantage. This has been particularly singled out in many of the growth industries of our age. At the same time, we know that HRM in these industries, in new organizational forms, and in knowledge-intensive industries in general, is relentlessly under pressure and criticized for not delivering value for money. As a case in point, there is an ongoing debate about the "value of HR" and whether firms should "do away with HR" (Ulrich, 1998). This critique attacks not only HR professionals and HR departments but also the fundamental ways and modes that companies have chosen for their entire HR organization and the delivery of their HRM practices. Hence, there seems to be a need for closer scrutiny of HR departments and HRM in general. In this book, however, we will look at a particular kind of firm, specifically the project-based firm.

This book takes a unique tack on HRM since it focuses on projects, project management, and, notably, project-based organizations as an important – and perhaps increasingly important – context for work and working life. A growing number of people spend more time in various types of projects and temporary organizations; accordingly, more HRM activities take place in project-based work settings. We argue that this project-based context is pertinent for the study of HRM and for the "contextualization" of HRM – putting HRM in context – because, as we will show later, the design and success of HRM depend on a host of contingency factors, including organization structure, problem-solving context, and the needs of individual workers. But what are the most important factors influencing the choice and design of HRM? And what are the most important factors in the context of project-based organizations?

Our journey in the land of HRM in project-based organizations began with a series of in-depth studies of what actually happens within the studied firms and what are the key challenges, problems, and novel solutions. This book is an attempt to summarize some of the findings from this journey. The book suggests a contextual framing of HRM in project-based organizations, especially project-based organizations employing engineers involved in solving complex problems – such as those problems found in the research and development (R&D) departments in the automotive and aerospace industries, the design of complex machinery and IT systems, or the development of a new drug, involving test activities around the globe. Exploring HRM in those settings should be relevant not only for people interested in "pure," project-based organizations but also for people who study and work in organizations and companies that, to a moderate degree, rely on projects in their everyday activities. In that respect, what is elaborated on in this book is a view of HRM that stresses the importance of organizational structure and problem-solving in their specific contexts. Later, we will extend this view by bringing in the complementary and configurational ideas recently developed in the HRM literature. This builds on recent theorization within the field of HRM that outlines an organization-theory interpretation of HRM which acknowledges the relationships between HRM practices and roles as well as the linkages between organization, work, and HRM.

In the present chapter, we outline the structure of the book and detail its guiding principles. Let us start with an overview of some of the challenges and changes that form the practical and theoretical underpinnings for the present book. We begin by identifying the competitive challenges. This is followed by a discussion about work, occupations, and boundaryless human resources, ending with an outline of the specifics of project-based organizations and their effects on HRM.

Competitive challenges

In the past few decades, we have seen quite a remarkable shift in the work carried out by professional workers. A higher degree of knowledge-intensity is generally observed as more work falls within the realm of complex problem-solving, where people are not engaged in autonomous labor but, instead, to a greater extent, perform their work in teams, working either with likeminded people, or with those who are not always so likeminded (DeFillippi et al., 2006). Many analysts argue that one of the most important drivers for this development of team production is the mounting complexity of products and systems, which forces firms to develop strategies and designs to reap the benefits of integrated solutions, systems integration, and project business (Davies and Hobday, 2005). This has spurred researchers to look into the significance and character of complex products and systems, complex R&D, and systemic innovation (Hobday, 2000; Teece, 2009), particularly in industries such as aerospace, automotive, and telecommunications. A common feature in these industries is the capability and importance of various integration efforts, including activities such as systems integration, project management, and technology integration (see, e.g., Davies and Brady, 2000; Iansiti, 1998).

This explanation centering on "complexity" stresses the strategic importance of integrating technologies and knowledge bases to be able to offer products and systems that meet new customer requirements. Being first-rate at integration, understanding a wide variety of technologies, and having a sufficient level of absorptive capacity within a broad range of technologies and fields have become increasingly important – somewhat paradoxically in an age when knowledge specialization is becoming more and more pronounced. Echoing the classic findings from the study of Lawrence and Lorsch (1967), a high degree of differentiation requires well-developed integrative devices and processes. Although, as Brusoni and Prencipe (2001) say, the key integration activities do not typically reside at the firm level but also at the project and team levels. This insight has wide-reaching practical and theoretical implications. Some writers even argue that the emphasis on project and team levels gradually leads to a dismantling of the role of the corporation as we know it, signaling the growing importance of projects and various types of temporary organizations as alternative chief economic agents. For instance, Castells (1996: 165) in his best-selling book *The Network Society* points out that "the actual operating unit becomes the…project, enacted by a network, rather than individual companies or formal groupings of companies." Similarly, Boltanski and Chiapello (2005) elaborate on the nature of the "project society" as a critical part of a new capitalism that dramatically changes the perception of people's orientation to the economic agents of the modern age. Instead, it seems that more and more loyalty, commitment, and energy will be directed toward projects, that is, moving from one project to another, meeting new people on a continual basis to pursue creative and innovative work.

Part of this futurology is emphasizing the role of projects and temporary organizations, and we believe there is an important message here. However, we also argue that firms continue to play a critical role and it is rather the balance between the projects (the temporary organizations) and the firms (the permanent organizations) that is perhaps most important and interesting. Accordingly, economic activity, to a great extent, will be performed in the interplay between companies and other sorts of permanent organizations, and projects and similar kinds of temporary organizations. Thus, we align with much ongoing research within the area of organization and capabilities. For instance, Brusoni (2005: 1898) points out that

> …projects appear to be the tool through which firms can integrate the capabilities developed by distinct communities of specialists that interact within, and across, their boundaries. In fast-changing environments, it is important that such integration does not lead to a permanent reduction in diversity…hence the importance of the "temporary" dimension of project-based activities.

In many ways, this development is also observed in the companies that we have investigated; systems integration, integration units, and activities have been singled out as critical for future competition.

Several of them highlight project management as one of their "core competences," and they state in public documents and annual reports that "projects are a core business." This development forms the background to the present book and establishes the relevance of studying project-based organizations in general, and perhaps, in particular, the type of project-based organizations investigated here – engineering and R&D-intensive organizations occupied with team production and team-based complex problem-solving.

Thus, making business out of complexity and integration capabilities seems to be critical these days. As a direct consequence, more people are involved in solving complex problems, and those complex problems often require more or less elaborate organizational responses comprising teamwork and mutual adjustment coordination (Thompson, 1967). One common response is the use of project-based structures paired with the use of in-house and external specialists who are drawn together to solve nonroutine, unique, and temporary tasks. This organizational solution forces companies to develop their problem-solving capabilities and team-working capabilities (cf. Brusoni, 2005). It also marks the weight of interpersonal skills among the individual project worker – to swiftly get started and rapidly engage in new problem-solving situations and, after completing an assignment, move to new problem-solving contexts. In other words, interpersonal skills and the ability to collaborate in distributed, cross-functional teams appear to be more important in today's work environment than in the organizational solutions of the past (Barley and Kunda, 2001).

Therefore, to thrive in this competitive landscape, the firm needs to develop its capabilities and resources along two parallel trajectories (Hedlund, 1994): (1) capabilities with a particular focus on complex problem-solving, knowledge, and technology integration, and (2) capabilities to ensure the continuous supply and development of human resources that can participate in complex problem-solving processes. In other words, the quality of complex problem-solving is largely determined by two separate, yet interrelated, lines of capability development. Analytically, these lines may be kept apart, but in practice they are tightly nested and interwoven. This means that human resources represent a way of bringing together a wide array of technical expertise representing different knowledge bases and areas of expertise. The integration effort would then be viewed in a variety of ways, as would its performance: firm-level evaluations, project-level evaluations, or even people-level evaluations. Firm-level evaluations comprise such issues as the value generated for the firm and new capabilities developed, whereas project-level evaluations entail matters primarily relating to project performance and project learning. People-level evaluations, for obvious reasons, are closely connected to the processes and design of HRM. They involve questions such as: What did the involved people learn from the integration activities? How did they perceive the encounters with new people, new technologies, and novel uncertainties, and, not the least, did they have fun doing it? Are they stronger and more capable now than when they began the project? The continuous supply and development of human resources could be seen as the critical task for HRM, which encompasses issues tied to the flows, performance, and involvement of human resources, as well as the continuous development of skills and competences of human resources.

Although we will discuss both challenges and capabilities, this book focuses primarily on the challenge of the supply and development of human resources. Given our focus on project-based organizations and the suggested approach to a contextual understanding of HRM, the integration capability is significant for a number of reasons. The quality of integration depends on the quality of the people involved in the integration process. A superior integration capability would have positive effects on the people involved – the human resources – and on the value and importance of HRM by improving the quality and accuracy of the management processes aimed at human resources. Hence, there are a number of important relationships between these two capabilities. Project-based organizations need to address both of them (separately and in combination), to distribute the responsibilities for maintaining and developing them, and to identify possible conflicts and synergies between them. In that respect, what might be good for one set of capability, such as the integration of new technology, might cause difficulties for the management of human resources.

Projects and projectification

Given this book's focus on project-based organizations, a few words should be said about projects and project organization. What kind of organization are we talking about when we refer to projects? What kind of organization is the so-called project-based organization? These are the questions addressed in this section.

There are many definitions available to help pin down the peculiarities of projects as organizational forms – ranging from textbook definitions to academic organization-theory definitions. Typically a project is seen as a task – a temporary, unique, and complex task of some form, or a collective course of action. This is the conventional definition. However, to an increasing extent, the term today encompasses the focal organization set to solve the task. In that respect, in everyday language we often think of the project as a particular kind of temporary organization (Lundin and Söderholm, 1995). In this book, we rely on this organizational definition of projects, and accordingly the project-based organization in our framing is an organization that is constituted by a number of such micro, temporary organizations.

The immediate work setting for people in project-based organization is that of the project. Drawing on Packendorff (1995), we distinguish four salient features of projects as temporary organizations. These features, listed below, are highly important for the studies reported here as they describe projects as:

1. being aimed at evoking a nonroutine process and/or completing a nonroutine product (i.e., associated with a certain degree of technical/task uncertainty; see Shenhar and Dvir, 2007),
2. having a predetermined point in time or time-related conditional state when the organization and/or its mission is collectively expected to cease to exist (i.e., typically work with some kind of time pressure and deadline; see Lindkvist et al., 1998),
3. having some kind of performance evaluation criteria (e.g., time, cost, quality, value creation, profit; see Shenhar and Dvir, 2007),
4. being so complex and uncertain in terms of activities, roles, and interdependencies that they require conscious organizing efforts (i.e., associated with task features of relatively high degrees of uncertainty and complexity; see De Meyer et al., 2002).

Of course, there are many reasons why project-based forms of organizing might be on the rise, such as fashion, institutional requirements, change for the sake of change, and so on. What we have suggested relates to the change in technology and solutions on how to best integrate technology. Modularization and standardization are important measures, but they are not sufficient; instead, the remaining complexities and interdependencies typically need to be resolved through some kind of interactive form of problem-solving, task force, projects, or whatever we decide to call them. Accordingly, projects could then be seen as a response to the limits of modularization and standardization on the one hand, and the need for novel knowledge combinations on the other.

Fact box 1.1 Projectification explored

The increasing use of projects has been analyzed in different ways in previous writings. However, in looking at the literature several different terms abound to capture this development. A few examples are given below:

- "Projectization" (Peters, 1992). In Peters' view, projectization revolves around corporate changes to turn traditional profit center organizations into temporary projects with dedicated teams, appointed project leaders, and fixed deadlines. Such teams are temporary and memberships change after project completion.
- "Projectification" (Midler, 1995). A change of the organizational structure, slowly moving the firm into putting more emphasis on the project dimension of the organizational structure, from strong functional units where projects have played a subordinate role, to projects playing at center stage with functional units acting as labor pools.
- "Projectivization" (Ekstedt et al., 1999). A general transformation of society that turns societies into more project-oriented ones, with companies carrying out an increasing amount of work in projects, and with sectors largely project-based being the ones that grow.
- "Project intensification" (Bredin and Söderlund, 2006). Increase in the use of projects as organizational form and increase in time-related pressure in the project process. Combined observations such as the ones reported in Midler (1995) with increased pressures on speedy development projects. Focus here is on the work level and human resource management practices.

The development of increasing reliance and use of projects, often referred to as "projectification" (Midler, 1995, see also fact box), could generally be talked about as a move from repetitive production to non-routine work processes and the use of temporary projects. Just think about the rise of R&D investments in modern firms, which spurred the development and deployment of the organizational configuration that Mintzberg popularized as the "adhocracy" with the following features:

highly organic structure, with little formalization of behavior; high horizontal job specialization based on formal training; a tendency to group the specialists in functional units for housekeeping purposes but to deploy them in small, market-based project teams to do their work; a reliance on the liaison devices to encourage mutual adjustment, the key coordination mechanism, within and between these teams; and selective decentralization to and within these teams; which are located at various places in the organization and involve various mixtures of line mangers and staff and operating experts. (Mintzberg, 1983: 254)

In many ways, the adhocracy constitutes the blueprint for the project-based organization, and many of the characteristics of the adhocracy are very much in vogue today: "emphasis on expertise, organic structure, project teams and task forces, decentralization without a single concentration of power, matrix structure, sophisticated and automated technical systems, youth, and environments that are complex and dynamic" (Mintzberg, 1983: 274). The idea of the adhocracy and the organization as an adaptive system has been a recurrent theme in organization studies since the classic studies by Burns and Stalker (1961) on "organic structures" and Bennis and Slater (1968) on "adaptive systems" in the temporary society, a prophesy that now seems to have become true. As formulated by Bennis as early as the late 1960s:

> Adaptive, problem-solving, temporary systems of diverse specialists, linked together by coordinating and task-evaluating executive specialists in an organic flux – this is the organization form that will gradually replace bureaucracy as we know it. (Bennis, 1968: 74)

In this book, we restrict our analysis of the project-based organization to the integrative dimensions of the adhocracy. We focus on those adhocracies found in R&D and complex systems industries. We center on a key issue of project-based organization, namely, the nature of the operational project-based work setting, including the type of project participation.

Project-based organizations and HRM

Investigations into project-based organizations typically begin with references to Woodward's (1958) description of unit production, Galbraith's (1971) typology of organizational structures, or Mintzberg's (1979) analysis of the adhocracy as a pure case of a project-based organization especially suited for innovation. However, the classics did not spend much attention discussing the everyday life and work situation of project workers. Several more recent studies on project-based organizations have, in a number of ways, documented the importance of more detailed examinations of the design and practices of HRM. Despite this, the interest for studies that focus explicitly on HRM in project-based organizations has been rather low. Over the past decade, this seems to be changing with the formation of research teams such as our own and Huemann, Keegan, and Turner (see, e.g., Huemann et al., 2007, 2004; Turner et al., 2008b, 2008a), who have made this topic into their main research area. In addition, a few recent writings about the project-based organization could be singled out to highlight the HRM challenges that are associated with this type of organization. These contributions will be summarized below.

Midler (1995) studied the projectification of the French automotive maker Renault and its evolution and change of project-based structures. One of his findings was that the increasing use of project-based organization generally puts greater pressure on HRM and complicates career paths at both management and engineer levels. Hobday (2000) came to similar conclusions in his study on the organization of production of complex products and systems. He compared the positive and negative sides of project-based organization and highlighted the difficulties of competence development and HRM in project-based organizations. In several ways, these publications echo the work within the contingency-inspired tradition of project-based organizations as described in Clark and Wheelwright (1992).

Lindkvist (2004) took an empirical point of departure and focused on an R&D unit that was transformed into a strongly project-based organization. His analysis is not strictly contingency based but rather focused on the individual qualities and the effects of implementing logics of project-based organization. Lindkvist argued that this has a few important effects on knowledge governance and individual responsibilities. The new organization promotes individuals to act in a more "mindful and attentive way than prior to the re-organization" (p. 4). This also fosters "mindful interaction" in teams although without teams becoming well-developed groups with shared knowledge bases, values, and understandings. This requires, Lindkvist demonstrated, specific individual skills and basic organizational and managerial support, but not necessarily the kind of strong organizational cultures that were popularized during the 1980s.

Whitley (2006) furthered the discussion about different types of project-based firms. The author adopted an institutional perspective and incorporated several aspects related to HRM in his comparative analysis. For instance, he demonstrated that there is a wide range of differences among them and that, given these differences, project-based firms struggle with rather diverse and specific challenges. In his institutional framework, two dimensions are singled out: (1) the extent to which firms focus on developing unusual, sometimes one-off, products and services for varied, and often uncertain, markets, and (2) the extent to which the organization of expertise, tasks, and roles is predictable and stable over projects. In particular, the latter is important for the analysis of HRM in project-based organizations. Stable roles is a signifi-cant HRM dimension that is primarily created outside the boundaries of the firm, however, it severely affects the possibilities of changing HRM structures and support in project-based firms. In a number of ways, Whitley's points have similarities with recent work in project-based industries where the role of the project is paramount, such as in filmmaking and TV production. In these cases, work roles seem to be critical for the development of "swift trust" – which is so impor-tant in getting the tight collaboration needed to take the project to its completion (Meyerson et al., 1996).

As mentioned, project-based forms of organizing constitute an important means for the integration of knowledge in firms dealing with complex problem-solving. Scholars and consultants praise the positive aspects of project-based organization, often using it as a normative tem-plate of what organizations should look like. Authors not only stress the qualities of this kind of organization when it comes to organizing integration efforts in knowledge-intensive work but also point out that it is a specific kind of organizing human resources. A typical quote is from Quinn, who argues that for many situations:

IDEAL ORG

> …the ultimate innovative organization is a free floating pool of tal-ent that moves into any project at any time based on market-like interactions. (Quinn, quoted in DeFillippi et al., 2006)

In developing these ideas further, Teece (2009) argues that these kinds of organization typically need to integrate a "temporary network of suppliers and customers that emerge around specific opportunities in fast-changing markets." In such contexts, he writes, recurrent "reor-ganization becomes the norm, not the exception" (Teece, 2009: 193). This is an important observation, since it leads to a slightly revised view of what actually constitutes the "human resources" of the firm; that is, will they be found inside or outside the conventional boundaries of the firm?

The above studies and examples of literature generally stress the tight link between project-based organization and HRM, and that conven-tional ideas about HRM are overturned through the effects of projectifi-cation and the increasing reliance on project-based organizations. Some of the challenges relate to human resources, how work pools are organ-ized, what work roles emerge, and the difficulties in handling some of the long-term HRM-related issues, including competence development, career paths, and sustainable staffing. The long-term issues are tied to

issue

the ongoing debate about the human problems associated with project work and project-based organizations. Such problems seem to be critical to handle if the organization is to build capabilities ensuring the continuous supply and development of human resources that can participate in complex problem-solving processes, such as those typically occurring in modern product and systems development projects. Below, we highlight some of the findings and observations in extant research.

The dark side of project-based organizations

Project-based organizing and boundaryless careers where people move from one "action locality" (Grabher, 2004) to another on a regular basis do not come without problems and tensions, although it might be difficult to distinguish the consequences that relate specifically to the increased use of project-based structures and temporary employment contracts. Typically, causes interact and projectification is only one of many interacting causes to effect HRM. Although more comprehensive views and treatments of HRM in project-based organizations have been called for relatively recently, the study of human problems associated with project work is rather extensive and goes back several decades.

Among the first publications are work from Wilemon and Cicero (1970), Gemmill and Wilemon (1970), Wilemon and Gemmill (1971), and Wilemon (1973) on the ambiguities of project management, project management and organizational conflict, and power in project management. During the 1970s, we also find the analysis of "temporary systems" and professional development (Goodman and Goodman, 1972, 1976), as well as a set of publications that later influenced researchers investigating projects as "temporary organizations" (see Lundin and Söderholm, 1995; Packendorff, 1995). The former set of studies document the problems with the matrix organization, the challenges of having two bosses who rely on competing authority systems, and the power struggle between project managers and functional managers that puts pressure on the individual project worker. The latter set of studies tackles the problems of competence development and the tendency to reuse people who already have the skills instead of seizing the learning opportunities of projects by engaging people who can grow with the task.

During the early development of this line of research, we also find contributions by Reeser (1969), Hammerton (1970), Melcher and Kayser (1970), and Butler (1973). Reeser (1969) analyzes the human problems in the "project form of organization" and zeroes in on the anxieties and frustrations of people working in a "projectized" organization, including the issues of phase-out and temporary relationships. He identifies the lack of formal procedures and clear role definitions to be major causes of frustration in project-based organizations. Hammerton (1970) stresses the difficult, yet important, balance between control and the freedom to be able to deal with the "entrepreneurial instincts" that are common for people working in a project context. Melcher and Kayser (1970) identify problems of cooperation in an interdisciplinary context, particularly highlighting the challenges of building a team in a project setting. This tends, according to Butler (1973), to lead to various sorts of "dysfunctional conflicts" in project-based organizations, which could have negative effects on job satisfaction and work conditions.

Keith (1978) found higher levels of role ambiguity, conflict, and overload in temporary systems than in permanent settings. This finding was developed further in a set of studies on "project overload" – a notion developed by a team of Scandinavian researchers (see, e.g., Zika-Viktorsson et al., 2006). Their survey reveals that project work, particularly in multiproject environments, enhances the risk of excessive workload with little time for reflection, learning, and recuperation between projects. The study also shows that these issues lead to stress reactions due to continuous deadline pressure. The latter, the authors argue, could also lead to a failure to make competence development efforts a priority. Together, the studies demonstrate that the inherent dynamics of projects often lead to severe pressures on the individual worker. In some cases, the long-term effects might be aporia, with a concomitant corrosion of character and burnout symptoms (see also Sennett, 1998).

However, there are even more substantial and fundamental critiques of this organizational solution. For instance, a group of researchers have set out to introduce more critical analyses of projects. Originally launched by a group of British and Scandinavian scholars, this network now spans the entire world and includes members who have published books and articles on the subject. Two early ideas underlying this network are the general criticism of project management as such and a discomfort with the portrayal of project management in academic texts. An early and important contribution is the study by Damian Hodgson on the "disciplining of project management". Hodgson argues that project management is launched as a way to free the individual worker to explore, to adventure, and to advance (see Hodgson, 2002, 2004). However, as Hodgson demonstrates, this has little to do with the reality or the actual results. He points to the opposing features of project management, namely, that project management is a way of instituting bureaucratic principles – control principles to keep the professional worker in place and to reduce creativity and freedom – through the use of the rhetoric of freedom. In that respect, project organizing could be viewed as a particular kind of subtle disciplining. Accordingly, a project then becomes an "unresisted mental prison for people, in the worst case a prison much harder to envision and escape from than those of traditional bureaucratic structures" (Lindgren and Packendorff, 2006: 125). This creates, Lindgren and Packendorff (2006) argue, a situation characterized by "stress, loneliness, disrupted family lives and superficial workplace relations." This line of critical analysis has also indicated that project-based organizing typically reinforces traditional masculine values and attitudes to work and life (Lindgren and Packendorff, 2006) – where projects are workplaces filled with impossible deadlines and overtime.

In several ways, these critical remarks restate some of the remarks posed by sociologist Richard Sennett (1998) in his book *The Corrosion of Character* and the call from Beverly Metcalfe (1997) to investigate the social and organizational impacts of project management. Sennett's critique in particular has attracted much scholarly attention. He stresses the risk of fluid organizational principles (such as project organizing) in terms of short-sightedness, lack of commitment, and lack of devotion. In his treatise, the emphasis on flexibility and teamwork leads to a superficial ideology where mobility and social skills are emphasized at the cost of loyalty and work ethics. Together, the studies zero in on the human problems of project work. The critical perspectives on project-based organizations offer important insights and provide a broader view of the nature and consequences of project-based organizations.

The above studies shed light on the "dark side of the project-based organization" – a side that managers and theorists should be aware of in order to properly design support systems and improve work conditions. It is, in our opinion, important to take these critical observations into account in order to be able to offer a fine-grained analysis of project-based organization and its consequences. We refrain from creating the illusion that project-based organizations are organizational designs without problems or challenges for the individual worker. In our work, however, we subscribe to a slightly different idea of project-based organization – not the purely rationalistic one but one that seeks to explore the positive sides of project-based organization and work against the negative sides. We believe that some of these critiques are based on studies of bad management rather than being the result of any inherently negative quality of project organizing per se. Things could have been handled differently, thereby ensuring a better work situation

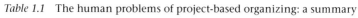

Table 1.1   The human problems of project-based organizing: a summary

Feature of project-based organization	Consequence
1. Matrix organization	Dual affiliations, loyalty problems, and unclear responsibilities
2. Cross-functionality	Lack of deep expertise, lack of affiliation
3. Deadlines and time pressure	Negative stress and burnout risks
4. Continuous work pressure	Limited time and opportunity for competence development
5. Task complexity	Feelings of chaos and insecurity
6. Technical uncertainty	Role ambiguity and role strain
7. Changing teams/temporary organizations	Lack of trust and social disconnectedness, corrosion of character
8. Fluctuating demand	Job insecurity

(Handwritten margin note: ✱ SUMMARY OF PROJECT FACTORS.)

for the project worker in combination with effectiveness and efficiency at the organizational level. We believe that, in contrast, several of the studies reported in our book provide examples of measures taken to improve the work situation of the project worker, thereby addressing some of the deficiencies reported in critical research on project management and project-based organizations. At the same time, as our studies of project workers show, there are positive as well as negative consequences of project-based organization and the acknowledgment and understanding of both is the first important step to implement appropriate improvements.

As observed in the above review of empirical studies on the consequences of project-based organization, project-based forms of organizing come with important human challenges. In Table 1.1, we summarize the most important challenges, according to previous research. The observations center on the matrix organization, the dual affiliations, and the possible knowledge effects of cross-functional work. In addition, the table highlights some of the effects of the task features commonly associated with projects, namely, time pressure, complexity, and uncertainty.

The bright side of project-based organizations

The above review of negative consequences might give the impression that project-based organizations are dangerous creatures that should be avoided at any cost. However, as indicated earlier, project-based organizations have qualities in handling integration efforts and dealing with complex problems which involve specialists from various areas of expertise. These advantages have been frequently referred to in the strategy and management literatures. This is, of course, also a key issue for the individual worker who has the opportunity to meet new people and explore new areas. Together workers can see where their combined knowledge can take them and learn from the integration of their expertise, finding out more about the areas of application.

Project-based organizations are also typically oriented toward deadlines. Deadlines are interesting for various reasons but perhaps especially important in a project context. Since almost all projects operate with a deadline, "making it in time" is a crucial aspect for people involved in a project. In many cases, this can lead to frustrations, high pressure, and stress. There are, however, also positive aspects. According to the work of Connie Gersick, deadlines can produce reflective thinking and cooperation, an insight that led Lindkvist et al. (1998) to argue that deadlines, as a particular kind of control mechanism, work quite differently compared to conventional structuring mechanisms, such as role allocations, job descriptions, and professional rules. Instead, they say, a deadline may produce a "rationalistic break" that induces people to think for themselves and make their own decisions before acting. In the words of Gersick (1995: 145), organizing by projects with explicitly stated deadlines is then a form of bracketing which "helps break the spell, facilitating strategic rethinking." On a similar note, Lindkvist et al. suggest that a deadline "generates recurrent glimpses of light, like the lighthouse, breaking darkness and making more global concerns possible" (Lindkvist et al., 1998: 947). Quite different from Sennett's (1998) analysis and the warnings about the "corrosion of character" mentioned earlier, these authors argue that project organizing leads to individual behavior that is responsible and reflective. According to Lindkvist et al. (1998: 947), this indicates that deadlines, if used in a shrewd way, may constitute an "unobtrusive" form of control that is possible to align with the ideas of "decentralization, autonomy and self-organization often invoked in the literature on knowledge management and concurrent engineering." This finding is also supported in the comprehensive study of engineers working in project matrix organizations presented in Hovmark and Nordkvist (1996). The authors identify a number of positive changes in terms of increased commitment, dynamism, support, solidarity, communication, and group autonomy. In that respect, studies have also identified a series of positive effects of task complexity and technical uncertainty and illustrated that these features might stimulate creative thinking and challenge the individual to perform a better and more rewarding job which involves meeting new people and moving to new social situations. Some of the observations presented in the book will show how HRM can be designed and developed to facilitate such results.

Responding to the challenges of project-based organizations

The above sections have demonstrated some of the challenges associated with HRM in project-based organizations. The intention has also been to highlight the value and importance of HRM in project-based organizations. From the organization's point of view, the management of the identified challenges seems to be a critical task. In addition, the skills and abilities of the individual project workers need to be addressed. What are the important technical and social skills required? What kind of integrative skills do the engineers need to possess? What kind of support do they need to improve their performance? What is the responsibility of the person assuming the personnel responsibility for the individual project worker? The latter question leads us into a whole host of questions tied to the organizational support and the organizational arrangements necessary to design HRM. The line manager may not be as involved in operational technical problem-solving as was common in the past. Instead, many companies try out new solutions. For instance, at one of the studied companies, Tetra Pak – a world leader in packaging systems and material – one of their project-based units abolished the traditional line management role and adopted a new one, called the "competence coach." Of course, many of the duties – such as recruitment, budgeting, human resource planning, and performance appraisal – were similar, but the new role was intended to be much more "HR focused." In one of our conversations, the company's CEO of the unit told us about the problems with the traditional line management role which often "ended up being all about supervising the work" instead of competence development and other HR issues, which were considered to be issues critical to the company's future. The new role also changed the role of the HR specialists and the HR departments. The role of the competence coach took over many of the responsibilities formerly held by the HR specialists. The HR specialists, on the other hand, had to focus more on the strategic issues: what kind of people do we need in the future, and what strategic collaborations are required to ensure a good and continuous flow of talent? They also had to focus on a set of operational issues primarily directed toward the competence coaches: what support do the competence coaches need, and what expertise can we give them to allow them to become even better at coaching their engineers? In Tetra Pak, project managers and project directors also played a key role. They were the managers with whom the individual project worker met on a daily basis. They were the ones who could assess the working situation of the project worker and detect any alarming levels of stress or discomfort.

HRM is not the sole responsibility of one department or one unit within the firm. It is a continuous and ongoing interplay among many players. Firms try to develop new forms of HRM to respond to the requirements of new organizational forms. The project-based form of organizing, for example, requires new skills and puts new demands on the individual worker. The traditional "personnel responsibility" takes a slightly different form: line managers become more HR-focused. In addition, a new cadre of managers enters the scene – a cadre that is vital for the integrative capability of the firm but that equally might have a key stake in the HRM performance of the company, namely, the project managers.

We have witnessed the advent of projects and project-based organizational structures which put increased pressure on managers to rethink and renew their HRM practices. The purpose of this book is to present findings from a multiyear research initiative covering the changes made in a number of leading multinationals. The focus is on R&D- and engineering-intensive companies operating in global industries such as pharmaceutical, aerospace, complex machinery, packaging systems, and automotive (for an overview of the case study companies, see Appendix). We draw from studies carried out in more than ten firms over a period of nearly ten years. Many of these studies have been reported in scientific articles published elsewhere, which will be referred to in the text for the reader who is interested in knowing more about the details of our empirical studies. In this book, however, we concentrate on the main findings in our studies relating to HRM in project-based organization. In particular we seek to:

- provide an enhanced understanding of project-based organizations and their consequences on HRM;
- present state-of-the-art of research and practice within the area of HRM, focusing on one particular type of organization – the project-based organization;
- present examples of novel and innovative forms of organizing HRM in project-based organizations.

- analyze the challenges to HRM in project-based organizations, identify the major changes implemented in the studied organizations, document some of the key challenges, and discuss how the firms have responded to these challenges;
- outline an elaborate understanding of the HR organization in project-based organizations and develop a deeper understanding of HRM in project-based organizations which acknowledges the collective and distributive character of HRM.

Improvement points

Our approach and arguments

Throughout the book we will argue in favor of a contextual approach to HRM. We will also, for obvious reasons, argue that project-based organizations offer a particularly interesting setting for contextualizing HRM and to explore the current challenges to HRM in modern contexts. We report on a series of empirical studies that will be presented in the various chapters. The intention has been to provide a holistic and in-depth understanding of HRM in project-based organizations. This intention rests on a number of basic arguments and field-study observations:

1. HRM needs to be contextualized. HRM differs among contexts; some similarities exist, but there are also important differences.
2. Project-based organizations represent one important organizational context. This context not only puts pressure on HRM but also, in many ways, leads the development among HR practitioners.
3. HRM is increasingly distributive and collective. HRM then is, to a large extent, carried out in collaboration among actors within the firm.
4. HRM is not the sole responsibility of the HR departments; other actors, including line managers and project managers, play important roles, particularly on the operational level. In addition, the individual project worker has a key role in laying the foundation for effective HRM.
5. The work setting is critical for the design of HRM. The work setting entails the type of project participation and project work, which in turn affects what type of HR support the individual project worker needs.
6. Individuals involved in project-based work play an increasingly important role in the design of HRM. Individual project workers develop skills that are critical for the entire HRM system to communicate to line managers, to work with project managers, and to

assist the HR department in developing their services to the project workers.

7. In project-based organizations, a key management role is that of the project manager. The project manager, however, is not only responsible for technology integration and operative problem-solving. To a large extent, he or she is also involved in HRM activities, such as performance appraisal, competence development activities, stress management, and related activities of importance for the working situation of the project members.

Outline of the book

The next chapter goes deeper into the kind of project-based organization addressed in this book. The aim of Chapter 2 is to pinpoint the major issues in these organizations that have effects on HRM. We then review the literature on HRM in Chapter 3. In this chapter we present a historical overview and try to show how this book relates to ongoing research within the field of HRM as well as to identify the particular contributions we believe that our work is making. Chapter 4 presents a framework for the analysis of HRM in project-based organization, referred to as the HR quadriad that we have developed in a series of studies of the design and change of HR organizations. The HR quadriad basically says that HRM, at the operational level in project-based organizations, is performed by four actors: HR specialists, line managers, project managers, and project workers.

Then follow four chapters that analyze in further detail each of the cornerstones of the HR quadriad. We begin with the line managers in Chapter 5 and a discussion about the devolvement of HR responsibility, which is discussed further Chapter 6 about the role of project managers in HRM. The individual project worker is the key topic for Chapter 7, before we turn to the HR specialists and the HR departments in Chapter 8. In the final chapter, Chapter 9, we summarize the findings that have emerged from the book and discuss the book's conclusions and contributions. In Chapter 9, we also point out some vistas for future research and lessons learned for managerial and organizational practice within the area of HRM in project-based organizations.

In the Appendix, we present the details of the various studies reported and the research methodologies used in the respective empirical studies. In the Appendix, we guide the reader who wants to learn more about the studies that form the foundation for the findings presented in this book.

Outlining the problems	**Chapter 1**	Competitive challenges and projectification
Defining the area	**Chapter 2**	Nature and features of the project-based organization
Painting the background	**Chapter 3**	History and theory of HRM
Presenting the framework	**Chapter 4**	The HR Quadriad
Part of framework	**Chapter 5**	Line managers
Part of framework	**Chapter 6**	Project managers
Part of framework	**Chapter 7**	Project workers
Part of framework	**Chapter 8**	HR specialists
Summing up the framework and findings	**Chapter 9**	Comparisons and contrasts

Figure 1.1 Outline of the book

2
Project-Based Organizations

Projects as cornerstones in the project-based organization

The preceding chapter gave a general introduction to projectification and project-based organizations. This chapter delves further into these issues and presents more details about the organizational context for the book and the challenges we address. This context is important to us firstly because we argue that there is a need to contextualize HRM and secondly because project-based organizations offer a particularly interesting, challenging, and, at the same time, promising context for the development of human resources. For most people working in a project-based organization, the project is an important work place: an action locality (Grabher, 2004) and a meeting place as much as a producer of emotional energy and job satisfaction. In this chapter, we will discern some of the salient features of the project-based organization, in particular, the kind of project-based organization focused upon in this book. Our intention is to clarify what kind of organization the project-based organization is and to determine the implications of its defining features for the practice and study of HRM.

> **Fact Box 2.1**   Turning to project-based organization: the case of Tetra Pak
>
> Tetra Pak is one of the leading players in packaging material and machinery systems. It operates on a worldwide basis. In one of the units, management has tried out a new organizational model giving emphasis to the project dimension. The entire organization was changed in the beginning of the 21st century not only to allow for better integration of technology and business processes but also to enhance HRM capabilities. During one of our interviews we focused on the reasons why the organization had changed its structure. The CEO gave us quite a number of reasons, such as improved integration across knowledge areas, enhanced management capacity, and better possibilities for project managers to do their job. In that respect, the CEO primarily emphasized the importance of strengthening the integrative capability of the firm. However, he also gave several explanations that touched upon the HRM dimension, including making it possible to better share knowledge among employees, improving the adaptability and resource allocation, and making it easier to build stronger teams. As we will discuss later on, this also had some important implications for the role of the line managers and HR specialists within the firm.

Project-based organizations

Research on project-based organizations often draws on different types of organizational designs along a continuum – with the pure functional organization at one extreme, the pure project-based organization at the other, and matrix organizations with varying degrees of project orientation in between. The main factor for deciding on the project orientation in such typologies is the level of authority over resources, such as personnel and finance (e.g., Hobday, 2000). Following Hobday's terminology, the project-based organization is accordingly defined as "one in which the project is the primary unit for production, innovation, and competition" and where "there is no formal functional coordination across project lines" (p. 878). In this type of definition, "project-based" inherently implies the total abolishment of functional coordination. However, it is somewhat indeterminate if this only concerns the functional coordination of core activities, such as production and innovation, or if it rules out all forms of functional coordination across the projects. For researchers whose main focus is on how project-based organizations deal with their permanent systems and processes, these definitions miss out on important counts. For instance, the definitions fail to acknowledge that project-based structures do not necessarily exhibit a complete dominance of the project structure over the functional structure in all aspects.

Lindkvist (2004: 5) suggests a broader definition when writing about project-based firms as those "that privilege strongly the project dimension and carry out most of their activities in projects." Similarly, Whitley (2006: 79) depicts project-based firms as those that "organize work around relatively discrete projects that bring particular groups of skilled staff together to work on complex, innovative tasks for a variety of clients and purposes." However, these definitions are vague, particularly concerning the nature of the activities that are being carried out in the projects.

Other attempts to delineate the characteristics of project-based organizations take into account factors such as employment contracts, affiliation, and the level of repetitiveness of project work. Söderlund (2000) distinguishes four ideal types of organizations depending, on the one hand, on the permanency/temporality of the work structure, and on the other hand, on the permanency/temporality of the employment contracts. In Söderlund's typology, "project-based organization" thus describes a situation where people have permanent employment contracts in an organization where work is carried out in temporary project constellations. Packendorff (2002) takes a similar stance and discusses four types of "project-based work" depending on whether project workers have their primary affiliation to the individual project or to the organizational context and whether project work is considered to be routine or the exception. In his typology, project-based work is regarded as that work in which project workers have a primary affiliation to the organizational context and in which project work is routine. Thus, Söderlund (2000) and Packendorff (2002) offer frameworks to better position the project-based organization in terms of the nature of work and employment affiliation. In that respect, they contribute to better addressing the project-based organization and the associated HRM challenges and work conditions.

One way to build on previous definitions, but define and develop them further, would be to interpret "project-based" organizations as organizations in which core activities, that is, the activities that are primarily directed toward the creation of products or services, which constitute the base for the organization's rationale and revenue stream (see Prahalad and Hamel, 1990), are performed by means of projects. When it comes to the organization of other activities and processes – for example, those related to HRM – some kind of functional coordination across projects is still highly relevant and required. The definition of project-based organization subscribed to here concerns a permanent organizational framework in which temporary projects are embedded (see also Sydow et al., 2004). Consequently, a project-based organization has a set of ongoing projects, architecture for its operational activities, and permanent employees who do most of their work in various kinds of projects. In other words, projects are core activities and are, to some extent, repetitive. There are important permanent systems and structures to make the project-based organization succeed, and employment is linked to the organization as such, not to the individual project. Following this line of reasoning, our analysis of the project-based organization does not center on so-called single-project organizations (DeFillippi and Arthur, 1998; Whitley, 2006), where the entire organization/firm is dissolved after completion of a project (see Fact Box 2.2 for examples of the kind of project-based organizations treated in this book).

Fact Box 2.2 Examples of project-based organizations

Over the years we have studied a number of project-based organizations in different sectors and industries. A majority of them are R&D or development units within larger multinational corporations. Below are a few examples of the organizations in our empirical studies (for details on code names see Appendix):

- Automotive R&D site with 4,000 employees. Primarily engineers with a background in mechanical and electrical engineering.
- Product and organizational development unit in a European logistics company. The unit under study has 2,000 employees working in various sorts of product development, service development, implementation, and change projects.
- Aerospace, main site for development of aviation technology. The studied unit has 4,000 employees, most of them educated within areas such as electrical engineering, mechanical engineering, software engineering, and avionics engineering.
- IT Systems, R&D unit with 2,000 employees, most of them working in various sorts of systems development and application projects. The typical education of the employees is within computer science and software engineering.
- Telecom R&D unit with 1,000 employees, specialized within one area of telecom and educated within the areas of computer science, electrical engineering, and programming.
- Complex machinery development unit for advanced plant design and automation solutions. A total of 155 employees work here, and most of them are engineers.
- Medical Systems, a unit for product and systems development. Approximately 100 employees, the majority of whom are engineers with a master's degree.

Distinctive features of the project-based organization: organization meets people

The preceding discussion suggests that project-based organizations have a set of common characteristics: their core activities are performed in projects, project work is common and part of everyday business, the projects are embedded in a permanent organizational context, and people are hired by the permanent organization, not directly by individual projects. Elaborating further on these characteristics, a set of features can be identified as distinctive for project-based organizations: (1) goal oriented, (2) team oriented and knowledge-intensive, (3) temporary, (4) interdisciplinary and cross-functional, and (5) tensional. These distinctive features are essential to the understanding of this particular organizational setting, and, therefore, equally essential to the success of HRM in project-based organizations.

Goal-oriented organization

Projects have quite specific targets in terms of delivery and completion date; they are processes intended to produce certain results (e.g., Archibald, 1992; Berggren, 2001). The intended result could be many different things: a product, a system, a technical solution, an installation, an event, an organizational change, etc. Some projects have an outcome that is very difficult to specify in advance. The outcome, as such, might be more or less impossible to reach. Others have a relatively clear end-state, but the process of getting there could be difficult to conceive and specify a priori. Still others might struggle with both these challenges: unclear goals and unclear processes (see, e.g., Turner and Cochrane, 1993). The typical project carried out by the organizations studied here is complex, involving a number of subprojects and knowledge bases. It is relatively uncertain with some degree of unknown technologies, although such uncertainty is not typically fundamental to the project. Even in the case of drug development, we address the clinical phase which in many ways resembles the organization of a large-scale development project. Other examples include the development of a new fighter aircraft, automobile, packaging system, telecom system, etc. Specifications are laid out a priori, and the completion of the project does not require research activities and exploratory work. Instead, most projects, although difficult and challenging, are examples of knowledge exploitation (March, 1991).

Team-oriented and knowledge-intensive organization

The project-based organization is one that is primarily engaged in various sorts of knowledge-intensive and collaborative project work, such as R&D projects, product and systems development, implementation projects, improvement projects, and change projects. The focus in this book is on the work of designers, engineers, programmers, and R&D personnel. These specialists, however, do not perform their work in solitude; they are, compared to many other kinds of knowledge workers, to a great extent working closely with other people, in teams and in joint problem-solving efforts. Contrary to conventional autonomous knowledge-intensive organizations, in the project-based organizations addressed here combined efforts and diverse kinds of teamwork stand at the fore. This means that the project-based organization needs to integrate knowledge resources in fast, flexible ways in order to reach a defined goal within a certain time period (Davies and Hobday, 2005; Whitley, 2006). Therefore, project-based organizations are likely to be characterized by knowledge-intensiveness, which means that that the competence and skills of employees have greater importance than other inputs, that the majority of employees are highly qualified, and that work involves complex problem-solving while working collaboratively (Alvesson, 2001; Swart and Kinnie, 2003). Accordingly for the management of human resources, both the flow and ongoing development of knowledge resources and their integration are critical tasks. The people occupying the organizations participating in our studies often have advanced degrees in engineering or natural science. In addition, several of them have also participated in internal training programs arranged and financed by their current or previous employer. In that respect, it seems relevant to speak of them as knowledge workers although their skills and knowledge are explored and exploited in close cooperation with other engineers and experts from both similar and dissimilar areas of expertise.

Temporary organization

In a project-based organization, project work, rather than being the exception, is routine, although projects typically require nonroutine technologies and solutions. The projects also tend to be designed for the special purpose, meaning that there is an ongoing reorganization of teams from one project to the next. The organization normally has a set of procedures and standardized processes in place to carry out its projects and, in many cases, quite advanced and well-developed frameworks for project management, including templates, process descriptions, role specifications, and instructions. In a project-based organization, then, people perform most of their work in projects, which are, by definition, temporary. As stated by Packendorff (2002) in his description of project-based work, "individuals working by projects experience a long-term trajectory consisting of a long series of projects." Since the projects are temporary organizations, which can be "characterized by the temporary constellation of people they entail" (Prencipe and Tell, 2001: 1374), project-based organizations are generally characterized by a short-term logic in which "new human encounters and relationships take place whenever a new project is started" (p. 1374). Therefore, a project-based organization is characterized by repetitive temporality. In a similar vein, Bresnen et al. (2005: 1541) refer to "the intended and finite nature of projects" as a key feature of project-based organizations, which often leads to a short-term emphasis on project performance. In that respect, it is not only the deadline and the goal orientation that could potentially come with it but also the ongoing reorganizations and new encounters that are in-built features of the project-based organization. As Sydow et al. (2004) point out, this is one of the most important rationales for the project-based organization, namely, to organize for specific purposes and allow for flexible resource commitment. Of course, this calls for particular integrative capabilities, but equally, also well-crafted capabilities to handle the flow and development of human resources.

The duration in time varies from project to project. Some projects last for a couple of weeks or months, while others might have life cycles spanning many years. The kind of projects carried out within the companies discussed here typically run for at least six months and in some cases three or four years, such as is the case in automotive and drug development. The existence of temporariness and time limits is fundamental to the organization of projects in the studied organizations. Typically, deadlines are tough and critical, frequently a matter of meeting a specific time for delivery and production ramp-up. Temporariness is also present since the typical project involves a combination of resources and knowledge bases that have not worked together before, although some of the participants might be familiar with each other from previous encounters in projects.

Interdisciplinary and cross-functional organization

To execute a project successfully generally requires interaction of people from a number of different of areas of expertise – it requires input from various knowledge bases and communication across functional boundaries. Therefore, projects normally cut across organizational lines, such as functional or departmental lines, or company boundaries (e.g., Archibald, 1992; Sydow et al., 2004). This implies that most projects consist of an amalgam of different areas of expertise, disciplines, and knowledge bases whose efforts need to be combined in various ways. This is also very much at the center of the integration issue addressed earlier, although it should be pointed out that the integration, as such, could be designed and handled very differently. Forms of integration could range from people collaborating intensely, communicating on a day-by-day basis, and being co-located in a shared office space, to their having far less communication and collaboration, and perhaps not being physically co-located, although still being deeply engaged in highly interdependent problem-solving. In either case, their work can be highly interdependent and can require advanced forms of integration for everyone involved to succeed in their efforts. A failed project producing a malfunctioning product or system is a failed project for everyone involved, at least in regard to the kind of project we are discussing in the present book.

The organizations discussed in this book are involved in difficult and challenging integration efforts. Relatively intense collaboration across functional boundaries is therefore critical for successful development projects. According to Bresnen et al. (2005), this type of work often relies on decentralized teamwork and relatively autonomous project managers, although, as we will see later, there might very well be differences in terms of the degree and nature of cross-functionality. In either case, the idea of cross-functionality is ultimately a solution to improve the integrative capabilities of the firm, to tap knowledge from different sources, and to better integrate knowledge across organizational and functional boundaries. However, there might be a range of different solutions to cross-functionality, and the project-based organization might choose different solutions depending on the complexity, pace, and uncertainty of the project at hand (Shenhar and Dvir, 2007). Thus, cross-functionality has important implications for the management of human resources, the development of expertise, and employment relationships.

Tensional organization

A project-based organization constitutes a permanent organizational framework in which temporary projects are embedded. Projects come and go and contribute to the evolution of the permanent organization. Sydow et al. (2004: 1477) emphasize the importance of acknowledging the "contextual embeddedness of temporary systems in the more permanent" and the related inherent tension between permanent and temporary systems logics in such organizations. On the one hand, projects enable the organization to integrate knowledge and competences across functional and administrative lines, focus the efforts on reaching the set goals within a pregiven time zone, and maintain organizational flexibility to respond to changing environmental requirements. On the other hand, as the study by Hobday (2000) indicates, a project-based organization with limited, or even a lack of, functional coordination is "inherently weak in coordinating processes, resources and capabilities across the organization as a whole." Consequently, the project-based organization incorporates the dilemma of the conflicting needs of the temporary projects and the permanent organizational setting that defends long-term development as well as routines and interorganizational coordination (Sydow et al., 2004). This could then generally be viewed as an inherent tension between permanent and temporary systems and logics residing within the project-based organization. This has some important implications for the management of human resources. The obvious one is of course that priorities within the temporary system, that is, the project, might be in conflict with efficiencies within the permanent system. The opposite is, of course, also true: what might be good for the permanent system, for instance, priorities made by the line manager, might be detrimental for project performance and the effectiveness of project management.

Multi-employment organization

Being involved in project work in this context does not necessarily equal having a permanent employment contract with the project-based organization. Even though human resources are employed or hired by the organization rather than by individual projects, some people might be involved on a temporary basis to carry out work in specific projects. Others might be hired to line units or competence pools within the project-based organization and involved in various projects over time, but they maintain their employment contract elsewhere, for example, with a technical consultancy. For many project-based organizations it is even a strategic issue to increase the ratio of "involvees" (total number of people involved in the organization's operations) to "employees" (I/E ratio, see Hedberg et al. 1997). Whitley (2006), for example, argues that project-based organizations that organize work around a series of recurrent projects "often rely on outsiders for completing individual tasks, but retain a core group of employees for initiating, organizing, and conducting separate projects." Similarly, Ekstedt (2002) discusses work contracts in project-based organizations and points out that consulting activities and the use of outside expertise increase as firms projectify their core activities. Ekstedt argues that in organizations where most of the "action" takes place in projects "small permanent organizations with strategic functions and a strong brand name harbor project teams for both development and production consisting of persons affiliated to a lot of different organizations" (p. 66). For most people, work in project-based organizations generally goes beyond the time horizon of the individual project. However, for the management of human resources, it is important to recognize that the work force that contributes to the organization's activities consists not only of "permanent employees" but also of a significant number of more "temporary employees" such as consultants, self-employed professionals, and others with temporary affiliations to the organization. Accordingly, the project-based organization can be seen as an organization characterized by multi-employment solutions.

HRM implications

The six distinctive features discussed above can be used as a foundation to elaborate further on the implications for HRM in project-based organizations. In sum, we might examine these features in regard to HRM and identify a few challenges for the practice and study of HRM. Returning to the initial idea of project-based organizations fundamentally engaged in two kinds of capabilities – (1) organizational capabilities with focus on complex problem-solving and integrative capabilities, and (2) the continuous supply and development of human resources that can participate in complex problem-solving processes – we might generally state that to a great extent the above features are direct consequences of improving the first set of capabilities. For instance, goal orientation typically leads to a narrow focus, perhaps even short-sightedness, which reduces the complexity for the actors involved and which could trigger knowledge integration and collaboration across organizational boundaries. Knowledge-intensiveness is tied to the development of new technologies and knowledge specialization typically critical for the success of the project-based organization. This calls for advanced integrative solutions, support mechanisms for teams to communicate both within and across team boundaries, and trained managers and engineers, such as project managers and systems engineers, who know how to design technical and organizational architectures to achieve system-wide efficiencies. The multi-employment feature is an effect of the same principle, that is, to be able to draw on resources that are best suited to solve a particular problem. In some cases, they are located within the same line organization, in other cases, in different line organizations, and, in yet other cases,

Table 2.1 Distinctive features of the project-based organization and its implications on HRM

Feature	HRM implications
Goal-oriented	Performance appraisal; difficult to evaluate individual performance due to teamwork qualities. Important to link goal-oriented efforts with each other and to create opportunities for reflection and recuperation between project assignments.
Team-oriented and knowledge-intensive	Need to build organizational capabilities to foster knowledge sharing; need to develop knowledge and competence continuously. High requirements on individuals to steer knowledge development.
Temporary	Continuous formation of teams which require an adequate management of the flow of human resources in terms of recruitment, staffing, and return from assignments (see Huemann et al., 2004).
Interdisciplinary and cross-functional	Work is typically carried out in parallel action localities; difficult to oversee work situations; difficult to control. Might lead to difficulties with regard to knowledge development, lack of knowledge depth, and affiliation (Allen, 1977).
Tensional	Different authority systems and priorities may be in conflict. What is best for the temporary system is not always good for the permanent system and vice versa (see Sydow et al., 2004). This is equally true for the individual performance: what is good for individual performance in a focal project is not necessarily good for firm-level performance.
Multi-employment	The workforce is constituted by people with different types of employment forms and affiliations. This means that the management of human resources is not equal to the management of the relationship to employees. Instead, it includes managing the relationship to all "involvees", regardless of their type of employment contract.

within different firms. To be able to swiftly establish a cooperation and coordination regime is of course critical for the integrative capability of the firm.

As is evident from Table 2.1 there is a strong relationship between the integrative capability and the supply and development of human resources. At the same time, it should be pointed out, there is a distinct difference between them since the integrative capability as such is goal-oriented: aimed for the specific attainment of client requirements, technological possibilities and solutions, and project performance. This capability is typically also steered and governed by people with roles such as technical director, project manager, project director, systems engineer, chief engineer, etc. There are, of course, many decisions taken within this area of management that have implications on HRM; however, the ultimate objective is not the management of human resources per se. On the other hand, the second capability is not directed toward specific problem-solving processes or project goals. Instead, it, in various ways, relates to the supply and flow of human resources, the performance of human resources, the involvement of human resources, and the development of human resources. To some extent, these activities are directly tied to the integration activities of the firm; however, a number of activities are, of course, also carried out without particular focus on a specific project. These are activities such as recruitment decisions, career planning, and competence development.

Crafting HRM in project-based organizations

Earlier, we discussed some of the human consequences and even problems associated with project-based organizing, including stress, feelings of insecurity, etc. The discussion did not readily address the problems associated with human resource management, that is, what should the organization do to handle the problems, what are the consequences for the management system set to take care of human resources, and how are the individuals going to prepare themselves for the ensuing consequences. In that respect, we believe some of the negative consequences associated with project-based organizing might be resolved with better management of projects (project management, project governance, project portfolio management, etc.), including improved structuring and coordination to make it easier for people to perform well in their projects. However, a major part of the solutions and improvement areas falls within the area of HRM. Generally speaking, this calls for further exploration into the landscape and role of HRM in project-based organizations.

Fact Box 2.2   Oticon: involvement and focus

One of the most famous examples of a project-based organization is that of hearing-aid manufacturer Oticon. Under the guidance of the new CEO, Lars Kolind, the company implemented a completely new organizational structure that was aimed to be much more focused on projects, teamwork, and self-organization. According to some analysts, the change of organizational structure was one of the decisive factors in the impressive turn-around of the company during the 1990s: innovation rates increased considerably, entrepreneurship was triggered, and work-life conditions were generally improved. "Departments, positions, titles and job descriptions were abolished and the previous functional structure was replaced with a project-based organization," writes Verona and Ravasi (2003: 586). In many ways, the authors argue that the change was driven primarily by the increasingly complex technologies involved. To a great extent, the change in Oticon was aimed at improving the entrepreneurial spirit among people and at broadening their skill sets. In that respect, managers wanted engineers and other employees to be much more involved in the identifying of new possibilities, product, and service ideas, and they wanted them to be more focused on particular projects. To be able to do so, individuals sometimes had to broaden their competences to be able to fill more than one role in a specific project. The possibility of having focused project participation was considered to be critical at Oticon.

What then are the challenges for crafting HRM in project-based organizations? A set of studies, as early as in the 1970s, elicited the potential difficulties of designing effective HRM systems in project-based and other kinds of distributed and decentralized organizations. For instance, Knight (1977: 181) argued that many project-oriented organizations "struggle along under the handicap of inappropriate systems which are more of a hindrance than a support." Knight continues:

> There are two main areas where this danger arises. One is the field of managing information and control systems…. The other is the sphere of personnel management. While it is possible to point out the problems that can arise in the latter sphere and while the answers to most of them do not even seem particularly difficult, I am afraid that very little hard information on company practices has come my way and I am reduced to speculating about the subject. (Knight, 1977: 181)

Despite these early insights and calls for research into HRM in project-based organizations, this has been a largely neglected area of research. It should be noted that the specific study of the nature of project-based organizations has attracted considerable scholarly attention in recent

Table 2.2 Project-based organizations and HRM: four previous studies

	Midler (1995)	Hobday (2000)	Lindkvist (2004)	Whitley (2006)
Aim of study	To study the change in Renault from a strongly functional organization to a project-based organization.	To analyze different types of project-organizational solutions and the advantages and disadvantages of organizing a project in a strongly functional organization versus a strongly project-based organization.	To study the logic of project-based organization, in particular the governance processes and how hierarchical principles can be combined with market principles.	To analyze different types of project-based organizations.
Type of investigation	Retrospective and longitudinal case-study over a period of almost 40 years. Comparison of the different types of project coordination used by Renault during the time period studied.	Comparative case study of two projects in the same firm. The projects involved the development and delivery of a complex technical system.	A single case study investigation of a unit with the Tetra Pak group, a Swedish company operating in the packaging material industry.	A theoretical treatise and model creation. Comparison of four different kinds of project-based organizations depending on their singularity of goals (unique output) and stability and separation of work roles.
Industrial context	Automotive, R&D	Advanced, high-cost scientific, industrial, and medical equipment.	Packaging material, market-based R&D	Multiple, including filmmaking, software engineering, construction, and R&D.

| HRM findings | Engineers were not prepared for cross-functional collaboration. Vague responsibility for the skill-based functional departments. Difficulties to maintain the long-term technical learning when organizational structures focused short-term and project-oriented objectives. Staff rotation had dysfunctional effects on project convergence. The dismantling of a team at the end of a project was a complicated issue, since a local focus, but on permanent structures or new projects rarely produced satisfactory job opportunities at the right time. | A strong emphasis on the project dimension can breed insecurity concerning career development. Cross-functionality leads to both opportunities and problems, including on the one hand learning from other disciplines and a local focus, but on the other hand, a lack of professional connections with experts in the same field and an ignorance of the global processes and systems within the firm. | Project teams hardly became "well-developed groups" in the traditional sense with shared values, shared understandings, and shared knowledge base. Organizational structure becomes "individualized," making the firm reliant upon the abilities of the employees to self-organize. Internal labor markets become more important and individuals feel more like "free agents." To build a reputation for a willingness to contribute and help others becomes essential. | Project-based firms come in different forms. The separation and stability of work roles are important to understand what challenges a particular project-based organization is struggling with and how it can build competitive advantage. It is when the project-based firm undertakes a series of similar kinds of projects with a core group of employees who remain with the firm for some time that distinctive organizational identities, knowledge, and capabilities may be developed and provide competitive advantage. |

years. These studies have one particular thing in common: they all identify a set of challenges for designing good HRM systems and that the success of the project-based organization rests, to a great extent, on how well the firm solves the HRM enigma. In that respect, the difficulty is not merely that of the integrative capability mentioned earlier but to a greater extent on the second set of capabilities of supplying and developing human resources. Table 2.2 provides a summary of the most influential studies and their findings regarding HRM.

As touched upon earlier, and as brought up in several of the previously mentioned studies of project-based organizations and firms, there is a dearth of focused analyses of HRM and HRM challenges in the project-based organization. In particular, there seems to be a need for more studies about the entire system and design of HRM in such organizations, what practice areas are critical, and how these practices are executed. In that respect, we attempt to fill the lacuna of empirical work on HRM in project-based organizations. Engwall et al. (2003: 130) formulate the issue as follows:

> As organizations move into project-based structures, human resource management, hiring of staff, and competence development all seem to be affected. This is, however, a virtually unexplored area of empirical research. Furthermore, issues concerning working life must be readdressed in this new corporate context design. From the perspective of the individual employee, factors like motivation, commitment, empowerment, job satisfaction, time pressure, and medical stress seem to be reconceptualized in the projectified context. Working life issues also include accounts of project work as a new career path and as ways of linking project organizations to individual goals.

Final thoughts

This chapter lays the foundation and outlines the chief arguments: why the study of HRM in project-based organizations is called for and what problem areas this study might help to improve. Despite the previous work on the positive and negative consequences of project work, which we brought up in the first chapter of the book, and despite the issues and characteristics of project-based organizations presented in this chapter, we know relatively little about what to do when designing HRM and HR organizations in such contexts. We know about the problems and the challenges and the potential dangers of project work, that careers might be affected, and that the competence development could become more problematic. However, the major questions of significance to management and, in particular, management of human resources, are barely touched upon in the extant literature. This is undoubtedly a major problem. It is a problem since more and more work is actually done in projects within project-based organizations, which naturally also leads to more HRM activities and processes devoted toward recruitment, appraisal, motivation, and all kinds of people-related matters taking place within the context of a project-based organization.

Another point to ponder is that much activity is going on within the field of HRM. New ideas are being tried out, and strategic decisions are being made, including the outsourcing of support functions and layoffs. However, we know relatively little about the reasons for these decisions and their long-term effects. One chief aim of research is, of course, to document the reasons and effects of such decisions. The ultimate goal, however, is that these decisions will be based on sound knowledge about HRM, that is, its place in the organization as well as its relationships with organizational structures and its problem-solving capabilities. In many ways, we dare say, today decisions are often made without such thorough understanding. This means that designers of organizational structures need to know more about the preconditions of creating the best organizational structures and related support systems to ensure the viability of project-based organizations. It means also that managers must be able to design HRM systems particularly suited to the needs of the project-based organization and the people who occupy them. Finally, the people and individual workers themselves must know how to live, learn, and create a good working situation in an organization that carries out its core activities in projects.

3
Human Resource Management in Context

Structure of chapter

- HRM: a vibrant area of study
- A brief history
- Research on HRM
- Managing the relationship between people and organization
- HRM practice areas
- Addressing the operational level in project-based organizations
- Final thoughts

HRM: A vibrant area of study

The former chapter explicated a number of distinctive features of project-based organization that have implications for HRM practice and research. The chapter also summarized the recent calls for further investigations into the management of human resources in this context. The present chapter gives a historical view on the evolution of thought around HRM, points out key contributions, and elicits development patterns that are important to addressing HRM in project-based organizations. By so doing, the aim is to relate our research and findings to the continuously developing stream of research on HRM.

The following questions are important for the present chapter: What are the current state-of-the-art research and practice within HRM in project-based organizations? What are the challenges for HRM in this particular type of organization? What interesting novel and innovative ideas currently prevail regarding the design of HRM in project-based firms? In order to have this discussion, it is important to introduce the concept of HRM, which will then make it easier to understand the way we use and operationalize the concept. Thus, this chapter discusses the roots and developments of HRM and gives an overview of current research. Moreover, it gives our view of the opportunities for developing knowledge about HRM through an enhanced understanding of the specific organizational contexts in which HRM is carried out.

A brief history

Most historical overviews of HRM position the concept, and its major breakthrough, in the 1980s and primarily relate it to North American management literature. However, the notion of managing human resources and HRM has a much longer history. Already in 1954, renowned management thinker Peter Drucker used the term "human resources" to emphasize the distinction between workers and other economic resources, and to stress the fact that humans are true resources from which the firm benefits – they are not merely costs. This resource idea overlaps with what later led to explorations of the capabilities and resources in a firm. A few years later the economist Edith Penrose (1959) published the seminal book, *The Theory of the Growth of the Firm*, in which she defined and discussed the firm as a collection of productive resources. Penrose made the distinction between physical resources and human resources and argued that it is the human resources that give the firm an opportunity to gain competitive advantage through the uniqueness and variety of the different services they can potentially render. This perspective would later come to be very important in acknowledging people's knowledge, experiences, abilities, and skills as strategically important resources of the firm, which are important topics generally in current research on HRM.

One of the main points Drucker made was that the worker should be seen as a "whole man," that is, a human resource which, unlike other resources, has control over whether he or she works, how well and how much he or she works and, which is "of all resources entrusted to man, the most productive, the most versatile, the most resourceful" (Drucker, 1954: 262–3). Hence, Drucker argued, "the improvement of human effectiveness in work is the greatest opportunity for improvement of performance and results" (p. 262). Drucker severely critiqued the two then-dominant and generally accepted streams of thought regarding the management of workers – Personnel Administration and Human Relations – for suffering from considerable "lack of progress," "sterility," and "intellectual aridity." According to Drucker, the Human Relations stream did, however, build on better basic assumptions when compared to Personnel Administration; for example, that people do have a willingness to work and can be motivated to perform well without coercive management control. Nevertheless, he argued that the Human Relations stream had stagnated, and that it relied on the false belief that people would be motivated only by being "happy"; it did not offer alternative ideas for positive motivation. Moreover, Drucker criticized its one-sided focus on interpersonal relationships and its lack of adequate attention to work and economic dimensions. Therefore, Drucker considered Human Relations, along with important insights from Scientific Management, to be important parts of a foundation for future development of the basic principles for managing work and workers.

Similar criticism of the Human Relations model were raised a decade later by Raymond Miles (1965). Miles stressed that, although the Human Relations model rightfully argued for participative leadership and for making employees feel useful and important, the applied rationale behind these arguments was wrong. This rationale seemed to build on the conviction that higher levels of job satisfaction and morale would lower resistance and improve compliance with managerial authority – not on the conviction that employees might make important contributions to the decision-making process. Instead, Miles suggested a "Human Resources Model" based on the assumption that all organizational members are "reservoirs of untapped resources," and that a manager's primary task is that of "creating an environment in which the total resources of his department can be utilized" (Miles, 1965: 150). Hence, the rationale behind bringing employees into the decision-making process should be to improve the quality of decision-making and, in turn, the performance of the organization – not primarily to make employees more willing to obey authorities. Higher levels of job satisfaction and morale was, according to his model, a byproduct of the process, which in turn would create an atmosphere for even more creative problem-solving.

During the ten years following Miles's contribution, the concept of managing human resources was not considered a hot topic in academic writings. A review of published articles, in scientific journals, focusing on "human resources" shows that research during the 1970s had a strong focus on "human resource accounting" and on the difficulties of evaluating human resources.[1] Interestingly, the term "Human Resource Management" was gaining popularity in managerial practice in the mid-1970s, and little by little it more or less replaced the term "personnel management" in many companies (Berglund, 2002). Nevertheless, the change in terminology did not really imply a change in approach or content. For example, Guest (1987) argued that many personnel departments were turned into human resource departments without any real change in functions or roles. For some time, in many cases, the two terms were used interchangeably, even though HRM terminology was considered more up-to-date (Kaufman, 2007). Many have retrospectively argued that the increased use of HRM terminology marked a qualitative shift in the view of employees and in the management of the workforce, resulting in a closer alignment to business, in the involvement of line managers, and in a greater focus on HRM outcomes (Brewster and Larsen, 2000; Paauwe, 2009).

The breakthrough of the HRM concept

In the 1980s, discussions of the differences between traditional personnel management and human resource management were intensified in academic writings. One line of thought argued that HRM terminology actually represented a new management philosophy, a new paradigm fundamentally different from the traditional approach on how to manage the workforce (Kaufman, 2007). The debate was particularly influenced by Japanese quality models and ideas of creating "excellent companies" (e.g., Peters and Waterman, 1982), which encouraged new ways of thinking about management in general and human resources in particular. At this time, many North American corporations were threatened by competition from rapidly expanding and highly efficient Japanese players. Japanese management traditions, based on strong relationships between employee and employer, lifelong employment contracts, and working methods directed at quality rather than cost management, strongly contributed to the rising interest in the HRM approach at this particular time (e.g., Guest, 1987; Hendry and Pettigrew, 1990). This rise of Japanese management models had a number of implications on the thinking about HRM around the world, which subsequently triggered considerable managerial efforts and research on corporate cultures, loyalty, and identity. The proponents of HRM increasingly proclaimed a strategic approach to the management of workers. In their view, employees should be seen as important strategic resources, not as costs that ought to be minimized. As a consequence, personnel/HR departments needed to get more integrated into the firm's operations, including strategic decision-making and organizational change. In many ways, the idea of strategic resources resonates with the original ideas Penrose presented 30 years earlier.

The emergence of the HRM concept was highly influenced by two intellectual developments: strategic management, on the one hand,

and human relation/organizational behavior, on the other (Hendry and Pettigrew, 1990; Kaufman, 2007). These two fields coalesced under the rubric of HRM, but they still had somewhat different basic assumptions and dominant viewpoints. The main argument for the strategic stream was the need to maximize the contribution of people to the organization. Fombrun et al.'s (1984) "Strategic Human Resource Management" is considered a key text in the early days of the evolution of this view. The authors wrote that the "untapped contributions of the human resources in organizations could make the difference between efficiency and inefficiency, death and survival in the marketplace" (Fombrun et al., 1984, preface) and that the HR system had to be aligned to drive the strategic objectives of the organization.

The Human Relations viewpoint, on the other hand, had more of a "developmental-humanist" perspective (Hendry and Pettigrew, 1990; Legge, 2005). One of the key texts representing this view was *Managing Human Assets*, written by Michael Beer and his fellow colleagues at Harvard Business School (Beer et al., 1984). These authors emphasized the importance to innovate in HRM practices to "build a relationship between the organization and its employees that will pass the tests of greater competition and the shrinking economic pie" (p. 7). They also stressed that due to the demand for a more strategic perspective on the organization's human resources, HRM should be a chief concern of general management rather than being seen as narrowly defined personnel responsibilities delegated to personnel specialists.

These two influential books were important for the diffusion of this thinking, and the HRM concept rapidly gained ground outside North America. With this diffusion, academic discussions about the subject also broadened. Sisson (1993: 201) argues that HRM was "the industrial relations issue of the 1980s and early 1990s," and Kaufman (2007: 36) speaks of a "veritable explosion of writing and research on strategic aspects of HRM" in those same decades. Guest (1987) discusses several driving forces responsible for the large impact of the HRM concept at that time. He particularly highlights the development of a workforce with higher educational levels that would have higher expectations and demands, and also the changing technologies and structural trends which would lead to more flexible jobs. Together, this required a new form of managing people in organizations.

In more recent research, several scholars have also considered the growing interest in knowledge, intellectual capital and other intangible resources to be a strong driving force for the development of HRM. For example, Brewster and Larsen (2000: ix) argue that:

> This qualitative shift was caused – and made possible – by changes in societal structure, in particular the transition from a mainly industrial, manufacturing economy to a service- and knowledge-based society. Providing service, knowledge, skills and know-how (at the individual and organizational level) implies a hitherto unseen focus on immaterial resources, core competencies, commitment and other features related to the individuals (that is, human resources) of the organization. The competitive strength of an organization is determined by its ability to attract and develop human resources, rather than optimizing the use of raw materials, machinery and financial resources.

Combined, these standpoints highlight the growth of HRM and resonate with recent calls for HRM having an even more important role in many firms. Recent discourse typically also emphasizes the interactive character of HRM and that HRM is not only in the best interest of the firm. It stresses that people have a larger stake in HRM generally, meaning that they not only expect more from the firm when it comes to HRM but are also expected to assume more responsibilities themselves for various HRM practices.

Research on HRM

Academic discussions in the 1980s and 1990s mainly revolved around definitions, approaches, and conceptual models of HRM, as well as criticizing and questioning its relevance and fundamental assumptions. For example, key themes included whether HRM is really so different from personnel management, or whether it is just a "new label" for the same activities; whether there is an "a priori definition" of what constitutes HRM, or whether it should be broadly defined as a range of activities that affect the employment and contribution of people; and whether HRM is a management model suitable for all types of companies. Another key theme was the link between HRM and firm performance, which continues today to be a key theme in research on HRM (see, for instance, Paauwe, 2009).

Looking at HRM research today, it is a nearly impossible mission to give a comprehensive and fair overview of its many streams, approaches, and subfields. *The Oxford Handbook of Human Resource Management* offers a useful grouping of HRM research into three major categories

(Boxall et al., 2007b): "International HRM," "Micro HRM," and "Strategic HRM." International HRM is concerned with HRM in companies operating in the international arena (such as multinationals), and internationalization processes. Micro HRM covers functions of HR policy and practice, including recruitment, training and development, remuneration, etc. Strategic HRM is viewed in its entirety as including overall HR strategies and their impact on performance, including the connections between business strategy and HRM. Important issues involve how the subfunctions of HRM might fit together as a system and their relationship to a broader context and to other organizational activities, which is largely in line with our focus in this book. We will, therefore, take a closer look at some of the fundamentals within the strategic HRM literature.[2]

The increased importance assigned to the strategic approach to managing people was an important driving force for the development of theories that addressed HRM as a potential source of sustainable competitive advantage (Kamoche, 1996; Lado and Wilson, 1994; Wright et al., 1994). This particular academic interest spurred the rapid development of research emphasizing Strategic Human Resource Management. Allen and Wright (2007) depict this as a relatively new research field that "represents the intersection of the strategic management and human resource management (HRM) literatures" (p. 88). The field of strategic human resource management was inspired and strengthened by theories on the resource-based view of the firm laid out by Wernerfelt (1984) and later popularized – particularly within the strategic management field – by, for example, Barney (1991). Drawing on resource-based theory, HRM can be understood in terms of how it contributes to an organization's growth and competitive advantage. Generally, the resource-based view has played an important part in providing a conceptual basis for asserting that people, and hence HRM, are of strategic importance (Boxall, 1996; Wright et al., 2001). The reason is that this view shifted the focus from external factors affecting and shaping strategy as sources of competitive advantage toward internal firm resources, which justified the strategic value of HRM (Allen and Wright, 2007). According to Boxall (1996), the resource-based theory improves the possibility of valuing HRM for "its potential to create firms which are more intelligent and flexible than their competitors over the long haul, firms which exhibit superior levels of co-ordination and co-operation" (p. 66).

Researchers have widely discussed strategic HRM and its different schools of thought, approaches, and models, and how HRM systems and practices increase performance (Huselid, 1995). Two main schools have dominated the debate: one advocating "best-practice models" and the other advocating "best-fit models" (e.g., Boxall and Purcell, 2000; Delery and Doty, 1996). These two schools will be discussed in the following sections.

Best-practice models: universalistic HRM

The research within the "best-practice school" is typically interested in patterns across sectors and industries and in determinants for success. In that respect, research identifies critical practices that tend to hold no matter the context. Two challenges are commonly addressed in this context. First, how to measure success – at the company level, work-system level, employee level. Second, how to identify key practices. One of the most influential studies is Huselid's (1995) work on so-called High Performance Work Practices and firm performance. This publication led to a host of studies and discussions among scholars regarding the difficulty of relating performance to individual practices. The argument is basically that there are so many other factors at play, such as economic cycles, decisions about technologies and innovation, formation of strategic alliances, internationalization processes, etc., that it would be nearly impossible to relate performance to individual and narrow practices tied to HRM. No matter what, the search for the performance and effects of HRM is, undoubtedly, important for practitioners and scholars within HRM, although there might be a need, as Boxall and Macky (2009) argue, to relate performance to output measurements closer to the particular practice, such as employee satisfaction, teamwork efficiency, and productivity improvements.

What then are the best practices identified in previous research? In Huselid's study best practices included, among other things, information-sharing programs, formal job analysis, internal promotion, Quality of Work Life programs, Quality Circles, incentive plans, training investments, employment tests, and formal performance appraisals. Pfeffer (1998) emphasized the importance of several practices: employment security, selective hiring of new personnel, self-managed teams and decentralized decision-making, comparatively high compensation contingent on organizational performance, extensive training, reduced status distinctions and barriers, and extensive sharing of financial and performance information throughout the organization.

However, other studies take a broader view on best practices. For instance, MacDuffie (1995) measures five practices: work teams, problem-solving groups, employee suggestion schemes, job rotation, and decentralization of quality related tasks. Also, Laursen and Mahnke

(2001) opt for a broader definition of best practices, including inter-disciplinary teams, integration of functions, delegation of responsibility, job rotation, collection of employee proposals, performance-related pay, and training.

Besides the already mentioned problems of performance and identifying specific practices, additional challenges are associated with research within this school. First, there is a problem with this kind of universalistic approach (Delery and Doty, 1996; Martín-Alcázar et al., 2005), since it positions certain practices as being superior in all cases, regardless of context. Second, it tends to ignore the relationship between practices – that some might be reinforcing another, and that there are important complementarities involved (Pfeffer, 1995: 57). Third, as was particularly apparent in the latter examples, the universalistic approach tends to adopt an all-embracing view of HRM – including everything that relates to management and organization as part of HRM and executed through HRM practices. For instance, we would rather locate interdisciplinary teams, integration of functions, and delegation of authority rights as part of management in general and not as part of HRM per se. We do not, however, claim these measures are not important to people or to HRM; rather, we emphasize they cannot be confined to HRM only because these measures are primarily taken to improve the integrative capability and the problem-solving processes within the firm.

Best-practice models are often criticized for ignoring contexts and differences among firms, the variations in goals among firms, and the integration and interdependence of practices (Boxall and Purcell, 2000; Martín-Alcázar et al., 2005). It should also be noted that the critique tends to be simplistic at times. For example, Pfeffer (1995) does point out that "it is important to recognize that the practices are interrelated – it is difficult to do one thing by itself with a positive result." He also suggests that very few companies can implement all the suggested practices, and that "which practice is most critical does depend in part on the companies' particular technology and market strategy" (p. 67). So a more nuanced description of this approach would be that it puts less emphasis on context and internal synergies among practices and more emphasis on the parts of HR management practices that seem more generally applicable than others. As argued by Boxall and Purcell (2000), there are aspects of "best practice" that are widely acknowledged and accepted among practitioners as well as researchers and, certainly within the category of project-based organizations, there are specific practices that are more successful than others.

Best-fit models: contingent HRM

The "best-fit school," sometimes referred to as the contingency approach within HRM, emphasizes instead the need of HRM practices to be aligned and integrated with the overall business strategy as well as with organizational and environmental contingencies (see, e.g., Delery and Doty, 1996). Authors within this school typically suggest different kinds of models for how a firm can achieve the best fit. One of the most cited works is that of Schuler and Jackson (1987), which links HRM practices to Porter's (1985) generic competitive strategies, and suggests three "archetypes" of combinations of strategy and HRM practices. Another is that of Guest (1987), who argues that HRM policies must be integrated into the strategic plan and that practices must be coherent when applied. Followers develop this line of argument and suggest models in terms of "horizontal" and "vertical" fit. Vertical fit refers to the fit between HRM policies and practices and firm strategy, while horizontal fit refers to the internal fit among individual HRM policies and practices (see overviews by, e.g., Boxall and Purcell, 2000; Legge, 2005). Interestingly, the fit between company structure and HRM has been rarely discussed, a topic of high relevance to the arguments of this book. One of the very few contributions is that of Begin (1993), who suggests a set of HRM systems configurations depending on the type of organizational structure.

According to Boxall and Purcell (2000), the first models of best fit were relatively thin since they largely failed to recognize both the importance of aligning employee interests with the firm and the complexity of HRM. Researchers within this tradition had, for methodological reasons, a tendency to search for correlations between two variables, which led them to fail to spot "much of the interactive, multivariate complexity of strategic management in the real world" (Boxall and Purcell, 2000: 188). The resultant models, as such, have also been criticized for being too focused on profitability, productivity, and cost efficiency and, hence, neglected other dimensions of performance such as values related to individuals and their relationships and interactions, and also the social responsibility of organizations. In response to this, the best-fit school has moved toward "configurational" and "contextual" approaches (see overviews by, e.g., Martín-Alcázar et al., 2005). The configurational approach is concerned with unique patterns of individual HRM policies and practices and how they are related to firm performance (see, e.g., Delery and Doty, 1996). This approach is accordingly interested in "unique-fit" models rather than "best-fit" models. One example is MacDuffie (1995), who argues that "research that focuses on the impact of individual HRM practices on performance may produce misleading results, with a single practice capturing the effect of the entire HRM system" (p. 200). MacDuffie, therefore, suggests it is more relevant to analyze a firm's HRM practices as an internally consistent "bundle," or a system of interrelated elements, which contributes to productivity and quality. Unlike many other contributions, MacDuffie also emphasizes the integration of the "HR bundle" with the "bundle of manufacturing practices." He argues that research "has overemphasized either the technical system or the HRM system without fully exploring the interaction of the two systems and how it can affect performance" (MacDuffie, 1995: 217). For the contextual approach, the focus is not so much on internal configurations or individual HRM practices but, rather, on the reciprocal relationships between the HRM system and its broader internal and external contexts. For example, Paauwe's (2004) "contextually-based human resource theory" aims at addressing the tension between economic rationality and relational rationality in the shaping of HRM policies and practices. Paauwe also discusses the "administrative heritage" and path dependency of HRM as important factors influencing the structure and design of HRM (see Barney, 1991). This contextual and unique-fit analysis then also draws attention to the difficulties of imitating HRM systems from other companies. This generally stresses that HRM systems need to be built on an understanding of the internal and external trajectories that have shaped the firm and its HRM practices.

The foregoing overview has shown the development of the field of HRM and the growth in research. It has also tried to point out the inherent differences between the universalistic approach and the contextual approach. The present book, as mentioned, is an attempt to draw attention to the importance of the context of the project-based organization. Thereby one might view the studies presented here largely as the natural progression to some of the work just discussed. We will return in the next chapter to the specific approach suggested and how this approach tries to reformulate the idea of context and contingency views on HRM. First, however, we need to frame and formulate the idea and definition of HRM that will be subscribed to and the inherent problems in arriving at a clear-cut definition of the complex notion of HRM.

Managing the relationship between people and organization

As the foregoing review demonstrates, the concept of HRM has its provenance in a variety of theoretical and practical fields, and the development of HRM research generally reflects a large spectrum of definitions and approaches. In the following, we will discuss the particular approach and definition of HRM adopted in this book. We consider HRM to include all activities directly linked to the management of the relationship between people and the organization in which they work. This definition puts a great emphasis not only on the "HRM system" as such but also on the organizational context in which it operates and on the people who offer their services to the organization. We believe there is an important distinction between HRM and other areas of management, although HRM, to some extent, will be affected by other management decisions, such as strategy, technology, and innovation; the reverse is also true – that purely HRM-oriented decisions, such as recruitment and competence development, will influence strategy, technology, and innovation. This, again, points to the relationship between the two sets of capabilities mentioned in the first chapter of the book.

As discussed, some of the initial considerations about the definition of HRM concerned whether it was a new "management philosophy" or just another label for personnel management (see Guest, 1987; Legge, 2005; Sisson and Storey, 2003). In fact, did not HRM basically cover the same activities as traditional personnel management, even though it had been renamed to capture new trends and the modernization needed due to a changing environment? Many proponents of HRM had argued that the concept and idea of HRM actually implied a new management philosophy that could offer an alternative approach to management, which departed to a much greater extent from the strategic importance of matching the needs and wishes of the individual worker to the needs of the organization. These arguments often implied that HRM did not necessarily replace personnel administration/management; it was rather an alternative to it that largely went against the old ideas of personnel administration. In his well-cited article from 1987, Guest stated that HRM was usually contrasted with personnel management, using the assumption that HRM was better, but without taking variations in context into consideration. However, Guest suggested there might be organizational contexts in which traditional personnel management could be more successful:

> Until convincing evidence to the contrary is available, this suggests that human resource management can most sensibly be viewed as one approach to managing work force. Other approaches are equally legitimate and likely in certain contexts to be more successful. (Guest, 1987: 508)

Thus, this view considered HRM to be "a special variant" of personnel management, reflecting a particular discipline or ideology regarding how employees should be treated (Legge, 2005: 107). It seems quite reasonable that this definition was dominant in the 1980s, when the ideas were new and posed a clear contrast to traditional personnel management. However, since then, the ideas of HRM have come to be the dominant ones, and today this is probably regarded as general knowledge about people management in any company. HRM can, in that sense, be seen as part of what sometimes has been described as a "paradigm shift" in the management of work and employees. Employees and human resources, as well as the way they are managed, have become recognized as key elements for success and, as Brewster and Larsen (2000: 2) stated, "It is, therefore, no surprise that the importance of HRM as an institutionalized way of handling the central issues of selecting, appraising and developing people has grown in prominence over the past few years." This institutionalization of HRM is also apparent in the *Oxford Handbook of Human Resource Management*, in which Boxall, Purcell, and Wright portray HRM as "a fundamental activity in any organization in which human beings are employed" (Boxall et al., 2007a: 1). They further argue that:

> HRM is an inevitable consequence of starting and growing an organization. While there are a myriad of variations in the ideologies, styles, and managerial resources engaged, HRM happens in some form or another. (Boxall et al., 2007a: 1)

Brewster and Larsen point out that one important aspect of the definition of HRM is that it is based on the assumption of an interaction between people and their organizational context:

> An assumption in traditional personnel management activities has been the perception of the organization as an extraneous, given and stable context for these activities – without actually interacting with them. Such a view on the personnel activities has lost credibility and legitimacy, because it disregards the contextual impact on human resource issues. By contrast, HRM rests on the assumption of an organizational interplay between individuals and their organizational contexts. (Brewster and Larsen, 2000: 2–3)

This interplay is at the core of the treatment of HRM in the present book. HRM can be defined as one area of management among many, others being innovation, finance, project, marketing, etc. More specifically, HRM concerns the management of the relationship between people and the organization in which they work. Accordingly, the term "HRM" can be seen as a descriptive label for a specific area of management. However, while traditional views of personnel management defined it as the "management of employees," the definition of HRM subscribed to in this book stresses that the area concerns the "management of the relationship" between people and their organization. Apart from Brewster and Larsen, quoted earlier, this definition builds on, for example, Beer et al.'s (1984: 1) work, referring to HRM as "all management decisions and actions that affect the nature of the relation between the organization and employees."

In sum, this book departs from the definition of HRM as the area of management directed toward the management of the relationship between people and their organizational context. "Relationship" here refers to a mutual professional relationship, in which the individuals offer the organization their services as a labor force, which include their skills, competence, knowledge, experience, contacts, etc. In return, the organization compensates the individuals in different ways, including with money, career opportunities, challenges, motivation, a good work environment, personal development, competence development, etc.

Three important implications

Defining HRM in this way has, at a minimum, three important implications for the study of HRM in project-based organizations. These implications can be viewed as key components of the definition of HRM relied on in the present book: organizational context, people, and relationship. In continuing, we will discuss the important implications which also point out the relevance of the chosen definition, particularly for the study of HRM in project-based organizations.

First, the organizational context is critical for the relationships and, thereby, also for the management of the relationships. The definition rests on the assumption of an active relationship between people and the organizational context, and, logically, both parties influence the nature of the relationship. This implication makes the organizational context highly relevant for our research. As mentioned earlier, the studies presented here are based on an overarching idea that HRM needs to be addressed and understood as dependent on its context. This is also a cornerstone in Boxall et al.'s (2007a) discussion of the academic discipline of HRM, in which they point out the importance of having a deep respect for context. The research reported in this book takes its departure from the basic assumption that the internal organizational context, particularly the operational work setting, has a major influence on the requirements placed on HRM.

Second, all people who contribute to the organization take part in performing HRM. Taking into account that individualization, empowerment, "coworkership," and the notion of "staying employable" are important trends in HRM and in contemporary working life (see, e.g., Tengblad, 2003), it seems more appropriate to regard all individuals who contribute to an organization as partly responsible for managing human resources. As stated by Heimer (1984: 305) in her study of career development in engineering project work, the individual needs to "fashion his or her work situation and career trajectory so that he or she develops in a satisfactory way, retains some control over his or her own fate, and has an acceptable day-to-day experience." If people want to stay with their current employer, they need to ensure they possess and develop the competences their organization needs and maintain beneficial relationships with the organization. She also points out that when an employer tries to stimulate loyalty by supporting their employees in building a solid experience base and "spreading the word" about their qualifications, this is also making the employees more independent. They are then able to rely more on their reputation and own capabilities and less on certification from the home organization. According to Heimer, this actually becomes a win-win situation in which both the organization and the individual gain better control. If the current employer does not offer the right challenges and development opportunities, however, individuals are likely to turn to seek other, more developing organizations. In sum, the definition of HRM subscribed to in this book expands to include employees as active participants in managing human resources instead of regarding them as passive receivers of HRM practices.

Third, HRM is about managing the relationship between the organization and the people who contribute to the organization, which might include more than permanent employees. Several studies reveal that modern organizations become increasingly flexible and project-based and that this also makes them rely, to a greater extent, on short-term and flexible employment contracts (e.g., Ekstedt, 2002; Whitley, 2006). The definition of who provides the human resources then becomes fundamental. As discussed in Chapter 2, project-based organizations often rely on a multi-employment workforce, meaning that the ratio of involvees to employees is relatively high (see Hedberg et al., 1997).

Whittington et al. (1999: 587) similarly discuss the changing boundaries of organizations and argue that competitive pressures force companies to "focus on 'core competencies', redrawing their boundaries around what constitutes or supports their true competitive advantage." Yet while the number of permanent employees might be reduced through such redrawing of boundaries, the number of individuals who offer their services to the organization is in many cases growing. Consequently, from the organization's perspective, it would be inaccurate to delimit HRM to cover only the management of the relationship with permanent employees.

HRM practice areas

HRM -
✳ Four Generic Functions

After having presented how we define HRM in this book, we now turn to the more operational parts of this area of management. What kinds of activities and practices are we talking about, and how is HRM structured? One of the seminal suggestions of HRM's core practice areas is presented by Devanna et al. (1984). They refer to four generic functions for HRM: selection, appraisal, development, and rewards. These functions "are ideally designed to have an impact on performance at both the individual and the organizational levels" (Devanna et al., 1984: 41). In contemporary HRM literature, the same functions are still considered to be at the core, although a review of mainstream HRM writings over the past 20 years depicts a more elaborate image of areas that have come to be considered key for HRM. For example, in the *Oxford Handbook of Human Resource Management* (Boxall et al., 2007b), the generic functions suggested by Devanna et al. (1984) are reflected in most of the core processes and functions discussed: recruitment and selection, training and development, competence, and performance management and remuneration. However, other areas are also highlighted, such as work organization, equal employment opportunities, diversity management, and employee voice systems.

In order to attain a picture of the core practice areas of HRM, we have reviewed the most well-cited publications covering the period from 1984–2007.[3] The HRM processes and activities focused in these works were listed and categorized according to their main functions and purposes. The intention was to group the different activities, practices, and processes into a few overall categories, here referred to as "HRM practice areas." We also focused on the narrow issues of HRM, leaving out the ones we considered were primarily within other management areas, such as technology management, project management, or change

[handwritten: ✳ Four Core Practice Areas]

management. As for the latter, there is of course a component of change in all activities, so also for the practice areas singled out here. As a result, four core "practice areas" emerged: Flows, Performance, Involvement and Development. In the following, we will briefly introduce these areas, as they will be a recurring part of the chapters to come.

[handwritten: 1.]

[handwritten: Flow of people.]

Flows: This practice area includes all management activities directed toward "managing the flow of people *in, through,* and *out* of the organization" (Beer et al., 1984: 64, emphasis in original). More specifically, the area thus deals with (1) in- and out-flows of human resources across organizational boundaries, and (2) internal flows, for example, job rotation and assignment to/release from project assignments and project teams. When it comes to the management of boundary-crossing flows, recruitment and selection are core activities. Moreover, the increased use of temporary workforce, flexible contracts (free agents), and strategic collaborations with consulting agencies (intermediary solutions) have come to be a paramount aspect of the management of flows. This has created new forms of "boundary-spanning" human resources and "boundaryless careers" which put greater pressure on organizations to develop their HRM practices concerning the management of flows (Arthur and Parker, 2002; Ekstedt, 2002; Garsten, 2008; Weick, 1996). Managing internal flows concerns the internal mobility of human resources. For this book, the flow between line units and project teams, and from one project team to another, is of particular interest. Although the temporary and cross-functional features of the project-based organization, discussed in Chapter 2, highlight the intense and continuous flow of human resources, only a few studies have addressed how this flow could be managed from an HRM point of view (see, e.g., Huemann et al., 2004). Nevertheless, we believe that a well-managed flow (boundary-crossing as well as internal) is critical – not only for the organization's capability to ensure the continuous supply of human resources but also for maintaining mutually beneficial relationships between mobile workers, be it free agents, intermediary consultants, or permanently employed project workers, and the organizations that benefit from their services.

[handwritten: 2.]

Performance: In a way, of course, all four practice areas aim at enhancing and improving the individual's performance – directly or indirectly. In this area, we include (1) influencing the design of work settings and support in order to ensure that people get the proper work conditions to perform a good job, and (2) appraisal and feedback systems, which in turn are closely tied to reward systems. With regard to the first set of activities, they range from dealing primarily with hygiene factors (Herzberg, 1966), such as physical work conditions and administrative matters, to enhancing more motivational factors, such as achievement, responsibility, job satisfaction, and "work itself" (Dunn, 2001). For example, in our research we have noted that line managers and project managers spend quite some time thinking of how best to design knowledge sharing/knowledge integration systems, and that many of them would appreciate more input from HR specialists in these processes. Studies of project-based organizations often stress the importance of capabilities for integrating different knowledge bases in order to perform well in their processes of complex problem-solving (e.g., Brusoni and Prencipe, 2001; Sydow et al., 2004; see also Chapter 1). In this book, we argue that HRM has an important role to play in the development of such capabilities. Turning to the second set of activities – appraisal, feedback, and rewards – their importance for employees' performance and motivation to improve that performance is hard to dispute. However, as we will see further on in this book, the project-based work setting creates a number of challenges with regard to how to ensure trustworthy procedures for these critical activities (see also Bredin and Söderlund, 2006; Hobday, 2000; Turner et al., 2008).

Involvement: The activities related to this practice area concerns the individual's influence over what happens in the organization, and participation in decisions that affect their work and work conditions. As discussed earlier in this chapter, such practices have historically tended to be based on a rationale that people are more willing to comply with authority if they feel they have had an influence (Miles, 1965). However, from an HRM point of view, the real meaning of involvement practices is instead focused on the mutually beneficial relationship between people and organization: to ensure people are given the opportunity to contribute with their knowledge and experience in order to improve and develop the organization. The area could be divided into at least two sets of activities: (1) those directed at employees' participation in decision-making processes, and (2) those directed at employees' influence over their work conditions. It should be clarified that, in the concept of "employee", we include all people working in the organization – regardless of employment form (cf previous discussions on "involvees", Hedberg et al., 1997). As to the first set of activities, these range from employees' direct and individual involvement in making decisions in dialogue with managers or by one's own mandate, to indirect and collective involvement through trade unions or work councils and through shared owner-ship schemes (Torrington et al., 2008). The second set of activities regards, instead, the employees' possibilities to influence, for exam-ple, working hours, future assignments, content of work, etc. Several studies indicate the ambiguities of project-based work relating to this issue. On the one hand, project workers often experience a greater freedom and more potential for controlling their own work (see, e.g., Hovmark and Nordqvist, 1996). On the other hand, project workers normally have to operate within strict deadlines, which might cause stress-related problems and diminish the feeling of control of one's own work situation. Moreover, project workers, particularly those in multiproject settings, often have the demand of coordinating their work with that of other members of the project and/or with other projects (Zika-Viktorsson et al., 2006). As indicated in the study by Zika-Viktorsson et al. (2006: 390), "The person in question may have autonomy with regard to technical solutions, but is still governed by what happens (or not) in surrounding projects." Earlier in this book, we also referred to some critical voices claiming that project manage-ment uses the rhetoric of freedom and autonomy, but is really a way of instituting bureaucratic control principles that actually reduce cre-ativity and freedom (Hodgson, 2004, see Chapter 1). There is clearly a bright side and a dark side of project management, both of which are of great importance for the HRM practice area of Involvement.

Development: This practice area deals with development of human resources on an individual level as well as on more aggregate levels (such as unit or organizational levels). In a way, the activities of this area aim at giving the "flow" of human resources a dimension of long-term development of competences and a career trajectory that is beneficial for both the individuals and the organization. In their seminal book, *Managing Human Assets*, Michael Beer and his colleagues clarified:

> Individual careers develop from an interaction between the com-petencies and career goals an individual brings to the organization and the work experience the organization provides. To the extent that the organization provides opportunities for the individual to use and develop his or her personal competence while moving through various jobs, functions, and levels, the individual will grow and experience satisfaction. (Beer et al., 1984: 68)

Consequently, in this area we include two highly intertwined sets of activities: (1) those directed toward competence development, and

(2) those revolving around careers. Competence development concerns a wide range of activities, of which some are the prime responsibility of the organization (such as competence mapping, strategic competence planning, support to employees in their competence development) and others are the prime responsibility of the individuals themselves (e.g., individual competence development plans, active participation in development programs, and striving for developing assignments; see, e.g., Jackson et al., 2009). Here, the interplay among individuals, managers (line managers as well as project managers), and HR specialists becomes crucial since "as an organization begins to embrace a philosophy of continuous learning and improvement, more active participation in the design and delivery of the organization's training system by all stakeholders is seen as both desirable and necessary" (Jackson et al., 2009: 208). Competence development activities normally include training programs and courses but, as Beer et al. (1984) also point to in the quote above, the primary part is the competence developed on the job. This is, of course, tightly linked to the individual's career development and activities concerning career systems, which are particularly interesting and challenging in project-based organizations. Several researchers argue that traditional "moving-up-the-ladder" career systems are not adequate to motivating project workers and supporting their career development. For example, a survey of "project-oriented engineers" performed by Allen and Katz (1995) showed that many of them were not interested in promotion in the traditional sense of moving up the ladder. What they aspired for was interesting and challenging projects.

> These engineers were motivated to perform well on current project assignments in the belief that superior performance would increase the likelihood that their next assignment would be an interesting one. Conversely, there was a belief that poor performance led to a less interesting future assignment. (Allen and Katz, 1995: 129)

Thus, it might be more important for project workers to develop a reputation of being good performers in order to build an interesting and challenging personal project portfolio for their careers. Similarly, Keegan and Turner (2003) discuss careers in project-based firms and argue that "there is a shift from viewing careers in terms of promotion and subordinates to viewing careers as continuous processes of learning and successful completion of projects" (p. 7). These studies, hence, document the importance of adapting career systems to the project-based work setting, and they similarly indicate the individuals' own responsibility for career development activities. As argued by Larsen (2002: 37), it is "a matter of one's ability to create one's own career path…based on knowledge, initiative, and the capability to employ oneself."

The four HRM practice areas are summarized in Table 3.1.

The categorization is primarily intended to offer a framework that can be applied for the analysis of HRM in project-based organizations. It does not rule out important linkages between the different areas. Instead, our configurational approach to HRM highlights the importance of seeing these linkages as interrelated and part of the HRM system. However, for analytical reasons, they are intentionally kept apart. Moreover, in some organizations, a few areas will be more strategically important than others, which points out that the significance of each area is contextually dependent.

HRM in an organization can, therefore, be seen as having a unique configuration in content, referring to the specific bundle of HRM practices. For example, what kinds of recruitment and selection processes are used? Which practices and activities are relied upon in the appraisal and reward system? Which practices and activities are critical for the organization's competence development system? What kinds of career structures are applied? As discussed in previous sections, one approach to HRM is that there are several "best practices" or best solutions regarding the management of human resources that generally lead to increasingly higher performance regardless of the organization's strategy or structure. However, drawing on the configurational and contextual

Table 3.1   HRM practice areas

HRM practice area	Focus
Flows	In- and out-flows of human resources across organizational boundaries. Internal flows: job rotation, mobility in line as well as in project dimensions.
Performance	Design of work settings that allow for high performance and enhancement of proper and motivating work conditions. Appraisal, feedback, and reward systems.
Involvement	Involvement in decision-making processes. Individual influence on work and work conditions.
Development	Competence development. Career systems and development.

approaches, HRM should depend on factors such as the characteristics of the organization and its work systems, of employees and their human resources, and of the employment form.

HRM also has a structural dimension, which refers to the role arrangement of players that is significant in carrying out various practices. This is a topic that has not been fully covered in extant HRM literature and reflects a general weakness in HRM research. Even though most HRM research and mainstream textbooks generally agree on the important role of, for instance, line managers and general managers in performing HRM, existing research tends to focus on the role of HR specialists and the HR department. The argument seems to be that since HRM is becoming increasingly recognized as central for the competitiveness of a firm, the HR department must change. For example, Lawler (2005: 165) uses the term "HR" synonymously with HR department when he argues that "HR can and should add more value to corporations. ... It needs to move beyond performing the many administrative and legally mandated tasks that traditional personnel functions have performed."

However, other players are critical participants for the outcome of HRM practices. The active role of all individuals who contribute with their human resources in managing the relationship to their organization has already been mentioned. Depending on the character of the organization, other players might also be crucial. For example, in organizations where projects play a key part, project managers typically assume a greater responsibility for some HRM practices. Our point is that HRM is organized in different ways and includes different key players, depending on the characteristics of the organization and the people in it.

Thus, when discussing the structure of the HRM system, we suggest the distinction between the "HR department" and the "HR organization." While the HR department refers to the unit of HR specialists within the organization, the HR organization refers to the entire structure of roles that are central in delivering value to the HRM system. The HR department is a player that might, but does not necessarily, have an important role in the HR organization. For example, the Danish hearing-aid company Oticon, studied by Larsen (2002), did not have a dedicated HR department when the new, purely project-based organizational structure was first implemented. Instead, project team leaders, coaches, and the employees themselves were the central players in performing HRM. This implies that an efficient and well-functioning HRM system does not rely completely on an effective HR department but rather on an overall effective HR organization. As will be shown later, however, our argument is that in most cases HR specialists have a role to play, although this role tends to depend on the activities of the other players in the HR organization.

Addressing the operational level in project-based organizations

In this chapter, we have given an overview of the rise and breakthrough of the concept of HRM and a brief introduction to HRM as a professional domain and research field. We have also tried to outline key theoretical and practical ideas underlying our take on HRM. This section extends a few of the basic points further and presents them in a series of trajectories to position our research in relation to extant theory and what key sources we draw upon to establish our view on HRM:

1. Human resources are resources. This calls on resource-based theory as an important fundamental analytical viewpoint of the thoughts presented in the book. This also stresses the fact that resources need to be made resources – and this is a mutual responsibility of the employer and personnel. In that respect, this mutuality and its dynamics illustrate that human resources are quite specific kinds of resources, for instance, and that they not only have the capacity to learn and adapt but equally have the capacity to change the organizational context as such.
2. HRM is seen as one area of management, and most management decisions have some implications on HRM, such as a decision to fund a particular innovative project, although some are uniquely and directly dealing with HRM, such as recruitment. In that respect, a host of management decisions have implications for HRM; however, not all management decisions are HRM decisions.
3. HRM is the management of the relationship between people and their organizational context, which means the individual workers themselves play a critical role in performing HRM functions. Successful HRM depends to a great extent, therefore, on the active involvement of the human resources.
4. Human resources are found both within and outside a firm's boundaries. This means that permanent employees are not the only part of the equation, as other human resources, such as temporary employees, might also be critical.
5. HRM is, from the organization's point of view, fundamentally a collective act among several players; the HR department is often one

important player; however, most functions are carried out operationally by others, such as line managers and project managers.

6. HRM is strategic, but much of it is performed at the operational level, and to some extent the operational issues and problems need to be sorted out in order for long-term planning and strategic vision to be facilitated.

These basic points require a few explanations and clarifications. The research presented in the present book follows the research tradition of strategic human resource management, with resource-based theories of the firm as an important cornerstone together with the important insights of configurational and contextual approaches. The latter will be discussed in further detail in the next chapter.

We presented our view on HRM and how it relates to present theorization within the field and what major practice areas are tied to this definition. The key issue was HRM as the area of management that in a broad sense relates to people and their work situation, specifically, the relationship between the human resources and their organizational context. This definition then emphasizes the importance of the organizational context which is an important message in this book – in particular the context of a project-based organization which we believe offers a host of interesting and important HRM topics. This means we basically align with much of the work that so far has been done within the area of strategic HRM and that we try to make use of many of the insights produced within this tradition. However, we differ from this tradition on an important count, namely, that we are not specifically interested in the strategy of the firm as such and, instead, we call for more operational grounding to better design HR organizations. Consistent with this stance, there exists a slight criticism of some of the literature. Several researchers have argued along similar lines – that the domain of HRM has tended to exaggerate the corporate and strategic levels (see, e.g., Francis and Keegan, 2006; MacDuffie, 1995) at the expense of everyday HRM and employee well-being. Thus, our concern is similar to MacDuffie's (1995), namely, that the strong focus on the strategic level has created a disregard for the basic operational work settings in which many HRM activities are performed. Therefore, we specifically address the HR organization at the operational level, closely related to, and even embedded in, the project-based work setting.

The way we define HRM also highlights employees as active performers of HRM instead of passive receivers, including those with permanent and nonpermanent relationships with the organization, given the risk of narrowing down HRM to only considering permanent employees when a large group of people with other types of contracts also contribute to human resources. Thus, when we refer to employees and workers, we are generally talking about all people supplying human resources to the organization, that is, permanent employees, temporarily hired consultants, employees of partner firms coming in to do critical work in an ongoing project, etc.

One important point we want to make with this book is to demonstrate the importance of regarding HR specialists/the HR department as only one of several players in the HR organization and not the only one, and in many cases, not even the most central one when it comes to carrying out HRM activities. In today's companies, there is a general trend to decentralizing HR responsibilities to line managers and of downsizing and centralizing HR departments. This trend can certainly be questioned concerning its foundation in the specific needs of the organizations. Is it based on the need to cut costs or on the need to improve the quality of the HR organization and what it delivers? Either way, it definitely changes the division of roles and responsibilities among the players in the HR organization. In this book, we report on studies that demonstrate changes in content as well as in structure of HRM in firms. However, the framework we use to analyze these changes is basically a framework for understanding the HR organization at the operational level in project-based firms. In our research, we have seen that very interesting and prominent changes at the operational level in our studied firms are tied to the roles and players in the HR organization and that these changes were also in many ways associated with the changes in the HRM processes and activities. In the next chapter, we introduce this framework, which we have named "the HR quadriad."

Final thoughts

HRM is a fascinating area of research and practice, which has value for all managers and workers. It is an area that has grown rapidly in recent years with many new journals, conferences, and solid publications. As Paauwe (2009) formulated it:

> HRM, as a field of study, is increasingly generating research approaches and conceptual frameworks of its own that are being explored, tested and examined using a range of both quantitative and qualitative techniques and drawing on a variety of theoretical and methodological perspectives. This is indeed a vibrant field of inquiry with

an impressive, and ever increasing, number of contributors. At the same time, it is important to remember that this is a young field of study. And like all new areas of inquiry there have been important advances that have been made over the past 20 years. But much, as is to be expected, still needs to be done. (Paauwe, 2009: 139)

At the same time, there are so many critical decisions taken every day that concern HRM. To some extent, many of these decisions are taken without proper analysis and understanding of their effects. In Japan, lifetime employment, which never applied to most labor markets in the rest of the world, is severely under attack. There are daily calls, according to Pfeffer (2010), for European countries to follow the US model and make labor markets more "flexible." Critical voices say that companies "should do away with their HR department," "outsource it," or at least change it fundamentally, as in the case with SAS Institute, advised by its potential underwriter to change its HRM rationale to look more like a software company which would increase the valuation of the company before going public. As Jeffrey Pfeffer argued in a *Newsweek* article, the more you examine some of these tactics of modern management, "the more wrongheaded" they seem to be.

We should say that we are of course not addressing all these issues. However, the ultimate raison d'être of the book is to contribute to the debate and the proper analysis of what firms do within the area of HRM, why they do it, how they should do it, and the consequences of their actions. The next chapter presents a framework we believe is beneficial to the proper analysis of HRM in one important context: the project-based organization. This organizational ideal is spread around the world, to a great extent driven by technological innovation and the new era of production, involving considerable flexible specialization and because more and more companies, at least in the Western world, do not make products – instead they develop and "initiate them" (Bell, 1999: xli). Although one might argue against the benefits of adopting a project-based organization, in most cases we do not really see a reasonable alternative. Instead, we need to work with what we have and develop knowledge about how to do it better, while accurately addressing the initiatives that will lead to improvements in HRM – initiatives that are good for people and good for their organizations.

4
Reframing HRM: The HR Quadriad

Addressing HRM in project-based organizations

The first three chapters documented some of the challenges and difficulties associated with HRM in project-based organizations. We have
discussed the context in which we are particularly interested: the
project-based organization and the specific reasons why we consider
HRM to be important to furthering the understanding of the challenges for the project-based organization. By so doing, we also emphasized why the project-based organization offers such an interesting
arena for the explorations of current and important HRM challenges.
In that respect, we have formulated the intention of combining and
contributing to two different and distinct areas of inquiry: HRM and
project-based organizations. In the previous chapters, we also tried
to lay the foundation for arguments outlining why the project-based
organization provides such important groundwork for theoretical
explorations within the area of HRM, that HRM needs to be contextualized, and that much can be gained from addressing specific forms,
designs, and types of organization. Thus, HRM differs among contexts;
some similarities exist, but there are also important differences. In

this chapter, we continue along these lines and present further arguments for the approach suggested in this book. We will also further develop some of the statements presented in Chapter 1. Returning to these initial statements, we argue that the "HR quadriad framework" presented in this chapter allows for a better analysis that responds to several of the recent calls for improved research in HRM. Table 4.1 presents the observations and the developed statements and their respective implications.

The initial observations in our research were quite simple: project managers seem to play an important role in HRM since they are increasingly the direct link between employees and the organization. Another observation, which might be debated, was that a project-based organization seems to put more emphasis on the responsibilities of the individual worker in assuming responsibilities for HRM; that is, the individual worker plays a key role in the HRM system of the firm. Of course, one might argue that other organizational contexts also lead to similar consequences that are dependent on people's unique skills. We also noted that the role of the line manager was taking on new forms in project-based organizations. In addition, we followed the debate in a wide range of sectors about the dubious role of the HR department – that it was considerably criticized and that many companies were considering outsourcing to be the next natural step. When consulting the literature, we could not find appropriate or good analyses of these observations, which spurred our interest to investigate them even further. Some of the discussions about HRM we found premature and lacking a thorough analysis. These include discussions such as those on the responsibilities of the line manager and on the plans to outsource many of the conventional HRM activities.

We had also been doing work on project-based organizations, their structure, management control systems, innovation processes, and strategy. We noticed that the context of project-based organization was quite unique, that conventional ideas about management control systems did not apply, that strategy needed to be looked at in a slightly different way, and that innovation was not necessarily the same in a project-based organization as it was elsewhere (see Hobday, 2000). These observations and conclusions naturally inspired us to further investigate the management of human resources in that setting. We also knew about the calls among practitioners and researchers alike for more detailed studies of HRM in project-based organizations. This was, of course, a further driving force for the research presented here.

Table 4.1 Studying HRM in project-based organizations: statements and observations

Statement/observation	Implications for research
Project-based organizations represent one important organizational context which requires new approaches to HRM.	The study of HRM needs to investigate particular kinds of organizational forms and identify variations within each category.
HRM is increasingly distributive and collective and largely carried out in collaboration among actors in the HR organization.	The study of HRM needs to investigate the interplay between actors and identify, more broadly, the significant players within the HR organization.
HRM is not the sole responsibility of the HR department; other actors including line managers and project managers play important roles.	The study of HRM needs to investigate in further detail the role of line managers and project managers in different kinds of project-based organizations.
The operational work setting is critical for the design of HRM in terms of type of project work and project participation. It influences the type of HR support the individual project worker is in need of.	The study of HRM needs to take more interest in the operational HRM practices and elicit the nature of project work, project participation, and what requirements they impose on HRM.
Individuals play an increasingly important role in the design of HRM. Individuals develop skills that are critical for the entire HRM system to communicate with line managers, to work with project managers, and to assist the HR department in developing their services to the project workers.	The study of HRM needs to acknowledge the role of the individual worker in the performance of HRM activities and the responsibilities, problems, and challenges that are involved.
In project-based organizations, a key management role is that of the project manager. The project manager, however, is not only responsible for technology and knowledge integration within the project. To a large extent, the project manager is also involved in the practice areas of managing the flows, performance, involvement and development of human resources.	The study of HRM in a project-based organization needs to specify the role of the project manager and develop the language to be able to address HRM responsibilities other than the formal responsibilities typically residing with the line manager. This would include activities such as performance appraisal, competence development, stress management, and related activities of importance for the work situation of project workers.

HRM at the operational level

During the course of our research, we realized that we repeatedly came across the same three observations concerning previous HRM research, observations that are particularly relevant for the analysis of project-based organizations. The first observation is the imbalanced focus on one actor in the analysis of HRM. Research has tended to emphasize the significance of studying the role of HR specialists, while downplaying other roles that are important for delivering HR value (line managers, project managers, etc.). This broader view seems particularly important to understanding the collective nature of HRM and the ongoing transference of HR responsibilities to line managers (e.g., Cunningham and Hyman, 1999; Larsen and Brewster, 2003; Thornhill and Saunders, 1998). A recent example supporting this broader view is given in Fact Box 4.1.

The second observation revolves around the level of analysis. As mentioned earlier, research on HRM has tended to overstress the corporate and strategic levels of analysis (see, e.g., Francis and Keegan, 2006; MacDuffie, 1995). In the study by Francis and Keegan (2006), this is also brought up as a problematic situation for HR practitioners. Their study shows that the heavy emphasis on the "strategic amplification of

---

Fact Box 4.1 Crafting project-based organizations and moving HRM responsibilities

Huemann (2010) reports on a longitudinal study of a telecom company that changed its structure during a period of 12 years. The company started out as a highly functional and traditional organization and decided to invest more leadership and management resources in the project dimension. By so doing, the company launched project portfolio management to improve the selection and overview of the entire project ensemble and created project management offices to give administrative and leadership support to project managers. The author concludes that the successful change of organizational structures into more project-oriented ones calls for new ideas about HRM. She provides evidence that many HRM tasks are even further distributed in a project-based organization – beyond the line managers, but at the same time a central HR function is required to ensure standardized processes, career opportunities, and incentive systems that support project-based work. Huemann also points out that, to an increasing extent, project managers carry out important parts of HRM for project workers – even if the project manager does not have any formal personnel authority. However, she adds that most project managers were largely unaware of their role in the HRM system.

HR work" has led to a situation in which "employee champion roles" that focus on the people dimension of day-to-day operational issues are less valued than "strategic partner roles" (see Ulrich, 1998). In response to this shortcoming, we specifically address the HR organization at the operational level, closely related to, or even embedded in, the operational work setting.

The third observation is of the consistently low interest in the context of HRM on an operational level. There is a dearth of studies that take the operational work setting into consideration when analyzing roles and practices that are significant for HRM. We expect that the way people are organized to carry out their work – be it in functional departments, cross-functional teams, projects, or other forms – should have a profound impact on the HR roles at an operational level. This viewpoint acknowledges the importance of context and contingency factors; however, our position is one that is more configurational – which acknowledges the interplay between organizational conditions and factors. In this chapter, we focus particularly on project-based organizations, a broad term denoting a variety of organizations with certain characteristics in common: they carry out most of their core activities in projects, and, thus, project work is routine rather than the exception for the people working there (see, e.g., Lindkvist, 2004; Packendorff, 2002; Whitley, 2006).

The intention underlying the framework presented here is twofold: (1) to improve the analysis of HRM in project-based organizations, and (2) to contribute to recent research that seeks to explore the contextual nature of HRM systems in new forms of organizations. Taking the contextual nature seriously would then, in the context of project-based organizations, embrace its collective nature and the observation that HRM is increasingly carried out as a complex interplay between several organizational roles, including the line managers and the individual workers themselves (Bredin and Söderlund, 2007). The "complementary" nature highlights the interdependence between practices and roles in the HRM system, which asserts that changes of one role (responsibilities, training, etc.) or one practice (reward, performance reviews, etc.) have implications on the other roles and the other practices. It would also need to take into account the "configurational" nature of HRM and the fact that HRM systems need to be designed according to a set of multidimensional organizational conditions (Martín-Alcázar et al., 2005). In that respect, HRM systems are better perceived as bundles of roles and practices (MacDuffie, 1995). In the following section, we review the extant literature to build the theoretical cornerstones of the HR quadriad framework, a framework particularly aimed at the analysis of the central HR roles at the operational level in project-based organizations.

Key roles in the HR quadriad

To address our dissatisfaction with these three observations, we have, over the years, been developing the idea of the HR quadriad, which has its foundation in the assertion that HRM is a collective act carried out and influenced by several players within the project-based organization. This point of view corresponds to the definition of HRM as the management of the interplay between employees (as providers of human resources) and the organization (employer). In a project-based organization, there are at least four key players involved: the project worker, the line manager, the project manager, and the HR specialist (Figure 4.1). These players build what we will address as the collective nature of HRM, and we argue that dysfunctions in the HR organization can be explained by the weak interplay between two or more of these players. The following model will lead the way through this chapter and the next four chapters – with a focus on each of the players in the HR quadriad. The HR quadriad as such is not only a model indicating four players; we argue that it is much more than that. It is a general view of how to design the HR organization of the project-based organization, the driving factors for the choice of design, and the interplay and complementarity between the involved players. As will be discussed in the final chapter of the book, we also believe that the HRM investments of the firm must be viewed in light of these four players and that outcomes

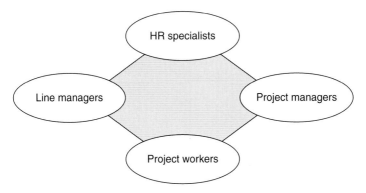

Figure 4.1   The HR Quadriad

might very well be seen by someone else, for instance, educating project workers to assume more responsibilities of competence development which has obvious effects on the work of the HR specialists.

Drawing on the results of our own studies, as well as on previous research on HRM and project-based organizations, we therefore suggest that the HR organization at the operational level in project-based organizations can be described as an HR quadriad consisting of four key roles: line managers, project managers, project workers, and HR specialists.

Line managers: As stressed in recent HRM literature, line managers are important players who deliver HR value to the company. Previous research suggests that the line manager's role in project-based organizations tends to move toward new forms of management (e.g., Bredin and Söderlund, 2007; Larsen and Brewster, 2003). When employees carry out most of their work in different kinds of projects, the line manager role shifts toward a "competence management" role that tends to focus on HR issues, including project staffing, competence development, and career counseling (see also Clark and Wheelwright, 1992).

Project managers: In the project management area, recent studies indicate that project managers play an important role in delivering HR value to project-based organizations (e.g., Bredin and Söderlund, 2006, Fact Box 4.1). This usually concerns direct feedback to employees but is also accomplished through contacts with line managers to give input to the evaluation and review processes. In some cases, the project manager is the project member's closest manager for an extended period of time. Generally, this would increase the HR responsibilities that rest with the project manager. Nevertheless, the HR role of project managers has been given only limited attention in previous research in HRM, and the topic is not an easy one. As Clark and Wheelwright (1992) state, the long-term career development and other long-term people issues cannot reside with the project manager, since project members are not assigned to a project team on a permanent basis. The project is, by definition, a temporary organization.

Project workers: Research on project-based organizing emphasizes the expanded responsibility for each individual employee in project-based work to stay "employable," to drive their own careers, and to develop competence. This development is discussed in further detail by, for example, Arthur et al. (2001) and Garrick and Clegg (2001). As it seems, individual project workers take on an increased responsibility for a variety of HRM processes and activities. This highlights the importance of regarding the individuals in project-based organizations as potentially active and important participants in the HRM process instead of just passive receivers. This development has also been discussed in recent research. For instance, Hällsten (2000) analyzes the decentralization of personnel responsibilities in a project-based organization where HRM essentially refers to the relationships among various parties, of which the coworker is one, and where all parties have a responsibility for maintaining and developing the relationships. This increased individual responsibility has some important positive effects. Nevertheless, there are studies documenting the difficulties and uncertainties that individual project workers must handle as a consequence of this transformation. Frequently, these studies report on the ambiguity and vagueness of HR responsibilities in project-based work settings as a fundamental underlying problem (e.g., Packendorff, 2002; Turner et al., 2008). As documented by Tengblad and Hällsten (2002), the unclear assignment of responsibilities among the different players in the HR organization, especially concerning the individual's role, repeatedly leads to issues falling between the cracks. In the end, many of these issues are left to the individual to handle. This further illustrates the role of the individual worker in the HR organization of the firm, and, consequently, we will regard the individual project worker as holding a critical role in the HR organization, a role that needs to be acknowledged and clarified.

HR specialists: Even though the general rhetoric in both theory and practice has stated that HR specialists and their work need to become more strategic and that operational HRM should be handed over to line managers, the value of HR expertise in operational work settings is highlighted in a number of studies (e.g., Guest and King, 2004; Hope-Hailey et al., 2005; Ulrich and Brockbank, 2005). For example, as stated by Francis and Keegan (2006: 244), "the neglect of people-centered roles is shown to have a negative effect on the sustainability of high firm performance, as employees feel increasingly estranged from the HR department." Previous research on HRM in project-based organizations has shown that access to HR competence that is integrated in the day-to-day activities and that has an understanding of the project-based setting is desired by many line managers and project managers (see, e.g., Bredin and Söderlund, 2006; Clark and Colling, 2005). In practice, however, the strategic focus pointed to above leads to a reduction of HR specialists who are integrated at the operational level, in favor of HR service centers and more strategic HR roles.

In sum, based on previous research into project-based organizations and HRM, we propose that the "HR quadriad" displayed in Figure 4.1 captures the critical constituencies of the HR organization at the operational level in project-based organizations. A quadriad is generally understood to be a group of four with an interest or a task in common. The term links with previous research on HRM. It starts out with the dyad between employer and employees, develops further with the triad including the worker, the HR specialist, and the line manager (Torrington et al., 2008), and finally adds the project manager as the fourth player.

Types of project-based work settings

One of the chief arguments in this book relates to the configurational nature of HRM. In our framework, this implies that the design of the HR quadriad would differ according to certain organizational conditions and contingencies, such as the type of project-based work setting. A number of researchers have developed different typologies or variations of project-based organizations (e.g., Clark and Wheelwright, 1992; Hobday, 2000). Most of them, however, distinguish between organizations with a stronger or weaker project focus, where the project-based organization is seen as one extreme. Instead, we distinguish between different types of project-based work at the operational level, based on the characteristics of the work setting from the perspective of project workers. We argue that two dimensions are particularly important and that, based on the combination of these two dimensions, one might identify two ideal types of "project-based work settings."

The first dimension relates to whether individuals carry out their project work primarily at their line unit, in collaboration with specialists from the same functional area (intra-functional project work), or in project teams, in collaboration with specialists from different functional areas (inter-functional project work). Both types of project work can exist within a project-based organization and the organization can still be equally "project-based," but the logics for organizing the operational work setting are different. Based on this distinction, we argue that different types of project-based work settings might require different designs for the HR quadriad. The first alternative, "intra-functional project work," can be compared with the project matrix, as suggested by Hobday (2000), and the "lightweight team structure," as suggested by Clark and Wheelwright (1992). The average project worker remains co-located in his or her line unit during the course of the project, even though a project core team from different functions may be dedicated and co-located. Line managers are often directly involved in the problem-solving activities in projects; they supervise the work and control key resources. However, this does not mean that project managers are "lightweight" coordinators or that the project dimension is less important than the line dimension. On the contrary, the vast majority of the activities carried out, also in the line units, are essentially project activities, and the projects are the fundamental source of revenue. The second alternative, "inter-functional project work," resembles that work carried out in the "project-led organization" (Hobday, 2000) and the "heavyweight team structure," or even the "autonomous team structure" (Clark and Wheelwright, 1992). In this setting, project workers have a basic long-term affiliation to a line organization of some sort, but they are normally dedicated to, and co-located with, the rest of the members in their project team during the project assignment. Project managers take on more of the management responsibilities concerning the technical problem-solving, whereas line managers are responsible for staffing the projects with the right resources as well as for long-term career development and competence development (Bredin and Söderlund, 2007; Clark and Wheelwright, 1992).

The second dimension that we believe plays an important role in the design of the HR quadriad is the type of project participation. This dimension centers on whether project members are primarily working on one or only a few projects at the same time, or whether their work is distributed over several projects. The first type is addressed here as "focused project participation." In the extreme case, it means that a project worker is assigned to one single project for an extended duration of time. This gives project workers the possibility to focus on one assignment and to build more solid relationships and ways of cooperation within the project team without having to rely on "swift trust" (Meyerson et al., 1996). Since this is normally combined with inter-functional project work in co-located project teams, it probably constitutes a dream scenario for many project managers, giving them dedicated resources co-located as a team to focus on achieving the project goals. At the same time, this situation has a set of challenges from a line management point of view, since it involves an increased distance between project workers, their colleagues with similar knowledge bases, and their personnel responsible managers (see, e.g., Bredin and Söderlund, 2006). However, a more common situation is that of the second type: "fragmented project participation." As the term indicates, this describes a project-based work setting in which project workers normally contribute to various projects at the same time. This is often a necessary way of staffing the projects, given that a project might not need a specific competence on a full-time basis during the entire project life cycle. Therefore, many project teams are more "fluid" in the context of personnel, as project members work part-time on several projects and come and go over the project duration. Several studies indicate that this might bring important challenges from the perspective of employee well-being, as there are risks of feelings of "project overload" and constant "firefighting strategies" which drain energy and reduce motivation (Gällstedt, 2003; Zika-Viktorsson et al., 2006). Similarly, the study by Perlow (1999) on the work patterns of engineers shows that they had difficulties finding "quiet time" to work on their own with "real engineering work," since the need for interaction with others led to constant interruptions. Equally, a fragmented project participation can be perceived by project workers as contributing to a positive variation of work and, hence, be a motivating feature for working in projects.

There could be several reasons for organizing the project work intra-functionally or inter-functionally and applying focused or fragmented project participation. The choice might be determined by such factors as task complexity, uncertainty, duration, and pace (see, e.g., Shenhar and Dvir, 2007). The main focus here is, however, not on the underlying reasons for choosing an organizational structure. Instead, we see the organizational structure as an important point of departure for the deeper analysis of the design of the HR organization and the responsibilities and relationships among the roles within the HR quadriad. Thus, we focus here on how the aforementioned two types of project work influence the roles and responsibilities of line managers, project managers, project workers, and HR specialists, in other words, the design of the HR quadriad.

Combining these two dimensions, we have four possible types of project-based work settings.

1. Intra-functional, fragmented: This is a project-based work setting in which project work is carried out in the line organization. The average project worker is involved in a number of projects and tasks simultaneously and is co-located with specialists representing the same area of expertise.
2. Intra-functional, focused: This is a project-based work setting in which project work is carried out in the line organization. The

average project worker focuses on one project during an extended period of time and is co-located with specialists from the same area of expertise. There is limited coordination across line units.

3. Inter-functional, fragmented: This is a project-based work setting in which project work is carried out in co-located projects, where the project worker is involved in several projects simultaneously, which means that work is carried out in several office spaces such that physical mobility becomes important. A lot of coordination occurs across expertise boundaries.

4. Inter-functional, focused: In this type of project-based work setting, project work is carried out in co-located projects, and project workers are involved in only one or a very few projects at the same time. A lot of coordination occurs across expertise boundaries.

In the analysis, we concentrate on the extreme types which will constitute two comparative types of project-based work settings:

Type A: This involves intra-functional project work with fragmented project participation.
Type B: This involves inter-functional project work with focused project participation.

These two primary alternatives are depicted in Figure 4.2 and are further outlined and compared in Table 4.2.

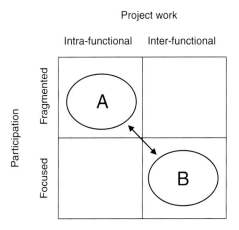

Figure 4.2 Types of project-based work settings

Table 4.2   Comparing the Type A and Type B project-based work setting

	Type A: Intra-functional project work and fragmented participation	Type B: Inter-functional project work and focused participation
Core activities	Performed in projects, although functionally distributed to line units	Performed in projects, interdisciplinary problem-solving processes
Characteristics of project participation	Fragmented, often many parallel projects simultaneously, working with colleagues with similar expertise	Focused, normally on one project at a time, working with colleagues with different expertise
Affiliation of project workers	Functional departments	Competence networks
Location of project workers during project assignments	Line/functional departments	Co-located projects
Manager of problem-solving activities	Line manager	Project manager
Personnel responsibilities	Line manager	Line manager/competence manager. To signal a different role, terms such as "competence manager" and "competence coach" are used instead of line manager

The HR quadriad and type of project-based work setting

The research reported here suggests that the roles within the HR quadriad are strongly influenced by the project-based work setting, particularly in regard to the type of project work and project participation. Returning to the HRM practice areas discussed in the previous chapter, a number of questions could be raised in light of the HR quadriad and its different roles. These questions are only a few examples of all questions that might be relevant to start exploring the relationships among the actors in the HR quadriad. However, already at this point they illuminate some of the unique questions posed within a project-based organization with regard to the management of human resources. These questions would then also be important to find answers for, for instance, what expectations the organization has for the project manager's contribution to HRM. Generally, several of the questions also point to the distribution of responsibilities among the actors in the HR quadriad. For instance, what is the responsibility of the line manager? What role should the project manager have? What skills are critical for involved actors to be able to play their parts in the HR quadriad? How should the various players work together to ensure a good supply and development of human resources?

Table 4.3   HRM practice areas: questions for the project-based organization

HRM practice areas	Some critical questions
Flows	Who is responsible for selection and recruitment? How are people recruited to projects? What support do line managers require to identify human resources needs? How is the management of phase-out handled? What are the responsibilities of the individual worker? What are the roles of the project managers in this process?
Performance	Who is responsible for performance appraisals? What can the individual do to facilitate a fair and instructive appraisal? What roles do the project managers have in the appraisal process? Should there be specific rewards for project achievements?
Involvement	How should projects be selected and what role does the individual project worker have in this process? What are the key motivation mechanisms for people involved in the projects? To what extent can project workers influence their work situation? What is important to get people involved in decision-making processes?
Development	What competences will be required to meet the needs of the future projects? What competence development initiatives are called for to meet the needs of future projects? What will people learn from participating in these projects? What role do project managers have in identifying these future needs?

This table will be used in the coming chapters for the analysis of each player in the HR quadriad. In that respect, we identify key areas of responsibility and particular activities within each practice area in which line managers, project managers, project workers, and HR specialists, respectively, are expected to play key roles.

Final thoughts

This chapter has presented the framework of the HR quadriad. Not only is this an acknowledgment of the collective nature of HRM in contemporary firms, it is also a way to better understand how roles interact, how HRM is adjusted to its context, and how different organizational conditions and factors interact to set the requirements and restrictions on the HRM system of the firm. As noted, the quadriad builds on the insight that HRM is carried out in collaboration among four roles, including HR specialists, line managers, project managers, and project workers. We have shown that the HR quadriad creates improved possibilities to study HRM at the operational level, something that has been underemphasized in recent HRM research which has generally, up to now, taken a strategic focus. The suggested framework emphasizes the importance of studying HRM on the operational level by understanding the functions and interactions of the variety of roles that deliver HR value, while previous research has tended to focus on HR specialists and, in some cases, line managers.

Important for the analysis presented here are the differences across contexts. To establish such an understanding, we distinguished different kinds of project-based work settings, based on two key dimensions: project work and project participation. We further suggested two main types of project work, separating between intra-functional, in which project workers carry out most of their project activities in a line function, and inter-functional, in which project workers are normally co-located in interdisciplinary teams. This separation was based on the insight that the operational work setting constitutes an important determining factor for HRM. In addition, we stressed the importance of separating between different types of project participation, as either focused or fragmented. Together, these dimensions display key characteristics of the two ideal types of project-based work settings: Type A: intra-functional and fragmented, and Type B: inter-functional and focused. The respective designs of the HR quadriad in these two types of project-based work settings differ considerably. As will be shown in further detail in the coming chapters, the analysis offers an advanced understanding of how the roles in the HR quadriad are shaped by the type of project-based work setting.

The framework of the HR quadriad is targeted for the analysis of the roles at an operational level that are vital to HRM in project-based organizations. It generally highlights the importance of taking different kinds of work settings into account when designing HR organizations because work settings influence the roles in the HR quadriad and, thereby, also each role's possibility to add value in the HRM system. These insights are well in line with recent calls for more HRM research into differences across contexts (Boxall and Macky, 2009). The combination of roles is also considered to be one possible way to improve the configurational approach of HRM (Martín-Alcázar et al., 2005) to see how roles interact and acknowledge that HRM practices are bundles and not isolated functional domains (MacDuffie, 1995). The research presented here, however, also gives rather strong evidence to the complementarity among HRM practices and the organizational variables affecting the design of the HRM system. The HR quadriad framework, we posit, is one possible way of strengthening the empirical analysis of the configurational approach in that it acknowledges the increasing collective nature of HRM and the transference of HR responsibilities to line managers and individual workers. The framework points out that changes in one area might have profound effects on changes in another area; for instance, transference of HRM responsibilities to the line managers affects the HR specialists. In that respect, the suggested framework points in the direction of developing HRM practices and conducting research that embraces the complementarity of practices and roles in the HRM system. The HR quadriad, therefore, is not only a way to address the four roles in the HR organization of the project-based organization but equally to address HRM as contextual, collective, contingent, configurational, and complementary. More on this will follow in the final chapter when we summarize the findings. In the next four chapters we will present findings from studies of each of the four roles participating in the HR quadriad. We will commence with the line manager and, thereafter, move to the project manager. After that, we center on the individual – the project worker – and end this part of the book with an analysis of the consequences for the HR specialists and the HR department.

5
Line Managers in the HR Quadriad

> *Structure of chapter*
>
> - Introduction
> - New organizational forms and HRM transference
> - Line managers in project-based organizations
> - Illustrations from two firms
> - Illustration 1: A new approach to line management at Saab
> - Illustration 2: Competence coaches at Tetra Pak
> - Line managers and HRM practices
> - Line managers in the HR quadriad
> - Final thoughts

Introduction

This chapter discusses the role of line managers in the HR quadriad. The chapter draws on a series of studies of personnel responsibilities in project-based organizations and the ensuing changes of the role of line managers in the HR organization of the firm.[1] Initially, the chapter revolves around the transference of HR responsibilities to line managers and the problems associated with this development. The aim is principally to shed light on what role line managers play in the HR quadriad and what support they need to improve their contribution to HRM. The chapter then presents some examples of what two project-based organizations have done in their attempts to rejuvenate the role of the line manager. The chapter reports primarily on two in-depth studies of R&D-intensive organizations: Saab, operating in the aerospace industry, and Tetra Pak, one of the leading companies in packaging systems.

One contemporary trend observed and discussed extensively in recent HRM research is the transference of HR responsibilities from HR departments to line managers (a trend often referred to as "devolvement" or "devolution" in research with a focus on this particular process). There are diverse views on the reasons behind this development. The reason most commonly emphasized relates to the increased acknowledgment of HRM as being strategically highly important rather than merely an operational support function. This singles out HRM as a critical general management responsibility that should not be handed over to, or left only in the hands of, HR specialists. The influential work on HRM by scholars at Harvard Business School in the 1980s argued forcefully for this view (Beer et al., 1984). Building on this argument, many have argued that HR specialists need to become more actively involved in strategy formulation, and some authors have even argued that they need to become "strategic partners" in order to add significant business value (see, e.g., Barney and Wright, 1998; Ulrich, 1998). This change in focus further implies that they should leave operational HR responsibilities to line managers. Another important reason for increased HR responsibility being placed with line managers seems to be the continuous need for rationalization, cost reduction, and streamlining which have struck support functions in most companies in the Western world. This typically leads to downsized and centralized HR departments and decentralized HR responsibilities to the line. Additionally, as we will discuss in this chapter, new organizational forms influence and redefine traditional line management roles, and, in many cases, these become inherently crucial in performing HRM at the operational level. As we discussed in the first chapter of the book, this is, we believe, one of the most interesting developments, especially if we are to understand the progress and changes of HRM in project-based organizations.

The aforementioned overview highlights a number of important change patterns and trajectories with regard to HRM and line managers. Figure 5.1 illustrates the underlying forces we believe contribute

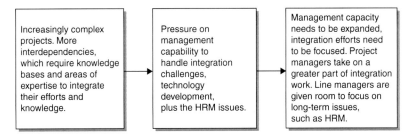

Figure 5.1   Line managers and HRM: some underlying forces

to the transference of HRM responsibilities in project-based organizations. In that respect, the identified trajectory centers on the nature and change of project operations as a key driving force. In line with our initial capability discussion, this creates a need to increase managerial capability, particularly with regard to integration efforts. Project managers accordingly assume more responsibilities for such work, which gives line managers more time to engage in long-term issues, including HRM, recruitment, competence development, etc.

New organizational forms and HRM transference

A number of studies suggest that higher degree of knowledge intensity and changes in organizational structures are important driving forces behind the process of what is generally referred to as "devolution" – a transference of HR responsibilities to line managers. For example, Larsen and Brewster (2003: 234) argue:

> Major changes within organizations will influence the allocation of roles in even more fundamental ways. As organizations become more knowledge intensive, dependent on know-how and services, HRM becomes a more critical part of the operation and a more critical role for the immediate manager.

The case study in Thornhill and Saunders (1998) demonstrates that organizational structure significantly influences the devolution process. In their case, a management buyout and privatization implied new, flatter, non-bureaucratic structures, which called for more flexible employees. After the buyout, the organization did not have access to the corporate HR department of the former owner, and no new HR department was set up. Instead, HR responsibilities were assigned entirely to line managers, who had already started to take on more HR responsibilities prior to the buyout.

Larsen and Brewster (2003) mention the probable impact of new organizational forms, such as matrix, network, and project-based organizations, on line management's involvement in performing HRM activities. The authors argue that:

> the line manager roles in organizations become increasingly complex because new organizational structures (e.g., virtual and network organizations) have less well-defined line manager roles than the traditional hierarchical, bureaucratic organization which

moulded the line manager role in the first place. (Larsen and Brewster, 2003: 230)

Furthermore, they state that the link between the HR department and line managers might lose relevance in organizations that rely on autonomous teams in which project managers and project workers themselves handle recruitment, pay, discipline, and resource allocation. In our research, such a high degree of autonomy of the project teams is very rare and, as we will discuss later on, most organizations choose to maintain, in some form of line organization, the responsibility for longer-term people management issues. When it comes to project workers, this task generally falls on the first-line manager; in other words, the management role with direct responsibility for the basic work units and project workers. This makes the first-line manager's role critical to HRM at the operational level, making him or her an important player in the implementation of overall HRM strategies and policies. When we discuss line management in this book, our primary focus is, therefore, the first-line management role, such as managers responsible for work pools and line departments. The studied line managers operate within a variety of areas, including aerospace development, complex machinery, engine development, and automotive development.

Line managers in project-based organizations

Various researchers have expressed a concern that HRM transference poses a threat to HR departments. If line managers take over HR responsibilities, what will be the role of HR specialists and HR departments? A number of studies strive to justify the prominent role of HR specialists in organizations. For example, in the case study by Thornhill and Saunders (1998: 474), the authors indicate that line managers have a limited strategic focus, arguing that:

> The absence of a designated human resource specialist role may therefore be argued to have had a significant negative effect on the organization's ability to achieve strategic integration in relation to the management of its human resources, with further negative consequences for commitment to the organization, flexibility and quality.

Similarly, Cunningham and Hyman (1999: 25) suggest that devolution of HR responsibilities to line managers makes HR departments

vulnerable, but that "the acknowledged shortcomings of line management, particularly with regard to the management of subordinates, may
help to confirm a continued presence for personnel as a discrete, if less
than strategic, function."

The studies referred to earlier not only express concerns about the
possible threat to HR departments but also articulate remarks about the
shortcomings of line management with regard to their HR responsibilities. Similarly, Larsen and Brewster (2003) question whether line managers really have the time, the ability, or even the desire to take on this
responsibility. The case study by Cunningham and Hyman (1999) also
suggests that line managers are frustrated at not having sufficient time
to deal with HR issues because of the dominance of "hard and measur-
able objectives," such as profit, lead time, and costs. These difficulties
with transference of HRM responsibilities has led several researchers to
the conclusion that to maintain high-quality HRM at the operational
level, HRM transference has to be seen as a process of increased partnership rather than a trade-off between line managers and HR specialists
(e.g., Currie and Procter, 2001; Renwick, 2003). This would imply that
HR specialists need to maintain an important but somewhat different
role in HRM, while line managers assume greater HR responsibility. As
argued by Dany et al. (2008) it is imperative to not only examine the
impact of HRM practices, but also to address the issue of influence distribution between HRM specialists and line managers, that is the question of who is involved in defining and implementing HRM practices.

> Indeed, while HRM integration [into the process of strategy formu-
> lation] should result in a higher level of consistency between HRM
> and business strategy, it does not, however, resolve the question of
> the quality of implementation of the espoused HRM policies (Purcell
> and Hutchinson, 2007). The relationship between HRM specialists
> and [line managers] in regard to HR policy is, therefore, an essential
> issue. (Dany et al., 2008: 2101)

In this book, we are setting out to obtain a deeper knowledge of
project-based organizations, and some might question whether it is
even relevant to speak of "line managers" in the traditional sense in
project-based organizations (see Midler, 1995, see also Fact Box 5.1).

A line manager is generally understood as the manager responsible
for a functional line unit which specializes in a specific function or area
of expertise in an organization (see, e.g., Clark and Wheelwright, 1992).
When the main operations are carried out in projects and temporary

---

Fact Box 5.1   Renault: a case of projectification

Christophe Midler – a French researcher who has studied the French automotive industry for decades – conducted an in-depth study of organizational changes at the automotive manufacturer Renault (Midler, 1995). The firm effected a transition from the classic functional organization in the 1960s to project coordination in the 1970s and, since 1989, to autonomous and powerful project teams. In many ways, the case of Renault has been singled out as one of the most famous cases of projectification – and many would say the projectification process, as such, very much laid the foundation for the overall improvement in the competitiveness of Renault. Midler argues that the projectification process in many ways led to a profound destabilization of the permanent organizational logics of the firm (task definitions, hierarchic regulations, career management, functions, and supplier relations, etc.). One problem Midler identified in his analysis is the difficulty of professionals trained for years in a compartmentalized corporate environment to engage more extensively in interdepartmental dialogue. It also leads to a number of critical questions, including the following: What is the future for "skill-based" functional departments in the firm? Are they going to disappear, scattered into different project teams? How is it possible to maintain the long-term technical learning process when organizational structures are focusing energies on short-term and project-oriented objectives?

---

project teams rather than in functional line units, is there really a line organization with line managers at all? The answer depends on how one defines project-based organizing and on what is included in the concept of line management. As discussed in Chapter 2, most definitions of project-based organizations depart from the relative strength and power of projects in relation to line units (see, e.g., Clark and Wheelwright, 1992; Hobday, 2000). Recalling the quotation from Hobday (2000), a project-based organization would then rely heavily on projects and have "no formal functional coordination across project lines" (p. 878). With such a view of project-based organizations, one might rightfully question whether there are line managers at all, or whether this actually is a management role only relevant for functional organizational settings. Clark and Wheelwright (1992) distinguish between different degrees of project orientation based on the level of authority over personnel, finance, and other resources. This also implies that the growing importance of the project dimension is inherently at the expense of the line dimension. A project-based organization would then, by definition, indicate a strong project dimension and a weak or nonexisting line dimension, and, accordingly, strong project managers and weak line managers.

However, our somewhat different view on project-based organizations indicates the relative strengths of the line dimension and the project dimension are not the main issue. Instead, we believe this organizational form, and its variety of critical roles, could be better understood when the degree of project orientation is based on where the core activities are performed. In that respect, we formulate a distinction between project-based organizations and functional organizations that is more adapted to the analysis of work conditions and HRM.

Accordingly, in a functional organization, where core activities are mainly performed in functional line units, line managers are naturally responsible for the performance of particular aspects of these core activities. However, projects might still be critical to the organization by focusing on solving specific tasks during a limited period of time. It could, for example, be change projects, technology development projects, competence development projects, implementation projects, etc. In a project-based organization, on the other hand, core production and development activities are mainly performed by means of projects. The activities people undertake in the organization are predominantly direct contributions to one or several projects, a fact that has implications for the line manager role.

However, we want to stress that project-based organizations, from an HRM point of view, do not necessarily have weaker line units or nonexisting functional departments. Several project researchers argue that the line dimension in project-based organizations needs, instead, to maintain a prominent position as a foundation for long-term technological development as well as for competence development and other HRM issues (e.g., Hobday, 2000; Midler, 1995). This can be seen as a change in focus and purpose rather than a loss in strength and importance. An example of the latter is described in the case study reported by Lindkvist (2004) of an organization's radical change from a functional structure to a project-based structure. Here, the line dimension in its traditional form was transformed from line units into what was referred to as "competence networks." We have seen similar transformations taking place to various degrees in the companies we have studied, and we can conclude that the line dimension tends to maintain an important, and often strong, position but its main purpose is different from the line dimension in a functional organization.

The line units in project-based organizations tend to take the form of work pools or competence pools – physical or virtual – which supply the projects with human resources with the right competences and ensure the long-term foundation and development for the company's project workers. The following illustration taken from Tetra Pak is a case in point where so-called competence centers play a significant role in the organization of the project-based firm. Their main activities relate to the allocation of people to projects, appraisal and performance reviews, long-term competence development of the unit as well as of individual project workers, career development, and other HRM-related issues.

This also means that the project-based setting molds the line manager role into one that might not be consistent with the traditional line manager role as we know it. Even though, as discussed above, line managers' expanded contribution to HRM seems to be a general trend in contemporary firms, our research indicates that project-based organizing might be an important driver for this development. While core activities are mainly performed by means of temporary projects, long-term management activities such as HRM, technology and competence strategies cannot be transferred to project managers, since their management responsibilities are limited to the duration of the project. This is also mentioned in the study of the "heavyweight team structure" by Clark and Wheelwright (1992), in which a core group of project workers are dedicated and physically co-located with the "heavyweight project leader." The authors remark:

> However, the longer-term career development of individual contributors continues to rest not with the project leader – although that heavyweight leader makes significant input to individual performance evaluations – but with the functional manager, because members are not assigned to a project team on a permanent basis. (Clark and Wheelwright, 1992: 13)

In the companies that have participated in our research, the changes in the first-line management role have been prominent, and we have come to understand that project-based organizations foster a new approach to line management, one in which first-line managers are not primarily the technical experts or direct supervisors but are rather responsible for competences and resources going into the projects and for the long-term competence and career development of individual project workers. And in knowledge-intensive firms that thrive on complex problem-solving this ought to be a highly important matter.

Illustrations from two firms

In the following, we provide two illustrations from our case studies that demonstrate how project-based settings mold a new approach to line management, and maybe even a new type of line management role. In both cases, the first-line management role is the one in focus. The first illustration comes from Saab, one of Sweden's most R&D-intensive companies, which develops solutions for defense, aviation, and space.[2] The company has approximately 13,000 employees and is internationally best known for its combat fighter Gripen. The organization that serves as an illustration here is the most R&D-intensive and project-based part of the business unit Saab Aerosystems, which focuses on developing and integrating airborne systems for civil and military aircraft. The work setting is primarily dominated by intra-functional project work and fragmented participation, although inter-functional and focused project work has been promoted in recent years. The line manager role over the past 20 years has changed from a predominantly technical role into a more HR-oriented one. In an interview with a senior manager at Saab Aerosystems, we focused on the emerging new role of the line managers in project-based organizations and increased HR responsibilities. He said:

> This is precisely what we are trying to do at Saab. We talk a lot about how the line managers have to view their work in a new way. This is very hard in a company with a strong engineering tradition, where the best engineer is expected to get line management positions. We are trying to get away from that now, and instead be clear with that the people with the best management skills should be the manager. (Senior Manager, Saab Aerosystems)

The second illustration comes from a unit at Tetra Pak, a Swedish company famous for having in 1951 developed the first system in the world for packaging milk in paper cartons. Since then, the business has developed and grown considerably. Today Tetra Pak is a multinational corporation that develops and produces processing, packaging, and distribution systems for foodstuffs, including software services. The company operates in more than 150 markets and has some 20,000 employees worldwide. The illustration presented here comes from Tetra Pak Plant Engineering & Automation – a unit that operates within the area of preparation and processing of liquid foodstuffs. It designs and delivers processing solutions and complete plants with integrated plant automation systems. The organization is highly project-based, applying mostly inter-functional project work with focused participation. The illustration depicts a relatively drastic organizational change that was implemented in order to improve the overall functioning of project operations. The former line units were transformed into "competence networks," and the former line management role was replaced with a new role: "competence coaches." The CEO of the company told us:

> Before, the [line managers] were the experts. They became managers as the carpenter became a foreman. The ones supervising the work were also the ones with the most knowledge. ... Today, no coach can be better than their coworkers. Technology develops so fast that it is impossible for us managers to stay current. We have to trust that they can do the work. We can direct how they should do the work, we can ensure that we develop competences, we can measure what they know and what they don't know, but we cannot do it better than them! That's what makes the whole difference. The manager knew everything before, but today he doesn't. (Managing Director, Plant Engineering & Automation)

Illustration 1: A new approach to line management at Saab

The Systems Development unit at Saab Aerosystems centers on further development and improvement of existing products as well as the pre-studies and the development of new ones. In 2003, the unit was part of a large organizational change, a reaction to the needs of the company to become more market oriented and competitive. Traditionally, the development of the combat fighter Gripen had dominated the operations of Saab Aerosystems, but during the close of the 1990s operations expanded into new areas and products, such as unmanned aerial vehicles, tactical mission systems, systems for the civil market, etc. Before the reorganization, the development of Gripen was carried out in a separate business unit in which each line unit had the technical responsibility for a particular part of the aircraft. After the reorganization, this unit was abolished and new units were structured according to competences instead of products. Systems Development became more project oriented, focusing on core competence areas that would provide competences to all the product development projects, not only to Gripen.

The intensive part of the empirical study at Saab was conducted in 2007. At that time, Systems Development had approximately 600 employees. In addition, there were about 300 consultants involved in various development work and projects. The unit had become a complex project organization with projects running within a number of large programs. The development of Gripen was still the largest and most important program, but not the only one.

Over time, the changes at Systems Development had increased the use of cross-functional teamwork, which resulted in the co-location of project teams. The line units had developed toward becoming resource centers for the projects, and the line manager role had slowly transformed into that of a resource owner rather than a technical expert. The increased number of products and projects, combined with an increasingly complex technology as well as the added requirements of line managers to take on more personnel responsibilities, made it difficult for the individual manager to handle it all:

> In the end it all comes down to what is a reasonable work load for a manager? You can draw whatever fancy structures you like, but in the end it is a human being there. And it seems perfectly unreasonable to have a technical specialist who should make all technological decisions in all the projects and at the same time develop their personnel. I would claim that there are no such individuals. You have to accept that you have to choose. (Senior Manager)

This development had been going on for many years, but after the reorganization in 2003, it became even clearer.

> For the line managers, this resulted in moving from being the technical manager for a part in the Gripen production to a more clear-cut role as resource- and competence manager. At the same time, we projected all the project milestones onto the performing line unit. That means that the line managers are now evaluated based on the performance of their coworkers in the projects. (Senior Manager)

Most of the line managers maintained important responsibilities for long-term technological development and for commonality in the technical solutions delivered to different projects. But, foremost, they expanded their positions as personnel-responsible managers for the project workers. Their responsibilities for recruitment, competence mapping and development, resource allocation, performance reviews, career planning, and the overall work situation of project workers were emphasized. Since most of the work was carried out in projects, all these HR activities needed to be tightly interrelated with project operations. Instead of being in their line unit, co-workers were increasingly being co-located with their project teams and in physical "project areas," which complicated the possibilities for many line managers to take on the increased HR responsibilities. For example, one line manager explained the situation at her unit, where project workers were normally assigned on a full-time basis to the projects and co-located with the project team during their assignment:

> My employees work on many different projects. ... We are extremely scattered at the moment. It's hard to keep a line unit together, and that is something that we have discussed within the unit recently. How do we keep together? ... If you don't have any form of home arena, you'll lose some of the cooperation that you can get from working with the same type of assignments. (Line Manager)

In response to this, many line managers developed new ways of handling day-to-day HR responsibilities. For example, the assessment of project workers' performance, development needs, and work situations became to a greater extent based on the line manager's discussions with the project workers, their project managers, and other team members, rather than on the line manager's own direct experience. Apart from the yearly performance review meetings line managers had with their employees, this was not a formalized process. It was rather a matter of integrating discussions of individual performance with other discussions. It could be, for example, resource allocation discussions with project managers, in which the line managers sensed whether coworkers seemed to be appreciated for their work or whether there was reluctance to getting someone on the team. In these discussions, line managers also tried to promote individuals who had expressed a wish to develop in a certain direction, or whom the line manager had identified as having certain potential. One line manager said:

> My job is to make sure that my employees have meaningful assignments and that these assignments are in harmony with their personal development. That they get attention for what they do and that they are in the right places. To help them get on the right track. (Line Manager)

The line managers were all engineers, and many referred to a strong historical tradition of powerful and influential line managers who were typically the most skillful and experienced engineers. To a large extent the line managers had been seen as the "heroes" in the organization. There were still some line managers who were primarily interested in the engineering aspect of their work and considered HR issues as the "boring part of their job." One line manager with a background as a project manager confessed:

> Being a line manager was something completely new to me, and honestly it was probably not the position that attracted me the most.
>
> *Why not?*
>
> Well, having to deal with personnel issues ... it's not really my main interest. But I've learned it along the way. It's a different way of working. You have to work on a more long-term basis. It's not all about deadlines; it's about competence and recruitment and personnel problems and those sorts of things. And that wasn't what interested me the most.

Most, though, were dedicated to their HR responsibilities, even though for many it was difficult to balance HR work with technological responsibilities. Moreover, they sometimes felt they needed to develop their HR competences further and that they would appreciate close and integrated HR support in some of the more soft management issues such as teamwork and commitment. One manager expressed she and her colleagues, indeed, were interested in such issues and had tried to solve them the best they could but, as she said, "You know, that's with the minds of engineers." Another line manager spoke about the need for more cooperation among line managers concerning HR issues in order to develop a common understanding of how to deal with issues and help each other out:

> I think that it is somewhat of a problem that we don't have a common line management competence. That is something we should develop. One way would be to get some kind of formal training in order to develop a common language among us, but what I really would appreciate is a structured network. I mean, after a while you realize that basically all line managers are struggling with similar hurdles. I think that it could be very useful to discuss these problems together, and maybe also with someone from HR. Things like "what do you usually do in these kinds of situations?" I think that would be good. (Line Manager)

The line managers at Systems Development had HR support in the form of a so-called "HR developer," an HR specialist at the local HR department with particular responsibility for Systems Development. The

HR developer had the responsibility to work with strategic HR issues, to improve HR processes, and to support the unit managers, area managers, and first-line managers in unit-specific matters. Apart from that, line managers could turn to a recently created HR support unit on a company level that offered support in subjects such as recruitment, profiling, wages, expatriates, and competence. However, recent downsizing and restructuring of the HR department caused certain initial frustration and uncertainty about HR support. Moreover, Systems Development had about 45 first-line managers, which made it hard for the HR developer to find the time to become involved with all of them and get a good overview of their needs in order to provide appropriate support.

Illustration 2: Competence coaches at Tetra Pak

Tetra Pak Plant Engineering & Automation is one of the centers of expertise for advanced plant design and automation solutions within Tetra Pak. It is a strongly project-based organization where people work on large client projects to design and deliver complete and custom-made plants for food processing and advanced automation solutions. The empirical study was conducted in 2004 and 2005; during that time, the unit employed just over 150 people plus approximately 40 to 50 consultants.

By the end of the 1990s, changes in the market and in technology led to an urgent need for new ways of working at Plant Engineering & Automation in order to make operations more efficient and to improve the integration of employees' competences in projects. At this time, the organization could best be described as a traditional "matrix." A number of departments were responsible for different functions within the unit. Each department was managed by a line manager in the traditional sense – resource owners with a strong technological focus. When starting a new project, the project manager would ask the line managers for resources in order to work in the project. However, this organization did not work in a satisfactory way, and the company's CEO told us about the difficulties:

> All the time there was a conflict about who was going to get what. The line manager was supposed to be the competence manager. He owned the resources. It was his responsibility to supervise the work and develop the competences. But it usually ended up being all about supervising the work and handling prioritization. (CEO)

To meet these difficulties, a drastic organizational change was implemented that would improve the work processes and routines as well as create a more defined distribution of responsibilities. The functional departments were broken up, and, instead, a number of cross-functional teams were set up as physical organizational units to create more permanent and efficient project teams.

In the new organization, each employee was affiliated both to a cross-functional team and to a competence center consisting of people within the same area of competence. These competence centers were not physical units but could rather be described as networks with a focus on individual capabilities and personnel issues. They handled competence planning, performance reviews, salaries, work situation, and career management. The traditional line management role was abolished and, instead, a new role was created to manage the competence centers: competence coaches. The competence coaches would leave the technical responsibilities behind and only work with capabilities and other personnel issues, issues that previously had tended to be somewhat neglected.

Initially, there were a lot of internal discussions about the competence coach's role. A general opinion was that they should be seen as "the HR department's extended arm" and that they should focus on "the soft issues." Even though competence coaches did not formally report to the HR manager, in practice they came to develop close cooperation. The HR manager called for monthly competence coach meetings to give information on new HR policies and other important issues that concerned the work of the coaches. These meetings were also an important arena for coaches to air their everyday problems, share experiences, and create a common platform for their work.

Indeed, the creation of the competence coach role was not easy. The first challenge was to find the right people for the job. At first, many of the existing line managers went straight to a competence coach role. However, it soon became obvious that, for many of them, adaptation to the new role was too difficult and they needed to move on to other positions. The qualities that had made them successful line managers were not necessarily the same as the ones needed to be successful competence coaches. It was a delicate balancing act. On the one hand, they needed technical competence and experience in order to stay close to the actual work, understand the coworkers' situation and speak the same language as them. On the other hand, the HR manager saw an obvious risk that the experience from being technical supervisors would make it hard for the coaches not to get involved in the technical development process.

As a coach, you have to leave the technical operations behind, but many of them kept that as sort of a side activity. Many didn't want to give that part up; they wanted to fiddle with everything that had to do with the technology. (HR Manager)

A second challenge was to find suitable competence development programs for the competence coaches. The new role was unconventional and difficult to define, so there were no training programs available for this kind of position. In many ways, the competence coaches themselves came to design the new role and develop the knowledge, competence, and experience needed.

A competence center normally included about 20 to 30 employees. The work of competence coaches varied to some extent, but generally all of them worked with resource allocation to the projects and with planning the employees' future project participation in a longer perspective. They also worked with competence mapping and performance reviews. The coaches were responsible for the overall work situation of the individuals within their competence center. Every week, the coaches gathered the members of their competence centers to provide an arena for discussions about common work issues and for the exchange of experiences. These meetings were also an opportunity for the coach to inform the employees of new work processes or system updates and to get information about the present working situation of the project workers and the general situation in the projects.

For many coaches, resource planning and allocation was the single most time-consuming part of their work. Whenever a new project was assigned to a project manager in one of the cross-functional teams, the manager had to design a project team with suitable competences for the project, preferably from within the same cross-functional team. They would then turn to the competence coaches to discuss available and preferred resources. As explained by one of the coaches:

> Resource planning for different kinds of projects takes up a large amount of our time. Things like who is the best man for the project and who belongs to which [cross-functional] team. You always wish that you were entirely free when composing the [project] teams, but you never are. It is mostly about who is available. It takes a lot of time!...Even if you try to be clever with your own planning, that plan does not always work out....You might have counted on that [a certain person] would be available a certain date, and it turns out he is not. Then all you can do is make a new plan, which might affect other projects. (Competence Coach)

Competence development was another area of responsibility that took a significant part of the coaches' time. This included competence mapping, competence planning, identifying the competence gaps in the competence center, and working to fill the gaps. An important aspect of this work was the individual development plans created in discussion with each member of the competence center. These plans constituted the foundation for supporting the employees in their needs and wishes for development and, at the same time, ensuring the competence center developed competences that would meet the future demands of the projects. One competence coach told us about the increased focus on competence development:

> We focus more on competence development now than we did before. We ensure that each individual has a personal development plan and that this plan is concrete. It is not necessarily all about attending courses even if that normally is one part of it. It is also about planning what kind of project you should try to assign a person to next time in order to develop in the right way.

> *How is that working out? Earlier you described the difficulties in planning their project participation.*

> This might be our greatest challenge. I do believe that we have become better at planning competence development, we put more time and effort into it, but we need to improve even more. But the next problem is to actually follow through with the plan.

The competence coaches were also responsible for evaluation and performance reviews. Regarding this matter, both the HR manager and the coaches saw warning signals early on that the system for this was questioned by the employees. They wondered about the ability of a competence coach to make a fair evaluation of their work. Employees who worked in long-term projects, often abroad, wondered, "How can the competence coach know how I work?" and "Has the coach even spoken to my project manager?" In response, the HR manager and another manager at the unit developed a new method for performance reviews. This method was based on a three-party meeting, including the employee, the coach, and a third party (usually a project manager or peer project team member).

Besides the performance review meetings, the competence coaches also had individual meetings with each employee once a year that focused on "well-being and efficiency." These meetings were open conversations about the work situation, colleagues, work-life balance, and other issues that needed to be brought up in the discussion. Following up and looking after the employees' well-being and general life situation were fundamental parts of the work of a competence coach. One coach told us about these more personal conversations:

> At these meetings we ventilate all kinds of things. We have templates and checklists to follow, so that we don't forget to talk about anything important, but I don't follow them very strictly. I keep to the formula, but if they want to speak about their private lives, I let them. Even though their private lives are none of my business, I want them to know that I am there for them. It's more for preventive reasons. If I see that a person is not feeling well, it would be professional misconduct not to ask about it. And they don't have to tell me if they don't want to. (Competence Coach)

On a day-to-day basis, the coaches were involved in everything that had to do with the project workers' work situations. It could be, for example, support in conflict solving in the project teams, helping out with constantly arising practical problems for project members, or discussions with project managers about working conditions and planning issues. Project planning issues were one of the most frequently discussed at the competence center meetings. Bad planning often created a stressful work situation, and if the project manager did not notice and listen to the warning signals from their project members, the competence coaches needed to bring them to the surface and deal with them. Even though the risks for stress-related illnesses were not alarming, the coaches saw that people tended to work too much rather than too little. There were many interesting projects to work on, and it was important for many employees to keep up a reputation as popular project workers in order to be hired for challenging future assignments. Generally, the competence coaches felt they needed to help the employees draw the line, to hold them back to some extent, to keep them from rushing too fast.

All the everyday problems and "firefighting," together with the complicated resource allocation puzzle, had the consequence that often much of the longer-term work had to be put on hold. Even though this caused certain frustration among the competence coaches at times, the new role offered an entirely new career path that suited certain kinds of people better than the traditional career paths:

> I'm far from being the best engineer, but my substantial technical background gives me an understanding of the different kinds of

problems that the coworkers bring up as reasons for needing more resources or more competences. I keep updated, but I know nothing of "bits" and "bytes." However, I know which the competences are, I can control that, but I cannot start tampering with what they are developing. ... I like staying close to the down-to-earth, practical operations. I feel that I've found the right job.

So, do you think that you would like to work in a position more towards HR?

Yes, I think I would, but I have always been hesitant towards the idea of becoming an HR manager; it is too far from where it all happens. Being a competence coach is just right. I'm close to the technology, but I'm not responsible for which technology to use. My job is to provide the right competences and to work with people issues. (Competence coach)

Line managers and HRM practices

What do these illustrations tell us about line managers and their HR work in project-based organizations? First of all, both are clear examples of the transference of HR responsibilities to line management, as discussed earlier in the chapter. Probably, part of this change can be due to the general trend of "devolution", a trend that has been highlighted in previous research and that is not specific for project-based organizations. However, an important driving force behind the change in these two companies seems to be closely related to the perceived need to improve project operations. The illustrations above show that two distinctive features of project-based organizations and project work seem to have a significant influence on HRM at an operational level.

First, project work normally involves cross-functional integration of knowledge. As pointed out in Chapter 2, projects integrate competences across functional lines – they comprise members who represent different specialties and different competence bases (this is discussed by, for example, Sydow et al., 2004). In both illustrations the increased focus on cross-functional work is clear. At Saab, co-located project teams had become increasingly applied even though intra-functional project work was still very common. At Tetra Pak, cross-functional teams became the new basic units to which project workers had a long-term affiliation. The management of technological activities and problem-solving was primarily a task for project teams and project managers, although at Saab many line managers maintained a long-term responsibility for technology development. However, despite this seemingly increased focus on projects and cross-functional project teams, line management has maintained an important role at Saab as well as at Tetra Pak. The role has changed considerably, though, as it has become more and more oriented toward coordinating, developing, and supporting the project workers' contributions to the projects, in the short term as well as in the long term.

Second, projects are by definition temporary, which creates a more transient work situation – people move between project assignments and project teams. This creates a need for the HR organization to handle this ongoing transition: assignment to a project, handling the relationship to and performance of the project worker during the assignment, assessment and evaluation after the project, planning of future project participation and competence development according to individual, as well as strategic goals.[3] If we turn back to the HRM practice areas, presented in Chapter 3, the line managers and competence coaches at Saab and Tetra Pak spend most of their time working with these on an operational level. Table 5.1 summarizes our suggestion of important roles that first-line managers in project-based organizations take on when performing the core processes of HRM.

Due to the temporary nature of project work, these activities follow the project cycles for the project workers. When a person has been recruited for the unit, the line manager is responsible for matching him or her with adequate project assignments. When people have been allocated to a project, line management seems to be focused on knowledge facilitation within the unit, so that people with similar competences share experiences and learn from each other. As was clear in both illustrations, an important role was also to collect input about project workers' performances to maintain a reliable performance review process. At Tetra Pak, where project work was highly interfunctional and the competence centers were dispersed, a new tool was developed to facilitate this process. At Saab, where project work was relatively intra-functional, line managers gathered this information through their day-to-day discussions with project managers and project workers.

During a project assignment, and particularly when an assignment is coming to an end, line managers have a key role in supporting the individual project workers. Here, the function seems to be acting as an "agent" for the project workers, rather than being a "supervisor." An analogy could be that of an artist's agent, who supports, promotes, and

Table 5.1   Roles of line manager in the HRM practice areas

HRM practice area	Role of line manager
Flows	Manage in- and out-flows of project workers to the line unit/competence center. Match project workers and project assignments.
Performance	Facilitate knowledge sharing between project workers within the same unit/competence center, also when they are dispersed in cross-functional teams. Make sure that work conditions in the projects are appropriate. Collect the input necessary for a reliable performance review process.
Involvement	Give project workers opportunities to influence decisions on future project assignments and advise and promote the project workers to project assignments that they strive for. Balance the work intensity for ambitious and "popular" project workers and support them in finding work-life balance.
Development	Match project assignments with individual as well as strategic competence development goals. Balance the short-term resource needs of projects with the long-term development needs of project workers.

finds "gigs" for the artist through their agency. The first-line manager, in this sense, promotes project workers for projects that are "right" for their career and advises them when it is time to take some time off to reflect or to slow down after a period of intense project work. We have also understood in our conversations with line managers that an important part of their work is to constrain the work intensity for ambitious and popular project workers and to support them in finding work-life balance.

When a project assignment ends, the cycle starts over with a new project assignment and the line manager tries to integrate competence puzzle-solving with resource puzzle-solving. As was seen in the illustrations, the line managers at Saab and the competence coaches at Tetra Pak indeed had an important task in handling long-term competence planning and building strategic competences. However, the increased use of co-located project teams and the tight deadlines of the projects complicated this task, given the distance between the project workers and their line manager, and the difficulties involved in finding the time for competence development programs. The illustrations depict a never-ending process of puzzle-solving to provide the projects with the right resources, while at the same time depicting projects as stepping stones in the competence development processes for the project workers.

The line managers and competence coaches in the studied companies spend a great deal of their time and energy on making this HRM cycle run smoothly in the short-term as well as matching it with long-term goals for individuals as well as for the organization. Although we believe that Table 5.1 above is useful for the general understanding of line management's responsibilities for HRM in project-based organizations, the illustrations also show that the line management role is influenced by the characteristics of the work system.

For example, firms that strongly favor inter-functional project work, which mostly organize project activities through co-located project teams, will probably develop a purer HR-oriented line management role similar to the competence coaches at Tetra Pak. The temporality of project work also makes this management role similar to a consultancy manager, with the primary responsibility for managing and developing a pool of project workers with similar competences. Hence, line units in a traditional sense (e.g., functional departments) might not exist, but this does not mean that functional coordination across projects is nonexistent. The functional coordination can rather be compared to the "competence networks" described by Lindkvist (2004), which constitute the backbone of the project-based organization and constitute "arenas displaying the specific competences, experience and personalities of network members" (Lindkvist, 2004: 15). Accordingly, titles such as competence managers, competence coaches, and the like, seem to become increasingly common in firms with a functional coordination in the form of competence networks instead of traditional line departments. Their key role in the HR quadriad is obvious.

In firms where project work is more intra-functional and where co-location of project teams are not that common but project workers perform their project activities from within their line unit, line managers still play an important role in the HR quadriad. However, the line management role in such organizations generally does not develop into a pure competence management role, as these line managers need to balance HR responsibilities with technological responsibilities. On the one hand, this keeps the line managers up-to-date with the developments of their competence area and of the technology used. Therefore, they can also, to a greater extent, act as technological mentors for the project workers. On the other hand, the technology-related activities tend to get higher priority than the HRM-related activities.

Line managers in the HR quadriad

This chapter has presented a few important observations about the roles and the changes pertaining to the line manager in project-based organizations. What have we then learned about the HR quadriad in project-based organizations, focusing on the first-line management role? Without doubt, the HR role of first-line managers in project-based work settings is prominent, and the HR work they perform is affected and shaped in various ways by the nature of project work and its temporary and cross-functional characteristics. The line managers manage human resource flows to and from their unit, they try solving the "resource puzzle" and the "competence puzzle" simultaneously, they work to facilitate knowledge sharing within the same competence area, they collect input for appraisal and performance reviews, and they act as "agents" for project workers, involving them and promoting them for future project assignments. However, it is also clear that it is difficult, if not impossible, to carry out these activities in a positive manner if there is a lack of cooperation and collective responsibilities among the rest of the players in the HR quadriad.

　Thus, to manage the human resource flows, line managers most likely need support from HR specialists in the recruitment and selection processes or in lay-off situations. It also seems reasonable to get input from project managers and project workers in the recruitment processes in order to get information on what kind of personalities or competences they ask for. To succeed in solving the resource puzzle (to match project resources and project assignments) and, simultaneously, the competence puzzle (to match project assignments with individual and strategic competence development goals), a line manager needs to have an effective process of collaboration and dialogue with both project managers and individual project workers. This was clear in both illustrations with Saab and Tetra Pak. Moreover, the line manager might benefit from an active and integrated support from HR specialists in their work with competence development processes and career planning for the project workers.

　The facilitation of knowledge sharing within the unit is a process that very much involves collaboration with the project workers. Several line managers we have met also appreciate the competence HR specialists can provide in developing well-functioning processes. Similarly, collecting information about project workers' performance, instead of relying on direct personal experience, requires well-functioning and trustworthy processes among line managers, project managers, and project workers. This is particularly important in organizations with inter-functional project work and where project workers are co-located with their project teams. HR specialists might have an important role to develop and facilitate these processes. Finally, acting as the project workers' "agent" requires a close relationship with, and professional knowledge about, each individual project worker in order to coach them and promote them in a positive way. It also requires building trustful relationships with project managers to convince them to sometimes accept project workers for certain competence development plans instead of project workers with the ideal competence for the project. HR specialists can, most likely, be important sounding boards for line managers when it comes to issues regarding this role. For example, at Tetra Pak the HR manager was, in practice, the coach for the competence coaches, providing not only HR competence but also an arena for experience sharing among the competence coaches.

Final thoughts

In this chapter, we wanted to clarify and discuss the important role of line managers in the HR quadriad of project-based organizations. The case illustrations from Saab and Tetra Pak describe line management in transition, moving toward an increased HR orientation. We have also suggested important roles that line managers need to take on to perform important HRM practices at the operational, organizational levels. Moreover, differences in the project-based work setting (type of project work and project participation) clearly affect how the HR quadriad is best shaped, as seen from the perspective of the line manager.

We believe that the line manager role is still underestimated when it comes to opportunities to improve HRM at the operational level in project-based organizations. The HR quadriad framework has made it possible to understand the line managers' HR role from a new angle, basing it on the collective and configurational nature of HRM. There is still much to learn about how the collaborative processes within the HR quadriad could be designed to match different types of project-based work setting (most notably Type A and Type B, mentioned earlier). We do believe that a better understanding of these matters could open up new approaches to line management and help to define these roles in various kinds of project-based organizations. In the next chapter we turn to the role of the project manager that is gaining importance in project-based organizations not only to sort out integrative challenges but also to manage the flow, performance, involvement and development of human resources.

6
Project Managers and HRM

Introduction

A new cadre of managers has begun to play an increasingly important role in recent years: project managers. This chapter focuses on this category of managers.[1] In the introduction of the book, we discussed the importance of the integration capability of the firm, systems integration, and project management. Project managers undoubtedly play an important part in delivering and developing that capability, and, as more and more companies realize the importance of this capability, they also realize the important role project managers play. This is probably one of the prime reasons behind the professionalization of project management and the boom of certification programs launched by institutions such as the Project Management Institute (PMI) and International Project Management Association (IPMA). The importance of the efforts of the project manager are further acknowledged by a wide array of management scholars (see, e.g., Clark and Fujimoto, 1991; Eisenhardt and Tabrizi, 1995; Meredith and Mantel, 1995; Pinto and Slevin, 1987). Studies have, for instance, pointed to the importance of management skills in delivering successful projects and have particularly singled out the significance of the skills of the project manager (e.g., Badaway, 1982).

There are several reasons why the role of project managers should be addressed. First, project management is the most frequent management assignment for professionals in contemporary organizations. Second, it is a management assignment which is often not based on a formal managerial position, but rather on a temporary assignment in which responsibilities typically exceed authority. Third, project management is rapidly undergoing a formal process of professionalization through the standardization of bodies of knowledge and certification. Fourth, failure rates and problems in projects are overwhelming and "many project leaders express feelings of stress, overload and a lack of control" (Lindgren and Packendorff, 2009: 286). Fifth, project managers tend to leave the role of project manager due to high pressure and decide to aim for other management positions, despite their interest in continuing with such duties (see, e.g., Ricciardi, 2001). Sixth, research has stressed the need to broaden the conventional project-level evaluation outside time, cost, quality, and client satisfaction and bring in such outcomes as organizational capabilities, team satisfaction, and competence development (see, for instance, Shenhar and Dvir, 2007). This generally illustrates the need for project managers not only to address the conventional performance measures but also, among other things, the management of human resources.

Notwithstanding these observations and claims substantiating the value of the work of project managers, so far only a limited number of studies have actually focused on what project managers do, particularly from an HRM point of view. Keegan et al. (2010) observe that the responsibilities of HRM are not only devolved to the line organization,

---

Fact box 6.1   The role of the project manager

Many of the firms that we have studied have some kind of role description for the responsibilities of the project manager. There are a number of both general and customized project management frameworks, such as the PMI's Body of Knowledge, PROPS, PRINCE, PPS, etc. Without reviewing them all, several of them include some definition of the role of the project manager – not only the processes for project management. Typically, they tend to focus on the formal decision rights of the project manager, but, to some extent, they also highlight the behavioral dimensions of project management and, to a lesser extent, the HRM dimensions.

but in many cases they are actually devolved "beyond the line," making project managers increasingly more important within the HR organization. The authors claim, however, that the "responsibilities for those beyond line management, including specifically project managers, are neglected, as are the relationships between HR, line managers, and other managers" (p. 2) with sometimes overlapping HRM responsibilities. Following the general claim that HRM research needs to focus more on HRM in practice (Legge, 1995), an obvious direction for studies of HRM in project-based organization would thus be to look in more depth at the role of the project manager. Therefore, in this chapter, we address such simple yet important questions as: What do project managers do? What are their responsibilities with particular reference to HRM? What is their role in the HR quadriad?

The chapter is structured in the following way. We begin with an introduction of the role of the project manager. The explicit ambition here is to take an historical look at the role and work of the project manager to trace the HRM responsibilities of project managers back to the original ideas. We also point out a few important development patterns which have contributed to the change in importance of the project manager in light of HRM. In that sense, the analysis documents some generic aspects of the role of the project manager. However, given our claim that HRM is context dependent, the differences across projects should also be highlighted. One way of doing this is to scrutinize the differences between project-based work settings. As our analysis shows, this contributes to the HRM responsibilities project managers tend to assume. We discuss the implications that these observations have on project managers and the responsibilities of project managers for HRM. The chapter proceeds with a discussion about the HRM practice areas and the role of the project manager. Final thoughts and reflections about important future research end the chapter.

The role of the project manager

Compared to the area of leadership – for instance, as presented in Yukl (1994) – project managers have not been as salient as company leaders in much of the previous research and literature. Stories of world-famous leaders are seldom protagonized by the leaders of large engineering projects (Miller and Lessard, 2001) or product development projects (Clark and Fujimoto, 1991). Yet, in his article "Why Does Project Management Fail?" Avots (1969: 78) stresses that among the most common reasons for project management failure is that "the wrong man is appointed project manager." Underlying Avots' conclusion are the observations that not only is there a lack of preparation for the job in terms of integration skills, but there are also several reasons for failure that can be traced to the HRM dimensions of project work.

One of the first academic papers on the subject of project management was published by Paul Gaddis (1959) in the *Harvard Business Review*. This paper is still considered to be something of a landmark in project management research (Packendorff, 1995). It was one of the first papers to highlight the role and importance of the project manager. Gaddis addresses the following questions: (a) What does a project manager in advanced technology do? (b) What kind of person must he be? (c) What training is a prerequisite for success? Gaddis clearly points out projects as organizational units and that project leadership can be understood as the responsibility of a group or an organization in charge of a relatively complex, but still concrete, task. In many ways, Gaddis's original contribution stands up even today to close examination. The author, for instance, highlights the importance of discussing which "personnel responsibility resides with the

---

Fact box 6.2　Project manager competence models

A set of recent studies have tried to identify the critical skills that the project manager must possess to do a good job. One example of such a model is presented in the "job-task competency model" by Cheng et al. (2005). The model centers primarily on responsibilities and competences linked to technology and task execution, but a few of them – such as health and safety, roles and responsibilities, and knowledge sharing – are located within the area of HRM. The authors identify the following competences:

- ensure that work is properly analyzed and planned
- deliver the job to client/sponsor satisfaction
- ensure that the quality of the end product meets stakeholder expectations
- ensure that the project is completed within the original requirements
- maintain budget control and to maximize company's profits
- ensure all staff and supervisors are aware of their roles and responsibilities
- ensure that information is appropriately and effectively communicated to project workers
- promote continuous improvements through team learning and development
- promote and share knowledge
- champion company standards and approaches
- schedule meetings, coordinate activities, and ensure cooperation with external partners

project manager" (p. 147). He also identifies several of the challenges that are problematic today, including the finite duration of the task, the interaction among professionals, and the difficulties of leading in unknown terrains: "the project manager often finds himself like a pilot flying blind, assisted by a relatively unproven set of instruments" (p. 149). Gaddis, despite the plea for a discussion about the personnel responsibilities of the project manager, primarily focuses on the importance of preserving a sense of momentum through all layers of the project and on the basic responsibilities, which are to deliver the end product "(1) in accordance with performance requirements, (2) within the limitations of the budget, and (3) within the specified time schedule" (Gaddis, 1959: 150).

In one of the first, in-depth empirical studies of leadership techniques in project organizations, Hodgetts (1969) addresses project leaders and how they deal with the "authority gap" because project managers "do not possess authority to reward or promote their personnel" (p. 211). He claims that project managers need to adopt a specific set of techniques and become increasingly "human relations oriented." These techniques include educating team members, providing credit, giving recognition, and making team members feel they play a vital part in the team. Reeser (1969) continues along these lines in his investigation into the specific leadership challenges facing project managers. He points out that the project organization, by its nature, has built-in capacities for causing unique human problems that call for specific leadership actions. For example, Reeser shows that the personnel working in projects suffer more anxieties about possible loss of employment than do other members in traditional functional organizations. In addition, career paths are singled out as particularly problematic in these settings, and they "worry more about being set back in their careers than members of functional organizations" (p. 463). Building on the work of Reeser, Butler (1973) argues that project leaders need to respond to a set of unique challenges since project management tends to violate established managerial practice with regard to "hierarchical authority and responsibility; procedural arrangements and accommodations, departmentation specificity; incentive systems; unity of command and direction; span of control; resource-allocation patterns; and establishment of relative priorities" (Butler, 1973: 90).

Lawrence and Lorsch (1967) made another early contribution to the analysis of the role of the project manager. In their article about the manager's role as "the integrator," they focus on the achievement of unity of effort among the major functional specialists in a business. The authors stress the importance of the "need for affiliation" to be able to become a good project manager, since "they pay more attention to others and to their feelings; they try harder to establish friendly relationships in meetings; and they take on more assignments that offer opportunities for interaction" (p. 150). Their empirical data also warn against assigning young managers who lack sufficient experience in all facets of the business to these positions, although "this may provide a useful learning experience … our evidence suggests that it really does not lead to effective integration" (p. 147). In addition, their evidence indicates that project managers are so tied up in day-to-day matters; they cannot look to the future.

As is well-known from studies of project management, a key part of the project manager's job is to focus on action, which, in many ways, is the underlying rationale for creating a project in the first place. This strong action focus has even led researchers to talk about an "action theory of projects" (Lundin and Söderholm, 1995) and to say that projects could be seen as organizing mechanisms established to trigger action and cooperation (Lindkvist et al., 1998). Hence, there are many underlying reasons for the project manager to focus on technology integration, task performance, time and quality evaluation, and a range of other issues that we normally would put in the technology and integration box of managerial responsibilities. Only a few of their responsibilities actually deal with issues that we associate with HRM, issues such as recruitment, competence development, team satisfaction, appraisal, reward, career planning, etc. Accordingly, many would probably argue that managing projects has little to do with HRM. Our viewpoint, however, is quite different. We suggest that projects have much to say about HRM, particularly since projects today constitute such an important action locality and learning arena for individual workers. In addition, team satisfaction and on-the-job training are as critical as ever and the person primarily assuming the overall responsibility for these issues is the project manager. Moreover, as we have seen in previous chapters, the HR process in project-based work settings needs continuous input from the project dimension concerning the performance and development needs of project workers. This might be particularly true in inter-functional project work with focused project participation, but it is also a crucial matter in other types of project-based work settings. The role of the project manager must, therefore, be seen as an important part of the HRM of the firm, and it is important for the project manager to develop skills and capabilities to assume this HRM-oriented role without compromising requirements on the integrative capability. One such area is the responsibility for feedback and performance reviews (see Fact Box 6.3).

Our evidence indicates a development pattern that revolves around the need to establish management capacity, primarily driven by the

Fact box 6.3   McKinsey and performance reviews

McKinsey & Co is probably one of the world's most famous management consultancies, reputed for only hiring the very best people from business and engineering schools around the world. Generally, many students list the company as their top pick among favorite employers. McKinsey & Co is a particular kind of project-based organization – typically engaged in various kinds of strategic analysis projects and implementation and change processes. Projects are a common work context, although the size and complexity of the projects vary considerably. Each project is headed by an engagement manager who has the overall responsibility for the project. To make sure that their employees get the right kind of feedback, the company invests heavily in formal performance reviews. The input for the biannual review comes from reports prepared by engagement managers, senior consultants, and knowledge area managers. During the project, the consultant also has several additional one-on-one feedback and coaching sessions with senior people managing and directing the project. According to management professors Christopher Bartlett and Sumantra Ghoshal (2002: 38), "The company maintains that its in-depth approach to development is one of the main reasons why people join McKinsey – and why they stay."

need for integration in and through projects. Therefore, in looking at the specific HRM responsibilities and from where they originate, one might consider two key drivers to be in play: increasingly complex projects in combination with the projectification of activities and work. These drivers obviously lead to more and more people carrying out project assignments. In some cases, projects are even co-located for an extensive period of time. In these cases, project managers become key players in the HR quadriad and, accordingly, have a prominent role in ensuring the quality of the various processes tied to HRM. Figure 6.1 explicates the underlying logic and the driving forces.

Project mentality and the "project man"

Typically, we tend to associate project managers with a particular sense of action orientation, which is made possible thanks to bracketing in time and a concomitant focus on immediate matters. There is, however, a risk to the strong focus on action and the negative effects this focus might have on project people. Gaddis (1959: 94) mentions the subject of "projectitis" as a common problem in project-based organizations, that is, "a seeing of all things as though a particular project were the center of the corporate universe." He warns that projectitis tends to lead to

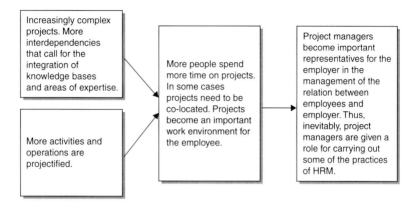

Figure 6.1   Project managers and HRM: some underlying forces

adverse results, including the reduction in efficiency and productivity of the human resources in the project.

> For those men with the mental and personal endowment for the project kind of work – the men of factual creativity, the applied scientists, the practicing technologists – there is no element of professional degradation in this work. On the contrary, this type of professional finds the project pace challenging and exhilarating as can be easily verified by observation – and far preferable to the apparent aimlessness of the pure research environment. (Gaddis, 1959: 97)

Several authors have argued that there is a need for a particular type of person to thrive in a project environment. Some have referred to this as having a "project mentality." Others have contrasted "the project man" with the "economic man" and pointed out that the project man is a person with a particular sense of action, a particular skill in developing social relationships, and the ability to move from one project to another (see also Bennis and Slater, 1968; Lindgren et al., 2001). Gaddis also suggest that "project people" are "inspired by more immediate, if less exalted, goals." One of the project managers interviewed for a study we conducted a few years ago expressed similar opinions. The project manager said:

> I love projects. You can work with anyone you just don't like because you know that it soon is going to be over, it's just temporary and I don't have to bother about this annoying person when this project is done. That is sort of a nice feeling. (Project Manager, IT)

This is a representative example that we have come across in several of our empirical investigations. Project managers view their primary roles to be "getting things done" and concentrating on the deadline, quality, cost, and output. Many of them have chosen the role of project

---

Fact box 6.4   Voices about project managers and HRM

In our studies, we have identified a set of developmental patterns related to the role of the project manager. The following quotations summarize some of our observations, which highlight not only what is expected of the project manager but also what are considered to be the project manager's critical responsibilities.

If it's a long project, the project member will get closer to the project manager and start developing a manager–coworker relationship with the project manager, and that is not desirable. Because then you are running long-term activities in project form and you get a strange hybrid where project managers cannot focus on what they are supposed to do. It becomes personnel issues that you should probably not deal with as a project manager. (Senior Project Manager)

I don't think that our project managers have any formal responsibility to give feedback to the project member after the completion of a project. I'm not sure, but I don't think so. Unfortunately. This should of course be done both to the individual and to the line manager. ... When someone leaves a project, I should get information about this person from the project manager. That's not a bad idea, it's a great idea. Feedback is extremely important and people cry out for it. (Line Manager)

I believe that project managers are a bit weak when it comes to feeding back information to line managers. While listening to me, you have probably noticed that I tend to point all the responsibilities to the line manager. But of course, if I have had a person working in my project, one would think that it is a hygiene factor that I evaluate the performance of this person. ... But, no, I don't think that this is done to any great extent. (Senior Project Manager)

Taken to its extreme, you could say that the project manager has one focus, and that is to deliver according to the specification, within budget. He could ignore that people are ready to drop with fatigue and resign, as long as he reaches the goals within time and budget. That's of course too harsh, project managers don't act that way, but from a crass point of view that's the way it is. But as a line manager I have to see to it that the personnel are well, that they don't work too much, ... that they find the project assignment interesting and developing and that the project manager behaves in a correct way. It's my responsibility to give the project manager a telling-off, even if I'm not his manager, if my personnel are not treated with respect or fare badly. ... A project manager shares much shorter periods of time with the personnel, depending on how long the project is, so he can drive the personnel much harder during that time, even though that does not necessarily mean that they behave badly. (Line Manager)

manager to avoid some of the mundane tasks that line managers must do. Instead, the project managers can focus on the "fun stuff" and on "maintaining momentum." The latter focus resonates with Gaddis's classic piece on the role of the project manager.

> As a man of action, his most important function will be the estab-lishment and preservation of a sense of momentum throughout all layers of his project. What he will strive hardest to avoid is "dead center" situations in which general inertia seems to become over-powering and his technical people for the moment see no direction in which to advance. Thus, the usual management function of trou-ble shooting, or of unraveling the knots, will occupy a great deal of his time. (Gaddis, 1959: 92)

The image of the role of the project manager thus seems not fit many of the conventional ideas about HRM. This observation, to some extent, corresponds with our empirical research, which shows that project managers tend to hold the view that long-term issues and HRM should be handled by others, allowing the project managers to focus on the important deliveries in the project. Although we have some sympathy for this viewpoint and believe that the underlying economic rationale makes sense, we feel that the project manager still has a role to play in the HR organization, a role which should not be neglected. Fact Box 6.4 presents some examples from interviews about the role of the project manager, how it has changed, and what expectations various actors have of project managers with regard to HRM. At the same time, it should be pointed out that there are important differences among different types of projects that need to be taken into account, together with the types of project-based work settings mentioned earlier.

The project manager and HRM responsibilities

Despite the emphasis on goal orientation, results-focus, and short-termism, there are still a number of HRM-related matters for which the project manager is partly responsible (see also Fact Box 6.5). Such matters have particularly attracted researchers to investigate the role and focus of the project manager. Turner (1999) identifies six traits of effective managers: problem-solving ability, results orientation, energy and initiative, self-confidence, perspective, communication, and nego-tiating ability. Meredith and Mantel (1995) categorize the skills neces-sary for a project manager into six primary areas: communication skills, organizational skills, team-building skills, leadership skills, coping skills, and technological skills. There are several other studies that investigate the traits that a person needs to be a good project manager. These studies also list many of the same task and technical orientations so typical to the image of the project manager, and they also add people skills. The focus, however, would of course depend on the type of project, in particular depending on the uncertainty, complexity, and pace of the project (De Meyer et al, 2002; Shenhar and Dvir, 2007). Although, we would agree that these factors are undoubtedly important, in the analysis suggested here, we will direct our attention to the nature of the project-based work setting to complement extant research.

There are several ways to identify and analyze the competences a leader needs to possess. Recently, several studies within the area of project leadership have relied on the set of competences presented (e.g., Dulewicz and Higgs, 2003; see also, e.g., Turner and Müller, 2005). Dulewicz and Higgs's (2003) framework identifies 15 leadership competences: seven emotional (EQ), three intellectual (IQ), and five managerial (MQ). This set of factors is used in an empirical investigation of 400 project managers to find out the relationship between project manager competences and project success. The major criteria for project success include not only the classic ones of time, cost, and quality but also client and team satisfaction. From an HRM perspective, one might, therefore, say that empirical studies within this area have moved toward including

---

Fact box 6.5   PMI and Project Human Resource Management

PMI (Project Management Institute) has compiled a rather extensive set of standards for project management, which is summarized in the book *A Guide to the Project Management Body of Knowledge*. In recent years, the book contains more information and guidelines about HRM. The concept of Project Human Resource Management is used to describe the processes to "organize and manage the project team". Four primary processes are distinguished: Human Resource Planning, Acquire Project Team, Develop Project Team, and Manage Project Team. Human Resource Planning involves identifying and documenting project roles, responsibilities, and reporting relationships, as well as creating the staff management plan. Acquire Project Team involves obtaining the human resources needed to complete the project. Develop Project Team involves improving the competences and interaction of team members to enhance project performance. Finally, Manage Project Team is described as the process of tracking team member performance, providing feedback, resolving conflicts, and coordinating changes to enhance project performance.

HRM performance measurements, which are often then broken down into finer categories, such as team satisfaction, skill development, team member growth, team member retention, and well-being. One of the most comprehensive discussions about the extended view on project success is found in Shenhar and Dvir (2007). This relatively recent contribution to the literature on project management highlights, in particular, the importance of evaluating project success from a broader perspective, including team satisfaction and other HRM measurements. Accordingly, it accentuates the HRM responsibilities of the project manager. The inclusion of team satisfaction as a success measure and the fine-grained categorization of HRM-related success measures are obvious signs of an increased awareness of HRM on the part of project manager. Another sign of development is the implementation of various "HR Gates" in the project management models (see Fact Box 6.6). This is an attempt to get project managers more focused and also responsible and accountable for HRM activities.

The recent call for transformational leadership is another sign of development. This call typically stresses the need for leadership centering on change, vision, and the mobilization of commitment. According

---

Fact Box 6.6   HR Gates at Volvo Car Corporation: Making projects human

Some companies have invested in improving the HRM dimension of their projects. One such attempt has been made by Volvo Car Corporation – a Swedish-based automotive company. The company has for many years invested in improving its development and project management processes. A few years ago, it also wanted to integrate more HRM features into the model. The solution became known as the, so-called, HR Gates, which was to complement the conventional gates in the stage-gate model. The gate model is intended to ensure that top management checks that not only the business and technical dimensions (system tests, tryouts, and quality, specifications, business case, design features, technologies, etc.) are at satisfactory levels but also that the people dimension is made part of the process. Top management must confirm that people have been recruited appropriately, plans for involvement exist, people understand their roles, the organizational structure is set-up correctly, human resource flows are scheduled, competence development is part of the project, and the role of the project manager in the HRM activities is clarified. In our conversations with the HR manager concerning the HR Gates, she emphasized the increased focus on project managers' involvement in the HR process: "This is an HR responsibility that all project managers have, regardless of where in the organization they work. They must follow through and check the HR Gates. I think that this is quite unique – that we are among the first to have it."

to Keegan and van den Hartog (2004), the literature on this subject suggests that transformational leadership may be of particular value to project-based organizations. This view acknowledges the growing importance of the emotional and motivational aspects of projects and accordingly the necessity for project managers to develop "faith in and commitment to a larger moral purpose" (p. 610). At the same time, even though transformational leadership might be called for in these settings, it might also be difficult to bring about since project-based organizations typically lack the necessary preconditions for transformational leadership. Among other things, this is due to frequently shifting or unstable relationships, restlessness, having most people report to more than one manager, low levels of belongingness, disintegrative tendencies and frequent changes (see, e.g., Alvesson, 1995).

Shared project leadership

One solution to the calls for HRM-oriented project management and transformational leadership is the increase of leadership capacity in the project dimension. One of the most significant developments in this area may be what has been referred to as joint leadership, shared leadership, or distributive leadership. Although some writers would argue that there are distinct differences between these alternatives, in the following section we will use the terms interchangeably giving preference to the term "shared leadership." According to Lindgren and Packendorff (2009), the growing literature on shared leadership, that is, investigations into circumstances where people share leadership duties and responsibilities (rather than circumstances where such duties and responsibilities are allocated to a single person), could be seen as a general critique of the conventional, superhero image of leadership. The distribution of leadership duties is also seen in project management contexts as a response to the underlying developmental patterns discussed earlier. For instance, Söderlund (2005a) posits that mounting project complexity and greater interdependencies typically lead to the formation of project management teams, often consisting of three persons who assume different roles to provide leadership in projects. This tendency is apparent in several of the companies we have investigated and seems to be critical to handling the administrative difficulties involved in large projects, such as the development of a complex telecom system, the development of a new version of combat fighter, the development of a new drug involving test activities around the globe, or the development of a new automobile model. In these cases, one project manager

Table 6.1 Perspectives on shared leadership practices in projects (Lindgren and Packendorff, 2009: 297–298 modified)

Perspective	Project-related arguments
Individual perspective: shared leadership practices as a way of enhancing the lives of those who work in project leadership positions	Solo leadership consumes people, and there is a risk of high levels of stress and anxiety.
	Enhanced balance of work requirements and personal responsibilities/private life.
	Better sense of security and stability in decision-making and implementation.
	Enhanced possibility to learn having the co-leader as a role model and provider of feedback.
	More enjoyable work.
Coworker perspective: shared leadership ideals as a source of enhancing the correspondence between employee expectations and actual project leadership practices	Young people are used to working in teams with some degree of shared leadership. When they rise to higher organizational levels, they are more likely to want to continue sharing leadership and resist traditional solo command.
	Expectation for shared leadership created by the experience of living in modern family models where both parents participate in decision-making, reinforced by experiences of working in teams.
	Young employees expect more democratic leadership in modern organizations.

Organizational perspective: shared leadership as a way of enhancing project effectiveness

Single-person leadership cannot reflect and handle the environmental complexity facing many projects. Several competences, skills, and roles are required.

Cross-functional communication can be enhanced through shared leadership since several departments, functions, and stakeholders can be represented at the same time at the managerial level.

Both control and improvisation can be represented by a dual leadership, thereby facilitating change, improvement, and communication.

Lower risk for suboptimal solutions if the leadership of an organization is truly shared by the project management team.

Less vulnerability in case of project manager absence or resignation.

Co-leaders can have a larger span of control together and more time for their project workers and for reflecting on the overall strategy and direction of their project.

Organizations can avoid losing project leadership talent because of stress associated with leader posts.

Projects can benefit from the cognitive and behavioral capabilities of a larger number of individuals.

When power is too concentrated, it may result in immoral and/or illegal actions taken by individual leaders struck by hubris.

Societal perspective: shared leadership ideals as a way of maintaining and increasing the legitimacy of leadership and management

Shared leadership increases the possibility of including minorities in managerial positions, thereby increasing the legitimacy of leadership.

typically assumes the overall, or total, project management responsibility, another focuses on the commercial and business sides of the project, and a third project manager assumes the technical project management responsibilities and the overall role as systems integrator. Of course, this is a solution implemented primarily to improve the integrative capabilities within the firm, but it could also be seen as a way to sort out some of the human problems associated with project management. We have not, however, seen instances of appointed project managers with the sole responsibility for HRM; instead, this responsibility, such as the responsibility for team satisfaction mentioned earlier, is typically shared by the members of the project management team, including the total project manager, the technical project manager, deputy project manager, etc. In that respect, the HRM issues, to a greater extent than other matters of project management, seem to be an area of management that tend to be shared among project managers. Of course, many of these matters need to be performed in dialogue and collaboration with line managers.

The focus on shared leadership indicates possibilities for new developments within project management with regard to how project leadership can be understood as a particular kind of practice and social interaction. Lindgren and Packendorff (2009) identify four perspectives (the individual perspective, the coworker perspective, the organizational perspective, and the societal perspective) of shared leadership that shed light on the reasons for adopting the shared leadership model (see table 6.1). These perspectives also sort out what project-related challenges might be resolved through the use of shared leadership in projects. The perspectives provide explanations for using such leadership, which improves the organization's capability to handle HRM activities linked to project-based organizations.

To sum up, the question of the HRM duties of project managers has been peripherally discussed by scholars for nearly as long as there has been research on the subject of project management. As shown in previous sections, a number of older as well as more recent studies underline the need to address the more people-centered capabilities of project management. An increasing number of studies also contribute knowledge about leadership and personality traits of "good" and "bad" project managers. However, there is still a dearth of studies centering on the role of project managers in performing HRM. The HR quadriad framework on which we elaborate in this book not only accentuates the importance of conducting more such studies to add to the knowledge of the roles in the framework, but it also stresses the importance to understanding the role of project managers in relation to the other players in the HR quadriad.

Upon reviewing the extant literature – such as the studies discussed above – we found quite a number of studies dealing with the project manager–project worker relationship, mostly in terms of team satisfaction, leadership, and motivation. While the relationship between project managers and HR specialists is virtually a blind spot (to some extent discussed in Bredin and Söderlund, 2006; Clark and Colling, 2005), there is a strand of studies on the project manager–line manager relationship in various kinds of matrix organizations. These studies deal with a variety of issues such as the locus of control and authority (e.g., Dunne et al., 1978; Gemmill and Wilemon, 1970; Katz and Allen, 1985; Wilemon, 1973) and comparisons of line managers' and project managers' influence on motivation and job satisfaction (e.g. Dunn, 2001; Keegan and Den Hartog, 2004; Pitagorsky, 1998; Turner et al., 1998). The review of previous research presented in Dunn (2001) about motivation by project managers and line managers shows that line managers has tended to be regarded as primarily focused on the needs of the individual (support, coaching, career and development, evaluation and rewards, etc.) whereas project managers are primarily focused on the team. On the other hand, Dunn (2001) reports on a survey among engineering-oriented project workers, which gives evidence of the project managers also having a large influence on the individual level. These results highlight three points of particular interest to the present chapter.

First, line managers are perceived as having a larger influence on growth and development and on "hygiene factors" (such as salary, administration, working conditions, job security, work-life issues, see also Hertzberg, 1966)), while project managers are more influential in regard to "motivator factors", such as recognition, content of the work, achievement, and responsibility. Second, Dunn points to the important partnership between project managers and line managers, indicating that "For several of the individual factors, the managers have a shared role. This provides an improved understanding of the work relationships and role responsibilities within the project matrix form…." (Dunn, 2001: 9)

(Dunn, 2001: 9) further specifies that this is reached, for example, by:

> Refuting the traditional model that the functional manager is solely responsible for addressing the individual needs of employees

Highlighting the interconnectivity of coordination (and communication) between project and functional managers relative to meeting the needs of team members

Establishing that the project manager has a clear responsibility for meeting the attitudinal needs of project team members.

Third, the study indicates important differences depending on the operational work setting. Project workers who spent more time on project work, while working on fewer projects (focused project participation) tended to look more to the project manager than to the line manager. The results of Dunn's investigation further strengthen our argument that the role of project managers with respect to HRM is important and is in need of focused attention from the research community. Moreover, the results prove the relevance of the collective and complementary take on HRM that we put forward in this book: HRM as a responsibility shared by several players (although Dunn only focuses on the project manager–line manager relationship). The results show that the work setting at the operational level matters and that the role of project managers with regard to HRM-oriented issues is to some extent shaped by the type of project work and project participation.

In the following, we will present examples from our research on project managers and HRM. This is a subject that requires more empirical studies in order to make a comprehensive analysis. With this chapter, we aim to raise the interest for such studies and to provide some empirical observations to substantiate our arguments. These empirical observations report on project managers' own stories about their work and commitment to the "soft side" of project management. Later, we will return to the collaborative and collective dimensions of the project manager role as well as the impact of the project-based work setting.

An inside view of HRM and the role of the project manager

We have chosen to illustrate a few observations by using interviews with senior project managers in large Swedish-based multinationals – automotive and telecom companies, for example – which are involved in the development of complex systems. These companies are generally thought to be good places to work and, among engineers, are considered to be the most popular employers in Sweden. It should be noted that the firms studied rely heavily on large projects, and projects are their normal business. Their engineers typically spend at least 60 to 70 percent of their time on project assignments. The project managers selected for our study were chosen because they were considered to be highly successful in their work. All had established themselves as among the very few who could take responsibility for managing and leading development projects of critical strategic importance to their respective companies. They had also been project managers for a long time and had identified themselves, and were perceived by others, as highly "professional project managers" among the few really "strategic project managers." The projects that they typically lead could be considered "temporary organizations" in their own right, although the teams working on them might change several times during the course of the projects. Most projects of this kind have a lifetime of at least two years.

PM I: Carl–The emergency manager

Carl is a well-dressed man in his late 50s. He immediately starts talking about his most recent project. He says that he is in love with the product that the company is producing. The atmosphere during our meeting is very relaxed and open. Carl is a graduate of the Royal Institute of Technology in Stockholm and, after earning his engineering degree, started working as a project manager for one of Sweden's largest steel producers. He believes this job was a good way to begin a professional career, especially since he graduated with a specialization in mining engineering. Early on, he took responsibility for a rather difficult and important project, sometimes reporting directly to senior management. He did a good job, which led to even more challenging projects and, after a number of successful projects, he was promoted to production manager. Since then, he has held various positions as production manager and top manager in several large manufacturing companies. Some years ago, he was headhunted by the company where he is currently employed. He wanted to try something new and different, thinking that he had been with the previous company too long. The previous company had experienced a few mergers over a short period of time, which meant internal politics had distracted him from doing what he liked most: "to do things." The frequent job changes resulting from these mergers also forced his family to move often, although he emphasizes that all this has given him a sense of self-confidence, an ability to meet new challenges and an interest in trying out new things.

Carl sees himself as a very ambitious and "energetic" person with a good sense of humor. He frequently laughs at himself and stresses the importance of maintaining distance from what you do and who you are. He also points out the importance of being a generalist when it comes to leading large, complex projects. He believes he is both a generalist and good at handling integration tasks, while also being a skilled "human engineer" with the ability to "manipulate people" to become good at what they do.

Carl became a project manager because of a combination of coincidence and talent. The advantages of working in projects, he says, is that one is able to run the full cycle, that is, to lead an organization from start to finish and to see the concrete results. In his most recent project, Carl was required to put in a good deal of overtime, spending long hours at the office. This latest project was important to him, however, since it provided him with the opportunity to do something he considered important.

Carl describes his work situation as very turbulent and stressful, but at the same time great fun. He explains:

> I have lived a turbulent life and I seem to have the ability to end up in such situations. Sometimes I get the feeling that I am the one creating this madness. I like things that are slightly chaotic because they create opportunities for change and I love change. To be in turbulent situations is more a normal way of working to me.

When we start discussing the general challenges of managing projects, Carl emphasizes the many positive aspects of project-oriented work. He mentions that one of the most fundamental issues of project work is the ability to look back on what has been done, to learn from it, and then to try it again and "learn from one's mistakes." He believes that seeing the end result is an important source of motivation both for him and also for the other people working on his projects.

> I come to think of a project that I worked on a few years ago in another company. Even though that was an almost impossible project with a tough budget and time plan, we were able to deliver on time, and I think we did a really good job, overall. When I see today what we managed to do, I am very proud of myself and the rest of the people who did it.

He says that project work is often a matter of emergency meetings and of fixing things that do not work. During very short periods of downtime and periods where things do actually work, he becomes restless. He needs a new challenge. A challenge, in Carl's mind, is a project that is fairly unstructured and unclear. It is only challenging when the budget and time plan are tough – if not, then half of the challenge is gone. He needs tough deadlines and difficult targets, because "it shouldn't be easy." He says that this pressure creates an opportunity for him to implement what he knows and to draw from his extensive experience in leading projects. He also says that a tough deadline is an important mechanism that makes it possible for him to do his job. Such a deadline puts pressure on the people and the managers who depend on the project. They must support the project in order to achieve the set targets and the deadline.

According to Carl, the role of a project manager is, to a great extent, a matter of structuring work and creating preconditions necessary for the project workers to do a good job. It is also very much a question of knowing exactly what needs to be done. For instance, he stresses that goals need to be clear, because "we need to know what to deliver." If the goals are unclear, no one, "no matter how talented they are, can succeed." He points out that among the most important tasks for the project manager are to make sure the goals are clear and understood, to clarify roles and responsibilities, and to force people to prioritize among conflicting objectives. He also believes he has an important role to play in reviewing the work conditions for those involved in the project. Carl says that management is a matter of balancing coaching and firm, clear direction.

One of the most important things, Carl says, is to not accept what top management says if they do not provide you with the necessary preconditions. He personally has a strategy of not getting involved in projects that do not have a fair chance of succeeding. If, however, Carl believes in something, he can work extremely hard in order to reach the targets. He says that he quite frequently is on the border of getting fired because he disagrees with the CEO, but despite the disputes, top management has continued to hand him the responsibility for several of the most important projects in the company.

Carl emphasizes the importance of creating a good team. However, typically it is a rather forced process in which the task at hand is the main focus. Carl describes the process in the following way:

> In the beginning everyone is very polite, then everyone is very rude and then you have a team.

The problem, he believes, is that you seldom have the chance to build a team in the conventional sense, because people are only there for a limited time and because some people participate in the project at an early stage while others enter later.

He singles out honesty as a key to this process and mentions that it would be unthinkable that every project would be a success – "they can't be." However, when failure is due to a problem in communication, which happens once in a while, then something is seriously wrong. In Carl's view, silence is the biggest threat to successful projects. It creates a sense of uneasiness and anxiety and should be avoided. In that respect, he points out, there are big differences between different kinds of projects. One such difference might be whether people are co-located and able to get to know each other while focusing on a single project, or whether the team members are scattered in different line units and must participate in several projects at the same time.

To a certain extent, Carl is in charge of staffing the projects together with the responsible line managers. Normally, the staffing decisions for projects are the result of negotiations with the responsible line managers and, of course, the individual project workers. There are often trade-offs because of the need to work with the people who are available. This leads to negotiations and, in some cases, to attempts to change the opinions of the line managers. Still, participating in the staffing decisions is important because, according to Carl, it creates an initial psychological contract with each and every one in the team. They were picked to do this difficult project.

The life cycle of the project is repeated – from start to finish and then by moving on to a new project. It is a process involving feelings, frustrations, and fear that starts over and over, time after time.

> I often get the question why I am still doing this. I must be stupid, but projects represent change to me, change and development, and I like that. I have tried to stay away from projects, but it does not work. You are sort of addicted to them.

PM II: John–The stubborn troubleshooter

John immediately steers the conversation toward the projects that he has been in charge of over the years. He is a mechanical engineer with a university degree and has worked for 25 years in the company where he is currently employed. Well known for his many successful projects, John is considered to be one of the company's very top project managers. Engineers within the company generally appreciate working in John's projects.

For the last 12 years, he has been working as a project manager. The major reason he opted for a project manager career was that he wanted to know more about the product – the trucks – that the company develops and produces. He says he has an almost "religious interest in trucks," and being a project manager for the development of new trucks is a perfect place to be for such a person. He has been offered a line-manager job several times but has decided to stay on the "project track" since, as he puts it, "I want to have a broader view and learn more about the entire truck." John says that his current project is a "dream project" with new and exciting technology and "funky features". At the same time, it is an important development effort for the entire company.

When describing himself, he frequently returns to his strong "results orientation" and his "stubbornness," which is generally considered to be a good thing among the rest of the managers within the company. He also considers time to be a critical issue.

> We have to move forward. The clock is ticking, and we will never get back lost time. It's a battle field out there and it's a matter of regrouping and just attacking again.

He believes the reason why many refrain from taking a project manager job is the high demands put on project managers. He adds that "working on projects is very much a matter of taking risks" and "dealing with uncertainty." Speaking about the pressures of being a project manager, John often returns to the many difficulties that must be solved. He often uses terms such as "troubleshooter" and "problem-solver" to define and explain what his work is all about. To a great extent, these troubles and problems are associated with technical issues or with problems that result from people not doing a proper job. He thinks that he is also generally viewed as being good at these things: "troubleshooting, that's what I do, and I'm good at it." At the same time, the constant flow of problems constitutes a considerable challenge.

> A project is only a matter of problems that must be solved. You never hear about what is working, you only hear about the things that don't work.

He believes that a successful project manager must feel total responsibility for what is done within the project and be able to solve problems quickly and make sure that the project is "moving forward." A project "can't stand still" since this leads to a "tremendous loss of energy." John mentions the critical importance of structure and planning to ensure that the project has the necessary preconditions to create action and progress. Clear roles and responsibilities are important to ensuring plans are understood and followed.

> It is very important to have clear roles and responsibility. As a leader, I have to be very precise about who is going to do what and what everyone is expecting of one another. It is a major problem in getting people to do what they should be doing, they often tend to do other things, not because they are evil, but because they are ambitious and interested, if you know what I mean.

He also stresses the importance of clear communication paths and being firm and consistent. In that respect, management and leadership are, in John's mind, very much a question of giving clear and non-ambiguous information and messages. He rarely mentions the people issues of his leadership tasks. When he does, it is primarily to state that people should follow the plans that have been laid out, that people must know their roles in the system, and that they must ensure that the project is moving forward. Motivation for John and for the other people involved is, in a sense, a matter of "doing a good job" and "seeing results." It is not, he adds, the role of the project leader to motivate people. Instead, in his opinion, it is up to each project member to find their own motivation or, if they are not motivated, to move somewhere else. At the same time, he considers recognition to be of great importance. People who do a good job in a project should be recognized within the organization. If someone is doing a good and an important job, "people in the organization should hear about it." He recognizes his responsibility for project members' work situation, but he believes that the joy of work is highly performance-related: "If we manage the project well and people have the possibility to do a good job, then these are the most important things." In that sense, John says, he does have an important role in people issues, but he believes that the prime role for most such matters "resides with the line manager."

Project managers and HRM: A few patterns

Looking at the interviewed project managers, a number of interesting patterns emerge. The project managers very much identify themselves as professional project managers and consider project management a lifestyle and a career option. Their goals and results orientations are key traits of project work in general, and project management in particular. This also seems to be an important motivation and momentum in their projects. By all accounts, they focus on time, cost, quality, and delivery, while building teams is more of a means to an end. In addition, time is important. Time creates a certain beneficial pressure that makes it easier for the project managers to carry out their job. As for HRM, they do not bring it up immediately. Instead, they mention the end result, the achievement, and the technical matters. They also talk about the importance of roles and responsibilities, having clear goals and how much time is devoted to various sorts of "troubleshooting". To some extent, one might say that these issues touch upon HRM: troubleshooting the need for competence development, troubleshooting the need for additional human resources and particular kinds of human resources, and troubleshooting difficulties in communication. Combining these matters with the participation in staffing decisions and discussions with line managers about future needs in projects clearly signals their role in HRM with regard to the practice areas of Flows, Performance, Involvement, and Development.

The above portraits, together with insights from the previous research discussed earlier in this chapter, shed light on a few of the issues critical to HRM as well as providing insights into the relationship between project management and HRM. Returning to the analysis, introduced in Chapter 3, of HRM practice areas, we might discern some of the activities that project managers are doing as part of HRM. Table 6.2 summarizes these observations, illustrating the role of the project manager as one of helping with managing the flow of human resources, giving feedback to better manage performance, clarifying roles and assignments to improve the management of involvement and communication, and finally, in a variety of ways, contributing to the management of competences and development.

Final thoughts

Project managers are important human resources, and they have increasingly come to play a role in the HRM activities of the firm. This chapter has attempted to shed light on both these dimensions, although the prime focus was the role of the project manager in the HR quadriad. We started out with an overview of the role of the project manager and how this role has shifted and developed into a much more HR-oriented position. This development certainly affects which skills and competences a project manager needs to develop. It is, however, associated with a set of challenges, since project management, per se, is a management task aimed at enhancing integration and problem-solving and not

Table 6.2　Roles of project managers in the HRM practice areas

HRM practice area	Roles of project manager
Flows	Participating in the recruitment and staffing of people to new projects
	Planning of human resource needs
	Building relationships with line managers to handle shifts and changes in projects
Performance	Facilitating knowledge sharing within the project.
	Detect and work to minimize problems in project work conditions
	Giving recognition and feedback to individuals on their performance
	Taking part in performance appraisals with line managers
Involvement	Clarifying assignments
	Clarifying roles and responsibilities
	Improving project workers' opportunities to positively influence their work performance and work conditions.
	Clarifying deliveries to trigger motivation
Development	Identifying needs for competence development
	Supporting project workers in their work, improving their skill sets
	Spreading the word on positive experiences with project workers

necessarily people issues. Adding too much responsibility for people-oriented matters might negatively affect the integrative capability and reduce the action orientation associated with the role of the project manager. Of course, traditional people-centered duties, including team building, motivation, and guidance of personnel, have played, and still play, important roles, and the responsibilities of long-term HRM might overlap with the role of the line manager. Our point in the present chapter has not, however, been to stress that the project manager is to take over these assignments from the line manager, but instead to point out the dual responsibilities for some of the HRM tasks. These HRM tasks are shared by the project manager and other actors in the

HR quadriad, perhaps most important, the line manager, but also the project workers themselves as emphasized in such recent developments as shared leadership. The latter could also be a measure taken to add leadership capacity to the project dimension without losing the action drive inherent in the project management function.

Another point made in this chapter is that many managers identify themselves with the role of project manager. They speak about the opportunities and uncertainties inherent in managing projects as key drivers and sources of motivation. They also emphasize the positive aspects of working in temporary organizations and that temporary relationships are more interesting and rewarding than the typical permanent organization. This seems to represent a specific kind of "project mentality." We also highlighted the fact that projects are different and that some projects require different kinds of "mentality," tasks, and approaches to the management of relationships. The portraits of successful project managers, however, reveal a type of stability to that project mentality: a focus on getting things done, time pressure, action focus, etc. Generally, this mentality tends to treat HRM as a secondary priority because "doing a good job" is, in itself, enough for people. Also, this description produces an image that the project worker is, to a great extent, responsible for handling HRM: to find motivation, to develop competences, and to stay current to be able to carry out one's duties in the project. The project manager can contribute by building a good team that allows for such developments and by participating in various kinds of activities to make it easier for the line manager and the project worker to carry out their HRM responsibilities.

This chapter has documented some insights into working life and HRM in project-based organizations. The specific focus was on the role and responsibilities of the project manager. In that respect, we focused on an increasingly common and important role that for obvious reasons has a paramount place in the project-based organization. Typically, the observations illustrate the project-based organization as a highly goal-focused and achievement-oriented kind of organization, in which people issues are primarily the results of challenges and "tough" projects. The observations also shed light on a modern topic, namely, that greater responsibility for HRM has been transferred to the individual worker. Most important, given our focus on the HR quadriad and the collective nature of HRM, we observe that HRM is performed at the operational level, involving project managers, line managers, and project workers. The next chapter focuses specifically on the latter.

7

Project Workers and Project-Based Work

Introduction

Project-based work, in the contexts dealt with here, is a special kind of knowledge work, and project workers are a special breed of knowledge workers. Project-based work typically involves close collaboration with other experts from other disciplinary fields and areas of expertise; it is, in this respect, a form of interdependent knowledge work. It is about applying and developing one's own knowledge in a conscientious way to produce a joint effort and achieve knowledge integration. Project-based work typically also involves meeting new people and continuously entering into new collaborations. Projects are, in this respect, highly interesting objects for the study of work and working life from the perspective of the individual project worker. This is particularly important in light of our view of project workers as active players in the HR quadriad. Hence, in this chapter our objective ambition is to summarize the main findings from previous research in this area while, at the same time, intermixing some of our own findings.

The starting point for our explorations into the world of project-based work is that career patterns are changing and fewer people attach their long-term prospects to the destiny of a single organization. This also leads more people to follow a "free-agent route" and, as suggested by Jones and DeFillippi (1996), it might enhance the development of a type of worker who "scrambles, bee-like, from opportunity to opportunity." Some of these individuals take this route primarily within the same company, while others instead develop routes primarily on the open market. In either case, in a certain manner their life resembles that of the free agent trying to maneuver in an organizational context immersed in market forces. And in either case, the changes in career patterns emphasize the individual's own responsibility for, and increased activity in, managing their careers and competence development (see Fact Box 7.1). In this book, of primary interest is the route taken by individuals within a project-based organization. However, we will draw on research conducted on both routes since we believe there are important similarities, and that the distinction between the two is more blurred than one would normally expect. In a project-based work setting, there are also important similarities since the immediate action locality in both cases is that of the project.

This chapter centers on two important implications that projectification has on the work situation of organizational members. Both stem from the inherent temporary and cross-functional features of project-based organizations, which lead to more work being done in various types of temporary projects. First, individuals are involved in work processes and structures with the salient dynamic of birth and death – they move from project assignment to project assignment, which means they repeatedly need to come to grips with new tasks, a situation characterized by a relatively high degree of uncertainty and complexity. Second, project-based work means frequent moves from one project team to another, which has important influences on personal relationships at work. An important driver underlying this is that project organizing per se allows for an organization designed for the occasion. The obvious consequence here is a recurring building and dismantling of temporary organizations, which means that social relationships also increasingly tend to be temporary (Meyerson et al., 1996). Hence, to fully understand the project-based work setting of project workers, we need to look into the consequences of both structure and relationships.

Fact Box 7.1   Individual responsibilities in project-based organizations

Lindkvist (2004) studied the transformation of a company within the Tetra Pak group. At the end of the 1990s the company was transformed into a more project-based organization in which work was to a greater extent carried out in cross-functional teams. According to the author, this change generally produced new rules of the game by fostering individual responsibilities and enabling market-like processes aimed to promote self-organized exploratory work. The company implemented a novel kind of line organization whereby competence networks replaced traditional line departments. Instead, individuals temporarily belonged to projects and were subjected to new project leaders as their assignments changed. Lindkvist argues that one of the fundamental results of the new organizational structure was the effort to make individuals more conscientious than they may have been prior to the reorganization. Relying more on projects, it was hoped, would increase individual entrepreneurship and flexibility as well as improve the adaptability of the firm.

This chapter offers insight into recent research on the boundaryless human resources, the boundaryless career, and the lives of project workers. We believe that much of the research about "free agents" and other kinds of "temporary workers" might give important insights into the analysis of project workers in general, as well as for those pursuing careers primarily within the same organization. As we have already stated in previous chapters, research points to both positive and negative consequences of project-based work for individuals. This should have important implications for the relationship between project workers and the organization they work in and, consequently, for HRM. We will further these discussions in this chapter and, based on previous research, deal with the role of project workers in the HR quadriad. However, we also want to take the discussion one step further by turning attention toward important skills individuals need to develop to master project-based work settings, and which coping strategies they tend to use to deal with problems and challenges in their work situations.

This chapter proceeds as follows: We first discuss the general challenges associated with an increasingly temporary working life. Thereafter, the chapter centers on projects as work context and sources of affiliation. These two topics are brought together in a discussion about boundaryless human resources, which indicates important consequences for both firms and individuals. We proceed with an analysis of the role of project workers in the HR quadriad and identify what skills and competences are critical in light of our framework. We will then relate our findings to the responsibilities of applied HRM practices. The chapter continues with an example of project-based work and project workers from one of our case studies that focus on the coping strategies people adopt to work in project-based settings. The chapter is summarized with a few final thoughts.

Challenges in temporary working life

Bennis (1968) forecasted an increasing need for ad-hoc or temporary groups to deal with current and future organizational problems. Such groups have a strong resemblance to the organic model, but with two additional dimensions, as noted by Bennis (1968): (1) Since such systems are formed for a limited purpose, they tend to include members who have never worked together before and who do not expect to work together again, and (2) similarly, since they are complex, they represent either a diversity of functions, such as finance, engineering, and marketing, or of skills, such as chemistry, electronics, and aerodynamics (Goodman and Goodman, 1976).

An often discussed aspect of project-based organizing is its potentially negative effect on project workers. Studies have, for instance, come to associate the increasing use of projects in organizations with relentless pressure on the individual worker: Deadlines are to be met, often extremely tough deadlines in conjunction with nearly insurmountable technological complexity. Additionally, these problems are to be solved in close, temporary and collaborative systems, with other specialists who represent different knowledge bases. Keith (1978) carried out a study of temporary systems and concomitant stress, strain, and altered role relationships. Frequent adaptation seems to reduce personal satisfaction and increase difficulties in adjustment. She argues that in temporary systems:

> individuals perform newly created roles of short duration. Newly created roles have frequently been found to lack clarity and concise definition (Schwartz, 1957). These aspects of newness are contributing factors to role ambiguity and role strain. (Keith, 1978: 196)

Generally, Keith's and similar studies document the many attendant problems with working in temporary systems. Role strain and ensuing stress are common, and "boundary-work problems" have been particularly highlighted: the need for socialization and familiarity; yet the difficulty of achieving these conditions is noted. This often results in perplexity and a vagueness of meaning for which no realistic resolution seems available. Another observation relates to the so-called corrosion of character reported in Sennett's (1998) famous treatise on contemporary working life. He criticizes the overuse of teamwork and places it at the center of praise for soft qualities, where listening abilities and adaptability are brought to the fore; and he states that the long-term effects of teamwork and flexibility are detrimental to the individual worker. In a similar vein, the study by Perlow (1999) documents what could be called, borrowing the language of Sennett, "corrosion of quiet work time." Perlow's study of software engineers shows that the frequent interaction needed in team-based problem-solving activities tended to fragment the individual's own blocks of work time, causing feelings of "time famine." To address this, Perlow points to the importance of synchronizing individuals' actions and interactions:

> To mitigate the time famine experienced by employees whose work involves both individual and team activities a new type of collective time management is needed – one that takes into account individuals' interdependent work patterns, the macro context in which they work, and the interconnections between this context and their work patterns. (Perlow, 1999: 80)

Others have put more emphasis on the learning aspects of project-based work. In one of the most comprehensive analyses of working life and temporary systems, Goodman (1981) demonstrates that effective use of manpower in project settings is seldom achieved. He also shows that people generally are recruited for past performance rather than for any "learning value" the assignment may have for them (p. 4). The latter situation tends to end up in a vicious reuse of competences and skills without, however, much competence and professional development, leading Goodman (1981: 9) to conclude that "professional development...is often either ignored or treated with a low priority." This observation is supported by more recent studies of project-based organizations. For example, Hobday's (2000) study of the effectiveness of project-based organizations in managing complex products and systems demonstrated that project-based organizations that have weak coordination across projects and a high-pressured work environment leave little space for formal training and staff development. This, Hobday argues, can also breed insecurity regarding career development and professional progress.

In addition, the type of project-based work setting seems to have important implications for the work situation of project workers. For example, several researchers point to fragmented project participation as being problematic from an individual point of view. This observation is supported and detailed in recent studies within the project management community and in the observations tied to "project overload" among project workers (see, e.g., Nordqvist et al., 2004; Zika-Viktorsson et al., 2006). This latter problem has also been investigated in research that explains the general overload in project-based organizations (see, e.g., Wheelwright and Clark, 1992) as well as the problem with resource estimates such as Brooks' (1995) "mythical man-month." It has also led a number of companies to better frame and investigate the working climate in their project operations – to develop special instruments to capture the work condition, job satisfaction, etc. for those people who are spending most of their time in various types of projects (see Fact Box 7.2)

In sum, we thus have a set of human challenges that the individual worker needs to handle or cope with. Table 7.1 summarizes the most important challenges identified in previous research. Of course, there is some variation across project-based work settings – whether we are dealing with focused, inter-functional project work, or fragmented, intra-functional project work. Although, to a certain extent, both these features involve uncertainties; the former tends to involve more uncertainties linked with temporary organization since work is primarily carried out in autonomous, temporary organizations.

Fact Box 7.2   Stress tests among project workers

In several companies in our studies, specific tests are carried out to evaluate the climate and stress levels in projects. A common approach is the classification of project workers into red (high stress levels, risk for burnout), yellow (high stress levels, some risk for burnout and illness), and green groups (satisfactory stress levels and no health risks). The members in the red groups are approached immediately and offered specific programs to improve their work situation. In addition, they are given a coach to help them reduce their stress levels and improve their skills for coping with a high-pressure work situation. Members in the yellow group are typically only invited to take part in some of the events, although the decision is very much left to the individual worker. In these cases, we have observed that approximately 50 percent of the members choose to participate in the support programs offered.

Table 7.1   The challenges of project-based work

Challenge	Implications
Complex tasks, uncertain assignments	Stress, difficult to estimate resources and time needed, project overload
Complex tasks, unique projects	Feeling of not being able to learn from the past
Temporary organization, time limits	Stress and feeling of not having the time to do a good job
Temporary organization, new people	Social insecurity, meeting new people, building trust
Temporary organization, complex tasks	Role ambiguity
Temporary organization, uncertain tasks	Reuse of people with "known" competences to avoid uncertainty, lack of learning
Temporary organization, temporary contracts	Increased flexibility of the employment contract, lack of employment security

Project-based work and HRM

A key assumption in our description of the changes in HRM is the underlying shift in the integration efforts within the firm and the ensuing administrative difficulties. At the same time, we have pointed out that many of these changes directly affect the individual worker, which implies, in the case of project-based organizations, that individuals need to assume a role in the HR organization of the firm. It also indicates that their contributions to the HRM practice areas are critical to making them viable and effective.

Let us first discern the development patterns observed in our research. The rationale follows the similar trajectory presented for line managers and project managers, although, of course the focus here is somewhat different. Three forces are singled out as critical, namely the increasing complexity of projects, more activities organized as projects, and the distribution of knowledge. These forces lead generally to individuals spending more time and performing a larger part of the work in various sorts of projects. As a consequence, project workers assume an expanded responsibility of HRM in the organization. This development has a set of importance effects on the context for work and the sources for affiliation, which will be discussed in further depth in the following section.

Projects as the context for work and a source of affiliation

In a study of technical contractors and independent knowledge workers who represent a specific case of project work, Barley and Kunda (2001) argue that projects are more salient as structural features than are hierarchies and functional departments. The authors, therefore, highlight projects as a primary locus of affiliation and, hence, as an appropriate focal unit of analysis for theorization. In their opinion, a comprehensive understanding of organizing would require greater attention to the dynamics of the life of projects. This observation has also spurred a host of theoretical and empirical investigations, since projects have become increasingly important action localities in which individuals pursue their careers (Grabher, 2004). Hence, a theory of post-bureaucratic work must put projects in a pivotal role (Barley and Kunda, 2001: 79–80).

Building further on these insights, the present chapter seeks to explore the real-life contexts and experiences of project workers – in that respect our intention is to explore projects in situ. We believe such studies have the potential to contribute to our understanding of both the management of project-based organizations and the working lives of project workers.

> As work becomes more project-focused, our sense of belonging increasingly builds on the project as the focus of commitment. From this perspective, the organization of work around project teams creates new forms of social capital that create network connections "within and between organizations" (Knoke, 1999: 18). (Tempest and Starkey, 2004: 511)

However, the terrain will be unknown in many projects since projects are frequently characterized by high degrees of systemic complexity (Lindkvist et al., 1998). In the most extreme situation, Slater (1968) argues, mobility in modern society cannot be captured by the metaphor of nomadic tribes. Instead, individuals are plucked out of their "cosical context" and transplanted; they must form new relationships, adapt to new physical environments, new norms, and so on (cf. Emery and Trist, 1965). This transplanting could be viewed as "pure occasions of organizing," in the words of Weick (1996):

> Projects are relatively pure occasions of organizing. And one way to view boundaryless careers is as a "project-based game as in a checkerboard" (Peters, 1992: 220). Boundaryless careers consist of the

repeated reaccomplishment of organizing in order to learn. And the reaccomplishment takes the form of a series of projects. People gain experience from both the content of what they do and the way they organize to do it. ... Boundaryless careers become defined in terms of movements among projects and within projects. (Weick, 1996: 49)

Despite limited interest in projects in conventional studies of work, one of the strongest voices within organization theory calls for closer examination of projects and the volatility of projects.

If projects are an important medium through which organizing is expressed, if projects take a more conspicuous social form in boundaryless careers, and if life in projects come to define careers scripts, then we may understand boundaryless careers better if we translate organization-level formulations into project-level formulations. (Weick, 1996: 50)

In particular, such formulations would lead us to investigate more closely the life and career of people involved in project-based activities and how the inherent dynamics of projects, with the project life-cycle being the typical road to follow, match with the career and competence development of the individual. In Weick's analysis, volatility arises as a consequence, primarily because timing becomes much more difficult, and the "chances that project stages will match the individual stages are lower because the length of time during which a match can occur is shorter" (Weick, 1996: 51). A more fine-grained analysis of projects would, for that reason, not only lead us to a better understanding of the work context as such, but also to an enhanced understanding of how individuals are motivated, how they develop their skills and competences, and how they pursue their careers (see also Fact Box 7.3). These are all critical questions for the role of individuals in the HR quadriad, the answers to which would then inform how the quadriad should be designed to best support human resources within as well as outside the formal boundaries of the firm.

Boundaryless human resources

With the increasing use of project-based organizing there follows, to some extent, a new view on and approach to human resources – what they are and how they should be organized. Since the inherent dynamic of work appears to be changing, and occupational clusters come and go

---

Fact Box 7.3   Projectification and careers

In Midler's study of Renault, the author addresses the difficulties of career management in project-based organizations. He argues that the dynamics of projects are not well-adapted to the traditional career models within the firm, such as yearly promotion, scheduled training programs, etc. Taking part in these programs makes it difficult to get involved in projects, for instance, since projects require complete attention at certain points in time and perhaps allow for downtime in other periods. However, this fluctuation is not necessarily linked to the regular cycle of HRM activities within the firm. Midler also discusses the issue of continuous dismantling of teams at the end of the development cycle and says, "permanent structures or new projects rarely produce satisfactory job opportunities at just the right moment" (Midler, 1995: 373).

---

and merge, the conventional concept of stable employment is decreasing. Contingent, temporary work is generally on the rise in a wide range of sectors and occupational strata, even among professionals and managers (Kunda et al., 2002). Quite a number of mature companies throughout the world in the manufacturing and engineering sectors have, independent of business cycles, laid off large numbers of employees and turned to labor markets and agencies to supply their human resource needs (Pfeffer, 2010). A number of empirical investigations have indicated that project forms of organizing trigger a higher degree of contracting. The obvious consequence of this is that a larger share of the human resources will be on temporary contracts. This fundamentally turns the employment contract or the "organizational affiliation" into a "temporary affiliation." This development is seen in a wide range of sectors and organizations as well as in organizations not occupied with projects; however, in project-intensive sectors and organizations, it seems to be particularly apparent. An example of a company that relies heavily on external human resources is given in Fact Box 7.4.

Permanence in temporary work

Garsten (1999: 607) states that so-called "temps" might be seen as strangers in the workplace, just temporarily passing through and thus running the risk of being "socially undermined." In many ways, these critical points echo the point made by Sennett on the corrosion of character. However, temporary social relationships in one area might lead the individual to develop permanent social relationships in others. This has been addressed in research on the embeddedness of projects and

---

Fact Box 7.4 External human resources – boundary-spanning HRM

At Jarowskij, a leading TV production company in Scandinavia, most human resources reside outside the firm. The company employs approximately 30 people on a permanent basis but has more than 3,000 people on the payroll. This makes an "I/E ratio" of 100, that is, 3,000 involved in projects/30 permanently employed. HRM in this company, then, becomes heavily focused on external activities, including activities such as network meetings and discussions about future projects. Even though this is in many ways an extreme example, the increasing I/E ratio is seen also in mature industrial companies, such as Ericsson, Saab, and Tetra Pak. In these companies increasing the I/E ratio has been a deliberate strategy in recent years not only to cut costs but also to increase knowledge development and improve knowledge sharing.

---

project ecologies (see for instance, Grabher, 2004). Empirical studies supporting this idea is found in Saxenian's (1996) research on IT specialists in Silicon Valley, and in Morley and Silver (1977) about filmmaking (see also DeFillippi and Arthur, 1998, for a more recent study on filmmaking). Saxenian argues that the region and its relationships, rather than the firm, are the key definers of the opportunities for individual and collective advances in Silicon Valley. However, the relationships are not like any labor market; instead, it is strongly socially embedded (Granovetter, 1995). Successful careers in many project-based industries are, therefore, largely dependent on participation in local networks of social relations, that is, the professional and social networks outside the firm and outside the focal project. These networks are important to building one's reputation and to searching for new opportunities. As an engineer in Saxenian's study stated:

> In this business there's really a network. You just don't hire people out of the blue. In general, it's people you know, or you know someone who knows them. (Saxenian, 1996: 27)

Furthermore, job hopping is not uncommon in project-based industries. In some industries engineers change assignments and employers so frequently that mobility has not merely been socially accepted but, in a few cases, has become the norm (Saxenian, 1996). For instance, a characteristic feature of the processes of technology development in Silicon Valley is not that the engineers have developed loyalties to individual firms; on the contrary, Saxenian reports, it is that workers develop loyalties to each other and to the advancement of technology and knowledge. As one of the CEOs interviewed for Saxenian's study claimed:

> Here in Silicon Valley there's far greater loyalty to one's craft than to one's company. A company is just a vehicle which allows you to work. If you're a circuit designer it's most important for you to do excellent work. If you can't in one firm, you'll move on to another.

This is further emphasized in the study by Delbecq and Weiss (1988), who argued that the critical unit is not the firm, but the set of individuals who come together around a project mission. A conventional description of the individual in this context is that of an "adventurer," moving from one temporary structure to another, always looking for new challenges and new learning opportunities. As stated by Morley and Silver (1977: 59–60), most temporary organizations, such as film units, exist to develop an idea, a plan, a product, a service, or to make something happen, such as a trip to the moon or an election campaign.

> In recognition of the tendency for organizations to bureaucratize themselves as they age, a variant has emerged – "the organizational equivalent of paper dresses or throw-away tissues" (Toffler, 1970: 133) – which might be called the temporary adhocracy. It draws together specialists from different organizations to carry out a project, and then it disbands. (Mintzberg, 1983: 266)

How then do these people cope with the continuous change in social relationships at work and how does this change affect the view of what a career is, or what skills and competences the individual must develop? The literature on career management offer some interesting observations with regard to these matters.

Intelligent careers in a world of projects

Boundaryless careers unfold as people move across firms, organizations, and departments for projects, develop "market niches" rooted in competences and strategies, and create opportunities based on prior performance and networks of professional contacts. For obvious reasons, the supply and development of human resources in increasingly fluid project settings has tended to emphasize the emergence of boundaryless careers and boundaryless people. This means, on the whole, that the emergence of temporary systems and the projectification of organization have been tied to the rise of boundaryless careers.

In a series of papers, Michael Arthur, Robert DeFillippi, and Candace Jones explore the requirements of the boundaryless career: what competences, skills, and knowledge do the individuals need to possess and develop in order to thrive in a work situation dominated by project participation. These skills are generally also relevant and interesting to consider for people pursuing a more conventional career within a large, mature corporation. According to our research, more people consider themselves to be "free agents" operating on an internal market, be it in Ericsson, Saab, or Tetra Pak.

Arthur et al. (1995) emphasize that to handle the shifting environmental, employment, and personal variables, the individual needs to develop a set of personal competences that reflect different forms of knowledge. These skill sets could be interpreted as requirements put on the individual in order for him or her to thrive in project-based organizations, which generally sheds light on the HRM responsibilities that are handed over to the individual worker. In the authors' opinion, intelligent careers primarily reflect the application of the following forms of "knowing": "knowing why", "knowing how" and "knowing whom" (see Table 7.2).

Knowing why relates to the nature and extent of a person's identification with the employing firm's culture. Knowing how refers to the skills and knowledge a person brings to a firm's overall know-how and draws both on formal occupational learning and experiential learning through on-the-job activities. Knowing whom refers to interpersonal relationships that an employee has which are also important for the firm's networking activities. This typology of knowing was further developed by Jones and DeFillippi (1996) in their study of career challenges in project-based industries who suggested an even broader framework, indicating the importance of "knowing what", "knowing where" and "knowing when". This framework is summarized in Table 7.2.

Liminality in project-based work

Due to high mobility, changing circumstances, traveling inside and across organizations, the situation of individual project workers can be described by drawing on the idea presented in Lindkvist (2005), that we might consider them as members of "knowledge collectivities." This idea of the project-based organization as constituted, in significant ways, by a number of dynamic project collectivities has some

Table 7.2   Competences, challenges, strategies, and implications for boundaryless careers (Jones and DeFillippi, 1996: 91, modified)

Competences	Challenges	Strategies	Implications
Knowing what: opportunities, threats, and requirements	Deal with uncertainty Remain "employed" Adapt to variations in activity and inactivity Produce quality work quickly	Move career across and up Learn industry and enhance exposure Use projects and roles to build reputation	Inter-industry mobility constrained by professional networks
Knowing why: meaning, motives, and values	Manage career demands Keep passion without burning out Balance career and family	Know your values and goals Commit to your craft Pursue your passion	Suited best for those whose primary value is the career
Knowing where: entering, training, and advancing	Create a career path Train and enter the industry Remain in the industry Enhance future opportunities	Gain credibility Get on-the-job experience	Be responsible for training, entry and advancement Expect limited support from industry or profession
Knowing whom: relationships based on social capital and attraction	Master relationships Be strategic and genuine in relationships Become more than a resume of credits and credentials	Manage social capital Offset instrumentality with friendships Use portfolios to showcase skills	Reassess whether to quit or continue relationships Know talent pool to assess skills
Knowing when: timing of roles, activities, and choices	Develop career timing Do not be trapped in role or status Extend or exploit skills Move quickly for opportunities	Reframe perceptions Break others' frames of reference Control pacing and choice of projects Make your own breaks	Synchronize projects and passion if possible Maintain passion in dry spells
Knowing how: technical and collaborative skills	Enhance collaboration	Expand communication skills Become cross-functional Develop and articulate vision	Evade commodity status by creating idiosyncratic value in one's skills and roles

important implications: for example, on the way we look at individual–organization relationships and HRM in project-based organizations. As Lindkvist argues:

> Typically these kinds of groups consist of diversely skilled individuals, most of whom have not met before, who have to solve a problem or carry out a pre-specified task within tightly set limits as to time and costs. As a result they tend to become less well-developed groups, operating on a minimal basis of shared knowledge and understandings. (Lindkvist, 2005: 1189)

What seems important, then, is to understand how individuals in these settings relate to less developed groups and organizational contexts and how they cope with higher demands on flexibility and mobility. This leads us to further investigate the notion of "liminality," a term used in related research on consultants and contractors, such as studies of "liminal spaces" (Czarniawska and Mazza, 2003) and "liminal positions" (Garsten, 1999). The term "liminal" was originally developed within anthropology, denoting the time and space of transition from one social status to another – for example, the passage between childhood and adulthood. The term originates from limen, a Latin word which may best be translated as "threshold." In the original usages, liminality was primarily conceived as a temporary, transitional phase denoting one's departure from one culture to another. The term has been used modestly since its introduction in the social sciences many decades ago, but it regained popularity through a series of studies of the work of consultants and temporaries (e.g., Garsten, 1999). Given its specific focus on transition phases, the concept might shed important light on the work situation of project workers, who continuously have to move in and out of projects – a process associated with feelings of anxiety and a blurring and merging of distinctions.

Thus, we use the notion of liminality to describe a particular working-life situation – namely, the feeling of not being part of an organization nor being completely outside (see, for instance, Garsten, 1999), but rather "betwixt." Earlier research has indicated that, in the context of work, liminality can more or less become a permanent condition in which individuals can develop a sense of belonging to various organizations, although without feeling any deeper commitment to any organization (Garsten, 1999). In project-based organizations, for instance, one may think of the engineer who moves from project to project, from team to team, and even from one client organization to another, having no solid roots in one team or department but continually moving between temporary projects and teams. Drawing on Garsten's (2008) analysis of "workplace vagabonds," it appears that to a certain extent people in project-based organizations might better be considered as "perpetual project vagabonds." Similarly, these individuals are supposed to be "lone wolves with a social talent, confident in themselves" (Garsten, 1999: 615).

Viewing project workers as "liminal personae" (Garsten, 1999: 606) forces us to explore the attributes and ambiguity of liminality and investigate how these threshold people deal with their liminal situation, how they seek satisfaction along the way, how they adapt to different situations and different people, how they balance emotional investments in new projects, and thereby learn to live with their liminality (Barley and Kunda, 2006). We believe these issues demonstrate in important ways the roles and responsibilities of the project worker in HRM.

Most individuals who have taken part in our empirical studies are highly skilled and well educated. The field research presented here is from a work pool of consultancy within a large high-tech corporation. The work pool itself is organized as a technical consultancy and employs more than a thousand engineers, most with master's degrees and some with PhDs. They work on various assignments and are typically on contract, working in complex telecom, aerospace, and automotive projects, and the like. We believe these engineers represent a template of project work in the project-based organization. In that respect, although their work might be viewed more as that of a consultant than, for instance, that of regular employees in Tetra Pak or Saab, they represent an increasingly common type of work-pool organization. Many of the firms that have been part of our empirical investigations are resorting to new kinds of line units, such as competence centers, competence networks, and project work pools – a development also reported in Midler (1995). This means the data presented here might be viewed as a prototype of what many of these line units are moving toward. We believe there is much to learn about their work situation in order to shed light on some of the general problems and challenges associated with project work in advanced, engineering-centric, project-based organizations.

The work pool in question, Workpool Engineering (WE, code name), operates in a range of areas regarding technical systems with engineers and experts within information security, software programming, systems security, systems integration, systems development, mechanical engineering, and electrical engineering. WE is known for its highly skilled employees and their knowledge within a number of specialist disciplines; it generally emphasizes having "better learning opportunities than our competitors" and that the company invests "more in personal and competence development compared to other employers and technical consultancies." Thus, these engineers play an important role in realizing the integrative capability of the firm, which requires them to assume responsibilities for systems integration but, perhaps more frequently and importantly, to take part in the knowledge integration process, which brings knowledge bases and technologies together in high-end products and systems.

> Competence and development around here are quite complicated things. But fundamentally it is about working with more and more advanced stuff. You start as a project member, you move on to become some kind of specialist, or you become a project manager. There are a few different paths, either deeper and deeper or broader and broader. (Project Worker B)

WE has a number of technological networks which, together with mentoring programs and continuous dialogues with their line manager, play important roles in steering them toward new assignments. Another opportunity for developing competence is to take part in various internal development projects where engineers are allowed to experiment and try out new methods and technologies. The continuous conversations with their managers and colleagues are considered important, primarily for developing in their role as project workers as well as for sharing ideas and concerns.

> We have also focused on opportunities to take part in conversations. These conversations, more like structured development talks, could be with senior mentors, with their manager, or with one of their colleagues. The most important thing is that it works and that we have regular support ... not necessarily who does it. (Manager III)

Being a knowledge-intensive firm, a critical issue for WE is to recruit the right people. A few managers pointed out during interviews that WE must have "good people" with a "certain attitude" and "personality"; thus, for these managers to succeed, it is important to possess not only the required technical skills but also the "social skills" that are critical to make it as a "project worker" who moves from project to project. The reason is basically that good people change assignments and enter new teams and new problem-solving contexts more easily than others. What managers emphasize is having people who know their limits and their areas of expertise as well as understand the reasons for, and take advantage of, the opportunities to move around. As one of the managers said, the worst situation is to have engineers "who enter assignments and projects they can't handle" (Manager III).

As to why people prefer to work for WE, many remark on the opportunities for moving across projects and across problem-solving contexts. They are essentially aware of the negative aspects of working as hired project workers, but still consider this to be a preferred alternative compared to working permanently in one of their client organizations. Some people refer to the possibility of working with exciting technology and others stress the social dimensions of consulting work.

The typical assignment lasts around one to two years, depending on the area of technology. Even though assignments can last for several years, they are frequently renegotiated, which means the WE engineer cannot plan for more than three or four months ahead. This brings in a certain degree of uncertainty and management stress. A career in the traditional sense is not considered to be critical. Instead, both managers and project workers emphasized assignments and projects.

> We want to talk about career as new roles and new assignments. ... We don't want our people to focus on a particular position or a title. ... This tends to get people more focused on position instead of knowledge and capabilities. That's not the focus we want. (Manager I)

From both the engineers' and the managers' points of view, changing assignments and the various approaches related to doing so were critical for long-term competence building. One challenge was to avoid getting overly specialized and locked into a particular technology. To several interviewees, this constituted a risk that compromised one's inability to develop the skills for moving across projects.

> It's good that you have the chance to see other places, work with other clients. It is only when you have had the opportunity to compare your previous experience with something else that you are able to see what actually works, what doesn't work, and why it doesn't work. Through this you might learn what is important. (Project Worker B)

During our interviews, we talked about the necessary skills and what experience one acquires from working at WE. These conversations were generally meant to shed light on the skills one needs to become a good project worker and the role the engineer has to fill regarding HRM practices. Several respondents return to the importance of establishing a "good reputation" and a "platform" to work from.

> When you start working here, it is very important that you build your platform, since this is the platform that you will be using for the rest of your career. You start with technology, and you move on from there, but we are a technology-intensive company so you need to have a strong connection to the tech stuff. (Project Worker B)

To be able to do this, the engineer has an important role to play. In that respect, managers and engineers themselves seem to agree that much of the responsibility for creating such a platform and reputation is the responsibility of the individual worker. Some of the interviewees return time and time again to the importance of "networking" within the company on all levels and within the clients' organizations. As one of the managers pointed out, "It is not the company's or the manager's responsibility to ensure that engineers are improving, do a good job, and stay current – it's their own responsibility." At the same time, however, this manager added that "what the company can do is to offer support services; managers can help build the reputation, steer the employees in the right direction, but it needs to be, to a great extent, driven by the individuals themselves."

New assignments tend to be coupled with positive feelings, with the opportunity to learn new things. At the same time, there is a feeling of newness that some believe is negative. One of the reasons for both positive and negative feelings is that newcomers rarely get clear and specific assignments, since they are delegated to contribute with a specific competence in a project. That means the role and assignment are created and developed during the course of the project as the engineers become familiar with the problem-solving situation and have demonstrated what they can contribute. Related to this problem is the continuous need to establish trust in new working situations.

> In many projects you need to spend a lot of time getting to know people, establish trust, and build your role and place to be able to carry out the assignment. You need to socialize, be nice, say the right things, and all that. (Project Worker C)

However, not everyone considers the major problem as being strictly social; others tend to view the problems primarily from a technical point of view, identifying problems associated with design features and technical specifications. When asked about the typical dynamics of an assignment, many referred to very loose and fuzzy beginnings that, over time, were sorted out through a variety of techniques and methods, and to the fact that the early stages of projects typically involve a lot of work to clarify things, sorting out all issues, before starting the hands-on job. This, however, does not have to be a final solution, but something that is good enough to get the work going and provide a "firm base that we can build on." At the same time, engineers do not only speak negatively about fuzzy technical situations and technical uncertainties in general, because they also feel that this aspect is the prime factor of motivation for them.

> I like assignments that are a bit fuzzy where you don't have the walls around you, where you can seek the opportunities and explore the open areas. But I don't think that the newly recruited can handle these situations. I guess many leave the company because they're not mature enough. (Project Worker F)

When entering a new project or a new assignment, the WE engineer normally receives a task specification and a role specification. In some cases, these are very brief and informal, in other cases, very detailed and formalized. Yet for many these descriptions and specifications say very little about their job.

> There is never a clear assignment specification when you enter a project. You get things as you go. The client checks out how good you are, what you can do, what you can't do. And then things change and you just have to respond to that – enter a new role because that client needs you to. (Project Worker A)

Leaving assignments and entering new projects is part of the everyday life of the engineers at WE. Managers generally argue that mobility could be improved, and they mention the dangers of staying too long at the same place, whereas project workers point out that they would like to have more opportunities – even change assignments at a higher pace than today. Still, leaving contracts is associated with a certain kind of stress or feeling of anxiety. In our interviews with the engineers, a recurring theme was the anxiety of finding new assignments. Some state that it is a mixed feeling involving "excitement, anxiety and a bit of worries." However, the engineers realize there is not much they can do about it; they just have to trust that new assignments and projects will be coming in and that "you can't worry too much because there is really nothing you can do about it." (Project Worker E). One respondent said:

> It always works out fine. Assignments come and go. Sometimes you don't have any assignment for a while and sometimes you just have too many assignments to choose from. That's how this business is." (Project Worker F)

Coping with liminality

After this empirical peek into the operational day-to-day situations of engineers in their project-based work, we will now discuss how they handle their liminality situations. As we will see, their actions with regard to this are important activities within the four HRM practice areas. We depart from a pattern observed in our empirical accounts, namely, the distinction between technical and social situations. In other words, engineers normally meet situations that are technically and socially challenging at the same time. By making this differentiation, we also emphasize the dual nature of complex problem-solving as consisting of both a social and a technical dimension. This generally echoes the two aspects of group development – where some researchers have explored group development phases in terms of climate, trustful relationships, friendship (Tuckman, 1965), etc., while others have looked in more depth into the stages of problem-solving, such as exploration and exploitation (Gersick, 1989). This distinction also mirrors the complexity inherent in many situations of problem-solving in project-based organizations. By this, we are calling attention to two aspects of the working situation of project workers: social and technical, and the liminality involved in both of these aspects. In the first dimension, it centers on the people in the project and their relationships; in the second dimension it is about one's assignment, responsibilities, and the specific technologies and technical problems involved.

In dealing with their liminality, we can discern a number of coping strategies that the engineers at WE use. The following coping strategies are discussed and analyzed theoretically: (1) "reputation reliance", (2) "role carving", (3) "relaxation", and (4) "redefinition".

The first identified strategy, reputation reliance, centers on the social capital of the engineers – how they are perceived when they enter the teams and how managers introduce them to new organizational contexts. In general, this also relates to the reputation of WE engineers and what features and characteristics of a candidate were identified during the interviews that, in turn, are attributed to his or her self-confidence and professionalism. Undoubtedly, a good reputation is a foundation for trust building in temporary groups (Meyerson et al., 1996), as it is also important in the engineering problem-solving contexts discussed here. However, what is perhaps more interesting is how individuals try to affect their reputation, how managers of the pool of resources "market" their people to build reputations, which ultimately makes it easier for the engineers to enter a new knowledge collectivity. For instance, managers here referred to the importance of talking to the client about the track record of an engineer, of convincing them that "this person will do a good job." The reputation reliance strategy is, then, tightly connected to HRM practice areas dealing with Flows and Development and, perhaps most important, with effective combining and matching of these two areas. The activities of individuals who rely on this strategy revolve around strategic use of the internal flow (past and future) to build competences and to create networks, making sure their "name" is known in the organization.

The second coping strategy, role carving, is important in situations where social liminality is the key factor. The importance of role carving has also been emphasized in previous research. For instance, the study by Barley and Kunda (2001: 249) emphasized the importance for contractors of carving out roles to be able to learn to live with their liminality. As the authors say, the contractors "carved out roles for themselves," which allowed them to "rationalize their status and resolve the practical dilemmas of life on the job." This strategy generally zooms in on the ongoing structuring and dynamics of roles in social settings and, perhaps most important, in dynamic projects. Meyerson et al. (1996) highlighted the importance of rather fixed and clear-cut role definitions to build trust rapidly. Whitley (2006) argued for the significance of stable and separated role definitions to form lasting project-based organizations. However, it might be difficult in these situations to have such clear role definitions. It might also be that project workers want to change role structures to affect the social or the technical problem-solving process. The negative side is, of course, that it might lead to "high costs in time, worry, conflict, and temporary inefficiency" (Stinchcombe, 1965: 4). During our interviews, engineers referred to too high expectations and that they had to respond to an institutionalized image of what was expected from them in their assigned role. They also mentioned the difficulty that project managers often do not know what to expect, because the problem to be solved is not yet fully explored. For instance, one respondent had been hired as a configuration manager, although this was not really what the project needed. Respondents also emphasized the importance of building platforms from which they could act. This is a typical scenario when they have just entered new assignments, although as they say, role carving is a continuous process. The role-carving strategy, then, involves important activities within the HRM practice area of Performance – engineers' aiming at improving their performance by actively influencing their immediate work setting and creating a role they believe is needed.

The third strategy, relaxation, zeroes in on the individual's ability to live with liminality and coping with the problem of entering new organizational constellations. This strategy centers on the technical aspects and is predominantly seen here as a passive attitude. The interviewed engineers referred to the importance of "wait and see," and that you learn that "things get sorted." Often in these cases, it seemed to them as though they could only moderately influence the situation and that it had to be dealt with by the client or other project members. Hence, this strategy is seen as a way for individuals to meet HRM challenges within the practice area of Involvement. However, instead of actively involving themselves in the decision-making process, they make the active decision *not* to get involved. In that sense, relaxation strategy is interesting from an HRM perspective since it indicates that high-involvement practices are not always the first-choice alternative for employees. Instead, this relaxed attitude to uncertainty might be a way for many individuals to cope with liminality in project-based work settings.

The fourth coping strategy revolves around the redefinition of tasks and technical problems. It is active and fundamentally focused on the technical type of liminality. We label it "redefinition," although it encompasses a broad range of skills and mechanisms. For instance, it covers how engineers reinterpret and reformulate the task, system properties, and functional specifications. It is viewed here as an active coping strategy because engineers in these situations reinterpret and reformulate complex problems more than is commonly done in everyday complex problem-solving. During the interviews, some referred to their role as being an advisor, particularly in situations where the client has a limited understanding of the problem at hand. This can happen not only in new projects but also in projects that have been running for years in which the approach has not been accurate. A problem could be defined either as something distant from the engineer or as something within his or her scope of responsibility, as something within a distinct domain of technology or as something more integral. In some cases, redefinition had quite extreme results, such as a speedy promotion to assume project manager responsibilities and, in other cases, having to leave the project because the client found another way of handling the problem or that they, in fact, needed a different engineer. In all cases, it could be seen as adopting a strategy to redefine the liminality situation. Fenwick reports on this type of coping strategy in her study of independent contractors, who say they often see from the beginning when a project for which they are being hired is poorly conceived or grossly shortchanged in resources and time, but "they must proceed delicately to determine how to shift management's thinking without jeopardizing the contract or their reputation" (Fenwick, 2007: 518). The strategy of redefinition primarily involves activities within the HRM practice area of Performance – in order to allow for high performance, the project worker takes an active position in redefining and clarifying what the problem is.

Finally, all four strategies include activities within the practice area of Involvement, since they in themselves are signs of employee involvement. The strategies of reputation reliance and relaxation can be described as strategies of a rather low degree of active involvement. However, it is important to note that this relative inactivity is due to the project workers' own choice and their "passive" strategies built on conscious and active decisions. Role carving and redefinition are, instead, strategies that include a high level of involvement activity. Here, the project worker takes an active part in influencing work conditions as well as content of work and includes himself or herself in the decision-making process.

Project workers in the HR quadriad

Turning the focus to the HR quadriad and the HRM practice areas, a few points should be made about the responsibilities of the project worker. These are based on the more general discussions earlier in this chapter as well as on the later parts that focused on individuals' strategies for coping with liminality as an important part of their HRM activities.

First, with regard to Flows, it is critical to handle the various aspects tied to liminality, entering into new assignments and signaling shifts in assignments. In particular, project workers with a strategy of reputation reliance need to be active in managing their "flow," so that they get the assignments they are interested in; they build a network and a reputation for being competent and useful project members, and thus minimize social uncertainty when entering a new project team. This requires a certain self-assurance and confidence in one's own competence and abilities. Managing their human resource flows is one way for project workers to cope with social aspects of liminality. Looking back on earlier chapters, this is to a high degree a close collaboration with line managers, normally the ones who can act as "artist agents," support project workers in planning their project trajectories, and build their reputations. Nevertheless, feedback from previous project managers is also crucial for future assignments, since their experience of having someone on a team can be valuable as a reference for future project assignments.

Second, management of Performance is primarily a matter of clarifying expectations, of knowing what is expected from the project worker in terms of both the social and technical aspects of problem-solving. Here, it seems critical to be able to carve out one's role and redefine complex problems – issues that were frequently brought up during our study of Workpool Engineering. In this regard, interaction with other project members and the project manager is crucial, particularly in inter-functional and focused project work. In intra-functional and fragmented project work, interaction with line managers in these matters will most likely be of higher importance.

This also brings to attention the third HRM practice area: Involvement – the importance of getting involved and ensuring the possibility of being able to do a good job in terms of having the right contact with significant people in the project and being able to improve one's working conditions. As pointed out earlier, the four strategies of coping with liminality are in themselves signs of Involvement, even though two of them actually have to do with conscious decisions to not get involved. These Involvement activities, we argue, compose an important responsibility for project workers; however, these workers need to be supported and encouraged by the other players in the HR quadriad. Otherwise, the valuable involvement of knowledgeable project workers might not take place, which means the organization might miss out on important improvement opportunities.

Finally, the practice area of Development is, as Figure 7.1 highlights, to a great extent a responsibility handed over to the individual worker. Although a company provides courses and other kinds of opportunities, the search for new assignments and learning from experience

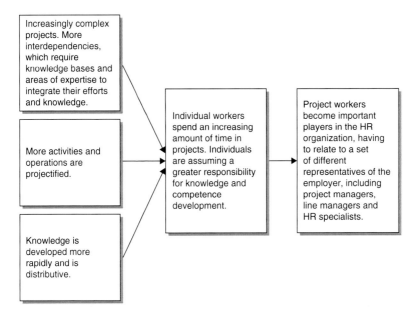

Figure 7.1   Project workers and HRM: some underlying forces

is chiefly the individual's responsibility. As has been pointed out in previous chapters, project workers collaborate closely with line managers in these issues. However, if many of the Development activities are the responsibility of project workers themselves, a direct relationship with HR specialists concerning development matters might be valuable.

Table 7.3 summarizes a few of the important patterns observed in our research concerning HRM and the responsibilities of the project worker.

Final thoughts

The ideas presented in this chapter are important primarily because of the need to better establish HRM with the needs and requirements of the individual worker. This chapter takes a starting point in the lives and careers of individuals and, based on that starting point, conducts an analysis of challenges the individual is facing and what type of HRM might be developed to improve the response to those challenges. One was discussed as a challenge in terms of "liminality." First, it was argued,

Table 7.3   Roles of project workers in the HRM practice areas

HRM practice area	Roles of the project worker
Flows	Knowing one's competence Adjusting assignments to competence Building reputation
Performance	Sharing knowledge Clarifying expectations Role carving and redefinition Seeking feedback
Involvement	Getting involved actively or deciding *not* to get involved. Actively influencing work conditions and the content of work
Development	Searching for new, challenging assignments Learning from experience Networking to build social capital, learn from others, and share knowledge with others

liminality is important to improve the overall efficiency of knowledge integration in projects that resemble "knowledge collectivities" – a type of project organization gaining popularity in complex problem-solving contexts. Second, the analysis of liminality may lead to an improvement of the working situation, to the development of skills for project-oriented engineers (see Allen and Katz, 1995), and to an understanding of how problem-solving skills relate to both social and technical issues. The latter, we believe, would be of equal importance to the firms in our investigation and to the individual project workers. In that respect, the exploration of liminality augments knowledge about an increasingly important organizational capability and individual problem-solving skills. Liminality further sheds new light on contemporary or even postindustrial HRM. Generally speaking, one might argue that HRM is increasingly occurring at the limits of organizations within networks and teams that often cross organizational divides. This was observed in most of the organizations in our studies – ranging from Posten and their reliance on external consultants, to the decrease of permanent personnel in Tetra Pak, and to the use of technical consultants in Saab (see Appendix).

The chapter also addressed the need for combining micro-level analysis with macro-level analysis. In that respect, it connects findings from institutional theory presented by Whitley with the "bringing work back in" ideas in Barley and Kunda (2001: 90). This also ties together the linkages between the two competitive challenges and organizational capabilities discussed in the introduction. In that respect, we build on Whitley's (2006) argument that there is a need for linking HRM with problem-solving contexts. In particular, our analysis highlights the dynamics and linkages between problem-solving contexts and individual skills and the strategies engineers use to deal with liminality. For instance, we identify the importance of role carving as a strategy the individual relies on to deal with liminality. The general role structures found on the macro level were, therefore, generally important, but insufficient, to help the individual deal with the problem of liminality.

We also emphasize the need to explore further the aspects and types of liminality to improve the analysis of project-based organizations as constituted by knowledge collectivity. Given their temporary, fluid, and mobile nature, liminality is a key attribute for project workers. At the same time, our main argument has been that coping with liminality is important to improving both working life and organizational effectiveness. Thus, it captures an important element in modern definitions of HRM: the dynamic interplay between employee/contractor and employer/client. Based on our empirical work, we identified four coping strategies: reputation reliance, role carving, relaxation, and redefinition. Through this analysis we argued that (1) liminality is not necessarily a negative state – positive effects can emanate from liminality; (2) liminality consists of primarily two types: social and technical, and these are intertwined, although for analytical purposes they should be kept separate; and (3) it might be possible to identify a set of strategies based on the dimensions of focus (social/technical) and attitude (active/passive).

8
HR Specialists in Project-Based Organizations

Introduction

In the previous chapters, we discussed the roles of line managers, project managers, and project workers in the HR quadriad. Bearing these discussions in mind, we now turn to the HR specialists and HR departments. Our view of HRM as being collective and complementary means the role of HR specialists at the operational level in project-based organizations is strongly influenced by the roles of the other players in the HR quadriad. For example, increased HR responsibilities for line managers – a trend we discussed in Chapter 5, which was intensified in project-based organizations – should, according to Larsen and Brewster (2003), have extensive effect on the size, role, and shape of the HR department. Moreover, the design of HRM suggests that the nature of the operational work setting affects the HR quadriad and its roles and, hence, the role of HR specialists and the design of HR departments. The underlying change patterns are summarized in Figure 8.1.

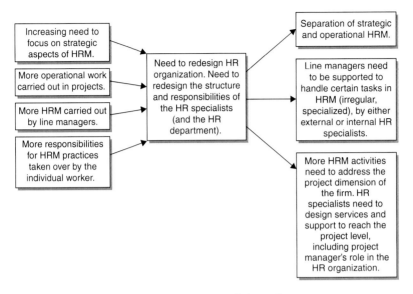

Figure 8.1   HR specialists and HRM: some underlying forces

As for the first set of factors on the left side of the figure, we identify a broad spectrum of factors that influence the role and responsibilities of HR departments. A key parameter is that as more work is carried out in projects more of the HRM responsibilities are handed over to others, including line managers and project workers, and to some extent, to project managers. Additionally, we also have the common factor discussed in the literature on strategic HRM, namely, that there is also a need to include strategic factors. In that sense, although we have pointed out the importance of addressing the operational work setting, the strategic factors cannot be ignored and, according to some scholars – a claim supported by our findings to a certain extent – HR specialists need to be involved in the strategic decision-making of the firm. These factors require redesigning the HR organization. The consequences will be explored in further detail in the present chapter, particularly how the operational HRM is supported, how line managers are supported, and how HR departments should be designed to better position HRM within the project-based organization.

In this chapter we draw on research that has suggested various roles and models for HR specialists, and we take the discussion one step further by focusing on the project-based work setting.[1] We commence with a summary of the ongoing debate about HR specialists and their role and value in contemporary firms. We continue with an analysis of the structure and design of HR departments and summarize some findings from a multiple case study comprising eight project-based firms. The role and structure of HR departments are discussed in further detail from these findings. The chapter ends with final thoughts and conclusions.

The role and value of HR specialists

Prior research into HRM gives an image of HR departments as struggling to find their role and defend their existence (Brockbank, 1999; Jamrog and Overholt, 2004; Torrington and Hall, 1996). In the earlier stages of our empirical work, we similarly observed problems facing the HR departments and saw several signs that the HR department was slowly "fading away," while searching for its place in a number of firms as well as being under severe pressure. For instance, one top manager interviewed in a firm where HRM is considered a strategic issue expressed the problem in the following words: "The HR department, I'm not sure what they really do, and I'm not sure I want them to do anything." Of course, this is an intentionally provocative statement and carries some irony; however, it reveals a general frustration with the role of the HR department, which should be taken seriously. Yet similar observations are reported in recent empirical research. One example is the study by Truss and Gill (2009) in which senior executives raise doubts about the performance of HR specialists.

Several HRM scholars have specifically argued that HR departments need to change if they are to contribute to the firm's success and create value for the firm. Otherwise, these authors suggest, HR departments might just as well be abolished. Along these lines, Ulrich (1998: 124) claims that "HR" tends to have a bad reputation in many organizations, and for a good reason: "It is often ineffective, incompetent, and costly; in a phrase, it is value sapping." In sum, previous research and practice undoubtedly offer a substantial critique of the HR department as we know it. One reason for the problematic situation of HR specialists could be the vague concept of "HR," which we believe is crucial to clarify. The expression "HR" is frequently used in an imprecise way, in practice as well as in the research community, creating uncertainty about to what it really refers. For example, Beatty and Schneier (1997: 29) state: "HR must be judged on whether it enhances the firm's competitive advantage...," and Ulrich (1998: 124) poses the rhetorical question: "Should we do away with HR?" In such writings, it is not clear whether "HR" refers to the firms' HR specialists or to the HR organization as we define it in this book: the entire system of players that carry out HRM practices in the firm. In the majority of cases, however, "HR" refers to the HR department and the HR specialists. This conceptual vagueness has several consequences for the analysis of HR departments. Among other things, it creates an underlying perception that the HR department alone is responsible for HRM in the organization and is also the one to blame when HRM practices are not working properly. The collective nature of HRM advocated for in this book, however, stresses that the function of HR specialists can only be understood in relation to the other players in the HR organization.

Despite the substantial critique directed at HR departments, most researchers argue that the HR department needs to be an important player in the HR organization of the firm. In fact, the HR department itself is often seen as an important basis for gaining competitive advantage (e.g., Brockbank, 1999). Some authors stress the importance of HR departments moving from administrative personnel units and, instead, becoming "strategic players" (Beatty and Schneier, 1997; Ulrich and Beatty, 2001). Others have argued that HR departments need to assume various roles such as "strategic partners," "business partners," and "change agents," as well as "administrative experts" and "employee champions" (e.g., Lawler, 2005; Mohrman and Lawler, 1997; Ulrich, 1998).

Taken together, arguments about the need to change the role of HR departments suggest the HR department is expected to make an important contribution to the development of core issues of management in today's firm. Nevertheless, it is at the same time recognized that HR departments are struggling with their current mandate. One of the seminal studies exploring the roles of HR specialists, conducted by Storey (1992), presents solid empirical evidence. This broad longitudinal study of the development of HRM in 15 British organizations identified patterns in the roles assumed by HR departments and suggested a conceptual framework of "types of personnel practitioner" based on the two dimensions identified as strategic/tactical and interventionary/noninterventionary. Storey's typology included (1) the strategic and noninterventionary "advisers," (2) the tactical and noninterventionary "handmaidens," (3) the tactical and interventionary "regulators," and (4) the strategic and interventionary "change makers." The author argued that the change-maker type was particularly consonant with the modern HRM model in which personnel responsibilities needed to be devolved to the line, and HR specialists should make a proactive and strategic contribution. However, the empirical work showed that having this type of HR specialist was not very common among the studied firms. Storey did not explicitly investigate the reasons for this, but suggested that the somewhat traditional character of many of the studied companies might be a possible explanation.

> It appeared then that the attachment to the traditional paradigm in the mainstream companies had something to do with the characteristic features of these organizations. It was in these large, unionized and proceduralized organizations that for a variety of reasons personnel had remained more attached to the traditional mode. (Storey, 1992: 187)

Consequently, Storey's study can be used only to speculate on the role of HR specialists in other organizational settings, such as project-based organizations. The research by Storey (1992) paved the way for a series of normative typologies of roles for HR specialists and HR departments such as the ones suggested by Ulrich (1998) and Mohrman and Lawler (1997). Although these typologies rely on limited empirical support, they have had a large impact in practice where positions such as "HR business partner" and the like have become very popular (Truss et al., 2002).

In sum, existing role typologies usually give normative suggestions of roles the HR department should take on, but they have two common weaknesses: (1) they do not consider differences in the organization of operational work settings, and (2) they generally do not discuss how such HR departments could be designed. In the following, we will briefly introduce what previous research has to say about the design of HR departments.

The structure and design of HR departments

Interestingly, the issue of structure and design of HR departments is not a very common topic among HRM researchers. This is somewhat surprising since some critiques against the HR departments have focused on their inappropriate structural solution. The importance of this issue is acknowledged by Mohrman and Lawler (1997: 161), who state:

> Clearly one of the most important challenges every human resource function faces is to reinvent its structure and organization so that it can deliver in the future the kinds of systems and business partnership behaviour that will make its organisation more effective.

Mohrman and Lawler point to the importance of analyzing the structure and organization of the HR department, but they do not focus on this particular issue in their study. There are, however, a few other important contributions on the topic. Beer (1997: 51–2), for example, discusses what the organization of HR specialists might develop into. Beer argues that "the administrative and strategic roles do not easily coexist in the same function or the same person" and that these activities, therefore, need to be separated if a strategic role for HR specialists is to emerge. Beer also foresees the birth of what he calls "geographically decentralized human resource service centers" that sell administrative services to the organization, and also "strategic human resource professionals" or "human resource partners" affiliated with particular business units. Furthermore, Beer argues that traditional HR services will be increasingly outsourced to external partners. A recent example is given in Fact Box 8.1.

Sisson and Storey (2003: 226) argue that outsourcing is one of four main structural options for delivering personnel activities within a firm. The other three options, according to the authors, are the HR department as an "in-house agency" (seen as a cost center), as an "internal consultancy" (selling its services to the parent organization), or as a "business within a business" (which may trade not only with the parent

---

Fact Box 8.1 In search of cost-effective HR departments

For the past decade or so, there has been significant pressure on HR departments to become more cost-effective. The result has been a shockwave of restructured HR departments among companies in all kinds of industries, involving downsizing, creating HR service centers, and outsourcing parts of HRM activities. This process is discussed and analyzed by practitioners as well as scholars under the term "HR transformation" (see, e.g., Ulrich et al., 2009). The main idea is that the competence of HR specialists should be used to add value to business instead of being wasted on administrative duties. A recent example is that of AstraZeneca, a global pharmaceutical company with over 60,000 employees. The company decided to outsource all the "nonstrategic" parts of HR, which actually implied outsourcing more than two-thirds of the HR function. The contract, with a value close to 5 million Euros, will run for 7 years, with the goal cutting the costs by around 1.2 million Euros per year. In the search for suppliers, the company opted for the one that was *least* willing to customize its services. An HR director at the company explains that the variety of specialized and customized practices, policies, and processes needs to be reduced: "The outsourcing gives us the possibility to deal with HRM more or less in the same way in 105 countries" (Dovier, 2010).

organization but also externally). The ideas of Beer (1997) and Sisson and Storey (2003) are interesting and highly relevant. Yet both studies discuss HR departments in very general terms. Beer suggests one possible wide-ranging development for HR departments but does not consider that different organizational contingencies could influence the HR department, as suggested by, for example, Storey (1992). Sisson (2001) acknowledges that a number of organizational conditions, such as size, sector, ownership, and whether the firm is joining, continuing, or leaving the business, are critical for understanding the justification for the HR department. However, he does not discuss organizational structure and the operational work setting as being among those critical conditions.

Ulrich and Brockbank (2005) present a framework that, in several ways, not only reflects the same ideas as those of Beer (1997) and Sisson and Storey (2003) but also takes into account organizational differences. They suggest that the HR department usually assumes one of three general patterns based on the strategic business organization (single business, holding company, or diversified business). According to Ulrich and Brockbank (2005), the three general patterns for HR departments are (1) functional HR departments (applied by single businesses) which consist of a strong central HR department at the headquarters that designs HRM practices to match the needs of the entire business, and HR generalists at the local departments who apply corporate-wide policies; (2) dedicated HR (applied by holding companies), which have dedicated HR departments embedded in the business units. These dedicated HR departments get tools and support from a centralized, corporate-wide HR department, but they are also responsible for designing business-specific HRM; (3) shared services HR (applied by diversified businesses, which are neither pure single businesses nor holding companies). The shared service HR is described as a way of balancing centralization and standardization with decentralization and flexibility. Here, transactional and administrative HR activities are provided through service centers, technology, and/or outsourcing solutions. The transformational and strategic HR activities are delivered by corporate HR professionals, by embedded HR partners who work directly with line managers and business unit teams, by centers of expertise that operate as consulting firms inside the organization, and by line managers.

Indeed, the three patterns of HR departments suggested by Ulrich and Brockbank are pertinent as a description of different HR department structures applied in many modern companies. However, one could question whether the strategic business organization is the only relevant organizational structure for determining the design of the HR department. Instead of this top-down perspective, in the present book we have favored a bottom-up perspective. This perspective suggests that the design of an IIR department should be influenced by the character of the operational work setting in which employees carry out their tasks, and by the overall HR organization needed for this particular organization. We maintain that previous research into roles and structures for HR departments has tended to overemphasize the corporate and strategic levels of analysis, and thereby has underemphasized the importance of the settings in which many of the HR activities are performed and to which HR specialists are supposed to contribute. This is particularly troublesome in the case of project-based organizations, which are often described as having flatter and more flexible organizational structures and in which project workers, first-line managers, and project managers take a more active part in HRM activities. It is equally troublesome since a number of recent studies have documented the limited explanatory value of strategies with regard to the design and structure of HR departments (Truss et al., 2002). Some studies have even documented the problems with overreliance on searching for a fit between the strategy of the firm and the design of HR departments with a particular emphasis on crafting its role in the strategy process. As formulated by Hope-Hailey et al. (2005: 63), one might question the "wisdom of focusing on the strategic partnering role. We have shown how the HR department may become more important strategically, but the human factor of people's everyday work experience may deteriorate."

The role of HR specialists and structure of HR departments: patterns from eight firms

Our research on HRM in project-based firms indicates that HR departments are in transition. In the majority of our empirical cases, the firms are trying to find new and more cost-effective solutions, and these changes are often inspired by role typologies such as the business partner models and service center models mentioned earlier. However, at the operational level we have identified a number of interesting patterns concerning the role and structure of HR departments in relation to the other players in the HR quadriad and the project-based work setting. Our empirical material draws on case studies of eight firms.[2] The firms belong to different industries (automotive, pharmaceutical, logistics, aerospace, IT, telecom, medical systems, and complex machinery) and their number of employees ranges from approximately 600 to 70,000. Our studies focus on project-based units within the firms, which in the majority of cases are R&D and development units. Some units rely heavily on intra-functional project work and fragmented project participation, while others are dominated by inter-functional project work and mostly focused project participation. As we have seen in previous chapters, the type of project work and project participation are important characteristics of the operational work setting which influence the roles and responsibilities among the actors in the HR quadriad. We take these conditions into consideration when discussing and comparing the role of HR specialists. In the following, we will present empirical material from our studies to give an image of the complex role of HR specialists in the HR quadriad and of alternative designs of HR departments.

HR-based and task-based logics

In the majority of the studied firms, HR specialists were dedicated to supporting line managers at the operational level. It could be in the form of a local HR department or single HR specialists dedicated to supporting a certain part of the organization. In the latter, there also normally were some sort of centralized HR service center to which line managers could turn when they needed particular HR support. This would be with regard to recruitment processes, competence development programs, sick leave, rehabilitation processes, and a number of other issues that may require specialist knowledge. The dedicated HR specialists had positions with titles such as "strategic partners" and "business partners," probably a sign of inspiration by the popular role of typologies discussed earlier. Normally, they were involved in strategic competence planning and leadership inventories, and participated in meetings at middle management levels.

In some cases, line managers wondered what HR specialists really did. They often questioned the value of the contribution of HR specialists, who were seen as being too far from the operational setting. Nevertheless, many line managers expressed a wish for HR competence to be more integrated at the operational level. One line manager, for example, talked about his good experience having an HR specialist involved:

> Our HR specialist wants to be more involved in our daily work, but she hasn't really got the time for it. She is responsible for a very large area. But I really appreciated the times when she has taken an active

part in, for example, leadership inventory processes. She brings another perspective and that is great! Sometimes you get a real eye opener. And since you are supposed to work more with people issues, it would be great with such a sounding board on other issues as well. That could give you more incentives to work with people issues and feel that it is rewarding. But it cannot be an HR department "on the side"; it needs to be more integrated in the daily work. Yes, that kind of sounding board would be really nice...to get the opportunity to discuss soft issues in novel way. I think that all line managers should benefit from that. It would be great. (Line Manager, Aerospace)

In other cases, line managers did not express such a clear need for integrated HR support in their daily work. Most thought they had developed the skills they needed to take on their HR-oriented roles, but that it was good to have an HR center or a dedicated HR specialist to call on when they needed special support or to stay up to date with current topics in HRM. There were also examples of HR managers creating and managing HR networks for line managers. For example, in one case with an inter-functional project work setting, the local HR manager saw the need for line managers to meet and share experience about their HR work, so he launched specific HR meetings for line managers.

The line managers need to have an arena where they can meet and discuss HR and competence issues and create a common language. This has been difficult, but for the last year, I have had meetings with all the line managers once a month. I call and run the meetings and prepare the agenda. It is intended to be an arena where the line managers can bring up questions, share experiences, and lessons learned. We discuss different issues to get a common view. (HR Manager, Complex Machinery)

The interaction between HR specialists and line managers was clear in all the studied firms, but the relationship between HR specialists and the project dimension was less well-defined. In one case, involving intra-functional project work, there was a special support unit for project managers that also included support for people issues. However, there was no real cooperation between this support unit and the HR department. In fact, the HR specialist's detachment from, and lack of knowledge about, the project operations were often mentioned by project managers, line managers, and project workers, and sometimes also by the HR managers themselves. For example, a senior project manager at the R&D unit of a pharmaceutical company told us:

> Actually, we have not had any organization to support the projects. HR has no idea of the situation of the project workers – they are quite detached from the project environment.

A top HR director at the R&D unit of an automotive firm had a similar opinion. Being a former senior project manager, she had a particular interest in these issues and said:

> The HR unit is very line oriented. When the employees have difficulties in the projects, the HR personnel don't seem to understand the problem. They don't speak the same language, because they are HR people and not engineers. It's a big problem and something we need to deal with. We have started, but we are not there yet.

In this particular case, there had been attempts to direct HR competences toward project operations, but these organizational solutions were soon abandoned. An HR manager gave us his thoughts:

> Even though we have been working on projects for a long time, the HR department has been organized according to the line, and some people think this is a weakness. On the other hand, it's kind of understandable, since the line managers assume the heavy part of the personnel responsibilities. We've tested solutions for, for example, HR specialists who worked with direct support to project managers, but we don't have that anymore. (HR Manager, Automotive)

This issue was also brought up by a senior project manager at a logistics company, who to some extent felt a need for more access to the competence of HR specialists in project management situations:

> I think that it's easier for HR specialists to see certain things [and] communication can also be the things that are *not* said out loud.…When you're in the middle of your project and you're completely hooked on what you're supposed to do, and you have a tough deadline, it's easy to forget about some things. And the backside is that we don't have a natural contact with HR; they are not a support function for us. It comes natural for line managers to turn to HR for

support, but not for project managers. And I don't really know why. (Senior Project Manager, Logistics)

Our case studies, hence, reveal a somewhat unbalanced relationship in the HR quadriad when it comes to the HR specialists. The interaction of HR specialists is almost exclusively with line managers and not with the other players in the HR quadriad. On the one hand, this might be reasonable and not problematic since, as the HR manager quoted above points out, line managers assume the main burden of formal personnel responsibilities at the operational work level. On the other hand, our collective and complementary understanding of HRM requires that it must be understood as being more than merely the formal personnel responsibilities. Looking back on the previous chapters, it is obvious that project managers have an important HRM role, be it as the closest manager for a longer period of time, or as one who provides crucial input to the process concerning project workers' performance, competences, and work situation. Similarly, project workers are, in many ways, "HRM developers" of their own and for colleagues; hence, they also contribute to HRM activities performed at the operational level in the organization. We believe there might be reason for project-based organizations to refine the role of HR specialists on an operational level and analyze what balance of interaction with the other players in the HR quadriad might be best, given the characteristics of the particular project work setting.

The analysis also showed that the firms seemed to rely on one of two main logics regarding the roles of HR specialists. In one group of organizations, the general perception of the role of HR specialists followed a task-based logic. This means their role was mainly seen as HR generalists who should provide general HR support adapted to the tasks of the specific line unit. In the remaining cases, on the other hand, the view of HR specialists' role followed instead an HR-based logic. Here, they were, to a greater extent, seen as a resource, providing services to line managers, when needed, within specific competence areas of HRM. The two logics are summarized in Table 8.1.

Recalling the discussions from previous chapters concerning the roles of the other players in the HR quadriad, the complementarity of the roles is interesting considering these two logics. A high level of HR orientation in the line management role, which seems more common in inter-functional project work settings, would probably reduce the need for dedicated and line-specific HR support. An HR-based logic for HR specialists – in which they are expected to provide specialist

Table 8.1　Logics for the role of HR specialists

Task-based logic	HR-based logic
The role of HR specialists is to be... • an integrated part of the line unit. • HR generalists who specialize in HR support for the tasks of a certain line unit. • close collaborators with line management.	The role of HR specialists is to be... • internal consultants • specialists in specific competence areas of HRM • resource and support providers who are available to line management when needed.

competences within certain HRM areas when line managers need their support – should thus apply primarily in such organizations. In intra-functional project work settings, on the other hand, line managers normally have a role that needs to balance HR orientation with task orientation. This means they have less possibility to focus on, prioritize, and develop comprehensive competences concerning HR issues. This, in turn, might call for a more dedicated HR specialist role.

However, these logics presume that HR specialists at the operational level only need to interact with line managers, which means they only apply to a limited part of the HR quadriad. The collective nature of the HR quadriad, however, calls for more inclusive logics for the role of HR specialists on an operational level, logics that acknowledge project managers and project workers as stakeholders and potential collaborative partners. Accordingly, the HR-based logic for HR specialists might need to include the possibility to make the "internal consultants" available not only for line managers but also for project managers and project workers. It might also be necessary to assign dedicated HR support to project management and co-located project teams, particularly in organizations with inter-functional project work. This would call for HR specialists with a specialization of HRM in project-based work settings. Similarly, the task-based logic for HR specialists could be complemented with an HR-based logic for HR support to project managers and project workers. It would also necessitate internal HR consultants being available for project managers and project workers.

In sum, we suggest that any project-based organization needs to analyze the character of its project work setting to find the right balance between the HR-based and task-based logics for the role of HR specialists at an operational level. This should, furthermore, have considerable impact on the organization of HR specialists and the design of HR departments. The possibilities for HR specialists to operate according to their role in the HR quadriad are most likely highly dependent on whether the design of the HR department facilitates it.

Line-based and competence-based structures

In several of the studied firms, the HR department had recently been restructured – from local HR departments and a central HR staff function, to more of a business partner model with shared service centers (see Ulrich and Brockbank, 2005). In these cases, local HR departments had been downsized and replaced by central HR service centers that gave support in specific HR areas (recruitment, competence development, expatriation, law, etc.) and a few "dedicated" HR managers who worked as direct support in strategic HRM for different parts of the company. Other companies had not converted to this model but kept a structure of local HR departments, although these had also been downsized. Table 8.2 summarizes how HR departments were designed in the studied cases (for the complete study, see Bredin and Söderlund, 2010).

A comparison of the cases leads us to identify two major structures for HR departments. Automotive, Logistics, Aerospace, and IT systems relied on the same type of structure, namely, one structured according to the line organization. We will call this structure "line-based HR departments" (Bredin and Söderlund, 2010). These four cases provided examples of both centralized and decentralized departments, but what they all had in common was that the HR department was basically designed to provide HR support according to the specific needs of the different line units. All these cases had a central HR department or a network of HR directors at the top level working with overall HR policies and HR strategies. Apart from that, Automotive and Logistics had decentralized structures for local HR departments at each line unit, focusing on the needs of the specific operations at that unit. Logistics had, however, chosen to downsize the local departments and complement them with a central support unit of HR generalists operating as internal consultants who could be hired by line managers to solve more difficult or time consuming HR matters. At Aerospace, all HR specialists were located at a centralized, global support unit, but they still provided dedicated support to certain line units. The solution at IT systems was somewhat different. Here, the company had not until recently had HR specialists. At the time of the study, HR directors had been appointed for each subsidiary and each business unit, similar to the dedicated HR model described by Ulrich and Brockbank (2005). However, there was no HR department. Instead, the dedicated HR directors cooperated through a network. The

Table 8.2 The design of HR departments in the studied firms

Company/organization		Type of project work setting	Design of HR department
Automotive	R&D site 4,000 employees	Intra-functional Fragmented project participation	Small central strategic HR department at the company level. A structure of HR department at each line unit.
Logistics	Product development and organizational development operations 2,000 employees	Inter-functional Focused project participation	Small, central, strategic HR department at a company level. Central unit for HR support. A structure of HR department at each line unit.
Aerospace	Main site for development of aviation technology. 4,000 employees	Intra-functional Fragmented project participation	Small, central, strategic HR department at a company level. The HR department is part of a larger central support unit, but there are HR personnel dedicated to supporting specific line units.
IT systems	Development site 300 employees	Inter-functional Focused project participation	No central HR department. Recently, the company appointed HR directors for each subsidiary and each business area, reporting directly to the top management. HR directors serve as HR support for team leaders and participate in team leader meetings. The HR directors form a network to discuss and collaborate in corporate-wide HR issues.
Pharma	R&D site 2,000 employees	Intra-functional Fragmented project participation	Small, central, strategic HR department at a company level. Centralized HR support unit providing support in HR specialist competence areas: staffing; compensation & benefits; contracting & legal issues; training Central department for "HR business partners," dedicated to supporting specific line units.

Telecom	Development site 1,000 employees	Inter-functional Focused project participation	Small, central, strategic HR department at a company level. Central department with HR specialist competence areas: staffing, leadership & culture, competence management, compensation & benefits. An HR department at each business unit with an HR director and "business partners," responsible for specific line departments. Business partners are also responsible for working with one of the four central HR specialist competence areas in the unit.
Complex machinery	Unit for advanced plant design and automation solutions. 155 employees	Inter-functional Focused project participation	Small central strategic HR department at a company level A central HR service center, "selling" services within HR specialist competence areas: recruitment; training; internal mobility. A central administrative unit, responsible for personnel administrative tasks such as legal rights and pensions. A structure of small HR departments in each unit (at the unit in focus, there is only one HR director and one assistant).
Medical Systems	Unit for product development 90 employees	Intra-functional Fragmented project participation	No HR department. The CEO believes that if the company grows with another 100 coworkers, an HR department might be necessary. In that case, the department would be structured to give specialized support in certain areas such as legal and contracting issues.

common pattern in all these firms is an HR department structure based on the design of the line units, and it is, therefore, labeled "line-based HR department" and singled out as a structure that is very much consistent with a task-based logic for HR specialists as discussed earlier.

Pharma, Telecom, and Complex Machinery are examples of another type of structure designed primarily to give specialized support within certain HRM competence areas. Accordingly, we will refer to this structure as the "competence-based HR department." Medical systems did not have an HR department at all, but if the company grew, a competence-based structure was what the CEO had in mind. At Pharma, Telecom, and Complex Machinery, most of the HR specialists had been centralized in HR service centers that provided services within specific HRM areas, such as Compensation/Benefits, Recruitment, Training, Contracting, etc. The local HR departments dedicated to supporting particular line units were very small, and in Pharma and Telecom they consisted of one business partner for each unit. Hence, the dedicated support to specific line units was limited. The general pattern in these firms thus points to a basic structure of the HR department primarily designed to provide services within specific HRM competence areas. We have labeled this structure the "competence-based HR department" because of the focus on areas of expertise as a key organizing parameter, which is also strongly related to the HR-based logic for HR specialists, as discussed earlier.

When comparing the cases that have adopted a line-based HR department to the cases with a competence-based HR department, an interesting empirical pattern was found concerning the character of the line units and the role of line managers. In most of the cases with a line-based HR department, the line units were the base for both technology and HRM, and hence, line managers had dual responsibilities for these two areas. Most cases with competence-based HR departments, on the other hand, tended to have line units that could be described more as project work pools that were strongly HR oriented.

Interestingly, the project work setting did not reveal very strong patterns related directly to the HR department structure. Two of the three cases with competence-based HR departments were primarily dominated by intra-functional project work and focused project participation. Here, the project workers either worked full time in a project or divided their time between one single project and various line activities. Among the firms with line-based HR departments, two had inter-functional project work and focused project participation, while the other two had intra-functional project work and fragmented project participation. In the latter two cases, project workers participated in several projects at the same time. Generally, the organizations with focused project participation tended to rely on co-located project teams more often than organizations with fragmented project participation, where the project workers carried out their project tasks while located at their line unit. As described in earlier chapters, the two different types of project-based work settings affect the roles of project workers, line managers, and project managers in the HR quadriad. We would assume that the character of the project work setting should have considerable impact on the actual structure of an HR department needed to enhance the possibilities for HR specialists to take on the appropriate role at an operational level.

However, the empirical evidence offers only limited support for such assumptions, which raises important questions. Does this evidence suggest that the type of project work setting is in actuality a less important factor in the design of HR department structures? Or is it rather a sign that firms should pay more attention to this organizational condition when core activities are performed in projects? We would argue for the latter. In the following, we will relate the discussion on the structure of HR departments to the previous discussion on roles for HR specialists.

HR specialists in the HR quadriad

We have in this chapter presented results from a multiple case study on project-based organizations, results that suggest firms rely primarily on one of the two basic logics for the role of HR specialists and on one of the two basic structures for HR departments. Our empirical studies further suggest that firms which rely on an HR-based logic for HR specialists tend to have a competence-based HR department structures. Here the role of HR specialists is perceived to be that of a specialist in specific competence areas of HRM, and they operate as internal consultants, giving support to the organization on demand. The structural solution is, then, primarily a type of HR service center that is often combined with a smaller network of HR business partners dedicated to specific line units, very similar to the configurations described by Beer (1997) and Ulrich and Brockbank (2005). Firms that rely on a task-based logic for HR specialists, on the other hand, tend to have a line-based HR department structure. The structural solution is local HR departments or a centralized HR unit with HR specialists dedicated to supporting specific line units. The role of HR specialists is then perceived to be an integrated part of the line unit as close collaborators with line managers and providing general HR support that is adapted to the tasks of the specific line unit.

These findings give rise to a new set of questions. For example, why have the organizations chosen a specific HR department structure, and why does one or the other of the logics for HR specialists prevail? Was the HR department structure designed based on the logic for the role of HR specialist the organization wanted to achieve? If so, what was the reason for the choice of this particular logic? Or was it the other way around – that the logic for the role of HR specialists has emerged because of the existence of a certain structure for the HR department? And if that was the case, what determined the choice of structure in the first place? Finally, the ultimate question would be what structure and logic would be most suitable under which circumstances.

Our case studies show that the differences in the operational project work settings coincided only to a limited extent with the differences in HR department structures and logics for the role of HR specialists. The operational work setting obviously does not seem to have had a large impact in the studied organizations. However, the discussions in previous chapters in this book suggest that maybe it should. More research needs to be done within this area in order to develop theories about the relationships between organizational contingencies, such as operational work settings and the different structural solutions for HR departments. Based on the research reported in this book, we take the first step in this process. We argue that the HR quadriad, in combination with the concepts of inter-functional/intra-functional project work and focused/fragmented project participation, offers an important analytical tool that gives us better possibilities to examine and make suggestions on how to align the role of HR specialists with the operational work setting, and how to design an HR department structure that supports and reinforces that role. In addition, the underlying argument in this book suggests that the configuration of HR departments at an operational level in project-based organizations should be based on what role HR specialists need to play in the HR quadriad. As the studies reported in this book show, the character of the HR quadriad – the role of its players and how they collaborate and complement each other – is, in turn, strongly influenced by the type of project work setting and project participation.

Recalling discussions in previous chapters, we have seen that in intra-functional project work where project workers normally have fragmented project participation, line managers are typically senior technical leaders who have dual responsibilities for technology and

HRM. Project managers normally have a role characterized by coordination and communication within the project, rather than by managing the problem-solving process for technological solutions, since most of the project workers perform their project assignments while located at their line unit. Project workers in intra-functional projects mostly collaborate with people from within the same line unit and, hence, reinforce and develop their own disciplinary specialization. However, their project participation is normally fragmented, which means they contribute to various projects at the same time; for some, this fragmentation causes inefficiencies as well as troubles with planning and prioritizing. Various studies also point to stress-related problems caused by too fragmented project participation (Zika-Viktorsson et al., 2006). We suggest that in such project work settings the role for HR specialists in the HR quadriad primarily follows a task-based logic and, consequently, that the basic configuration for the HR department is line-based. Here, HR specialists are important as an integrated part of the line, collaborating with line managers. The HR personnel have special competences regarding the operations of the particular line unit and also HR support for project workers with fragmented project participation. In addition, the line-based configuration could be complemented with a smaller, competence-based, structure for specialized HR services available on demand to all the players in the HR quadriad.

In focused inter-functional project work, on the other hand, the roles in the HR quadriad are quite different. Here, line managers are almost entirely HR oriented, with none or very limited technological responsibilities. Project managers get a more prominent role in the HR quadriad in inter-functional project work settings compared to intra-functional project work settings. They are project team managers who manage a temporarily co-located and dynamic team of relative strangers, and they have a critical responsibility to feed the HR process with information about project workers' performance, competences, work situation, etc. Project workers operating in inter-functional project settings with mostly focused project participation also have a more prominent role in the HR quadriad; this happens, on the one hand, by their handling the liminal conditions of their own work situation and developing appropriate coping strategies, and on the other, through mentoring systems in which they act as back-up and support for less experienced project workers so they can perform in inter-functional teams.

In inter-functional project work settings, line managers, project managers, and project workers all have more prominent and active roles in the HR quadriad, which requires a constant interaction among these roles to make it work. The HR specialist role then becomes more important for providing specialist competences when needed. The dedicated and integrated day-to-day HR support might be less essential as long as line managers and project managers are well prepared for their HRM responsibilities. The multiple case study revealed a somewhat unbalanced interaction in the HR quadriad, which in turn showed that the HR specialists at the operational level are, in all cases, mainly focused on providing support to line managers. However, in light of the previous chapters, we would suggest that the HR specialist's role in inter-functional project work settings should also be oriented toward supporting project managers and project workers in their HR roles. This could be done by providing specialist HR competences as well as by coordinating and creating platforms for efficient collaboration and experience sharing among the other players in the HR quadriad. Thus, we suggest that the role for HR specialists in the HR quadriad of inter-functional project work settings primarily follows a HR-based logic. Consequently, the basic configuration for the HR department should be competence based, but preferably complemented with a smaller, line-based structure in which HR specialists are assigned the role of supporting collaboration among the other players in the HR quadriad.

Returning to the HRM practice areas, we would describe the role of HR specialists in the HR quadriad as outlined in Table 8.3.

Final thoughts

The role and value of HR specialists has been widely discussed in the research community, and new forms of HR departments and HR specialist roles are emerging. With this book, and particularly with this chapter, we emphasize the need to avoid focusing excessively on the strategic levels when designing HR department structures. Instead, we suggest, to make a sound analysis of the operational work setting and what kinds of needs it has is an important starting point. We would argue that this is particularly important in flatter and decentralized organizational forms, such as the project-based work setting. The HR quadriad framework singles out the important role HR specialists have on an operational level in project-based organizations. It also clarifies that this role can only be designed to bring value if it is understood in relation to the other players in the HR quadriad with its collective, complementary, and collaborative character. This chapter particularly highlighted the relative imbalance in the HR quadriad when it comes to HR specialists; we, therefore, suggest developing more relationships

Table 8.3 Roles for HR specialists in the HRM practice areas: comparison between intra- and inter-functional project-based work settings

	Intra-functional project-based work setting	Inter-functional project-based work setting
Overall orientation of HR specialists	Line-based HR department and task-based logic	Competence-based HR department and HR-based logic
Flows	Assuming shared ownership for recruitment processes Planning of human resource needs on an operational level Providing integrated support in the collaboration between the line managers, project managers, and project workers concerning assignments to, and shifts between, projects	Being available as a service on-demand in recruitment processes Being available as support in human resource planning activities Providing tools and processes for collaboration between the players in the HR quadriad concerning assignments to, and shifts between, projects
Performance	Facilitating and improve knowledge-sharing processes within the unit Working with diminishing possible negative consequences of fragmented project participation Being involved in feedback and performance review processes	Providing support on-demand on issues concerning knowledge sharing Providing HR competence concerning focused project participation Providing tools and forms for effective feedback and performance review processes
Involvement	Facilitating the involvement of project workers in the process of planning careers and future assignments Working to ensure project workers' possibilities to influence their work conditions in order to minimize problems due to stress and to achieve work–life balance	Developing tools and processes for the effective involvement of project workers in the planning of careers and future assignments Providing support, tools, and processes for increased project worker involvement
Development	Working with the process of matching project assignments with individual as well as strategic competence development goals. Championing the balancing of projects' short-term resource needs with the long-term development needs of project workers	Developing general tools and processes for matching project assignments with individual and strategic competence development goals

between HR specialists, project managers, and project workers. Moreover, HR specialists have an important part to play in supporting collaboration among all the players in the HR quadriad. This could be done by developing general tools and processes for collaboration with the core HRM practices (HR-based logic) or by direct involvement in these operative collaboration processes. An interesting example of the expanded scope of responsibilities of HR specialists is presented in Fact Box 8.2. This example also accentuates the increasing importance of boundary-spanning HRM, not only within the firm, but also to outside parties – parties that might have important roles as managers for projects and/or as critical human resources.

The chapter generally addresses the design of HR departments but gives more emphasis to a number of issues that have been only limitedly addressed in previous research. First, we argued for the importance of context and, more specifically, the need to address the operational work

---

Fact Box 8.2   HR Director and Projects

A few years ago, Posten – a major Swedish logistics company – wanted to speed up product and service development. Management decided to implement various measures to improve its project management capability, including forming a pool of senior project managers and establishing project management support units. The company also created a set of new roles for its very top HR directors and gave one of them the key responsibility of overseeing its project operations from an HRM perspective. The HR director focused on two primary issues: the working situation of people involved in project operations, and the relationship with key outside partners, such as consulting firms, which played important parts in ongoing development projects. During one of our interviews, the director particularly stressed the importance of having a broad view on human resources in the projects. He said, "Many of our employees are actually managed by consultants from other companies – we bring in outside project managers to handle, for instance, some of our major IT projects. To me, it then becomes really important that these people are aware of their role in our HRM system." He also stressed the importance of having someone who can take an HRM view of things, such as on major development projects and IT implementation projects underway. "We know that they will affect people, but we don't know how. My role is to make sure that we consider these issues in our projects." Besides this, during his meetings with the external partners he also became more and more aware of the fact that their own employees were also important human resources for the benefit of Posten. If they left, were ill, or did not like their job, this would have severe implications on their projects. He summarized his thoughts in the following way: "Just looking at the projects and HRM gives you a rather different view on what HR directors should be doing, doesn't it?"

setting as a basis for the requirements placed on the HR department. Second, we argued for the need to focus on the operational level, instead of following the general tendency in previous research to position HRM primarily in terms of strategic considerations. In line with Hope-Hailey et al. (2005), we argued that flawed analysis of HRM requirements at the operational level could possibly have severe strategic effects. Third, we stressed the need for novel concepts to examine the requirements, conditions, and possible solutions for HR departments. In that respect, we built further on the differentiation of project-based organizations in terms of their operational work setting, in combination with some fundamental structural alternatives, such as the logics of HR specialists and structures of HR departments. With regard to the latter, we then also suggested an improved framing of the HR department as one player within the HR quadriad. Accordingly, the analysis presented here advances our understanding of HRM in organizational terms and that the design of the HR organization and the role of the HR department are fundamental for the theorist trying to comprehend the challenges of HRM in project-based organizations as well as for the designer attempting to improve the value added of investments in HRM.

9
Comparisons and Contrasts

Structure of chapter

- HRM in project-based organizations: bringing the pieces together
- Connecting to contextual HRM
- Connecting the pieces and patterns
- HRM practice areas and the HR quadriad
- From context to configuration
- Improving the HR quadriad: managerial implications
- The future of HRM in project-based organizations

HRM in project-based organizations: bringing the pieces together

This book has come to its final chapter and it is time to summarize the main messages and ideas, compare the different observations, and look into the future. In the various chapters, we have had the chance to meet a number of companies: engineering, R&D-intensive, project-based organizations that very much resemble the image of the kinds of organizations that, many would say, will populate an increasing variety of sectors and industries in the years to come. This is particularly true in the industries where complex problem-solving and the integration of technologies and knowledge stand at the fore. When we have talked about project-based organizations, we have primarily addressed a particular engineering-intensive organization with the following shared features: most work is carried out in projects using temporary teams and the like; integration efforts and capabilities are critical to the success of the organization; and, as a result, different sorts of cross-functional collaboration play an important part. In some companies this collaboration might require co-location and focus, while in others co-location is not required; instead the different members in the team will be dispersed across units and maybe even countries. However, even in these situations collaboration might still be intense, requiring frequent communication, and advanced forms of integration of knowledge across disciplinary boundaries.

We argued that some of the most critical business challenges relate to the capabilities of managing integration activities and complex problem-solving. These challenges have been evident in the companies that participated in our empirical studies – companies operating in a wide range of industries, for example, complex machinery, automation systems, aerospace, high-tech engines, and automotive, to name a few. In previous research, the challenges have been addressed in terms of the value and significance of technology integration (Iansiti, 1998), the role of knowledge integration (Hedlund, 1994), or the building of project competence (Söderlund, 2005). In this book, we have suggested taking an allied, yet different approach to this fundamental competitive problem. We have chosen to address HRM – the supply of human resources, the development of human resources and the organization of HRM systems and processes – to make the company better prepared to deal with the earlier mentioned integration challenge. In so doing, we have positioned our research against three streams of literature: (1) capabilities literature, (2) literature on the project-based organization, and (3) HRM literature. It is, of course, a difficult feat to combine these different strands of literature. Still, we believe such combinations are necessary to accurately frame HRM in contemporary firms – to better understand the ultimate goal of HRM and, accordingly, to address some of the challenges facing managers in charge of developing and improving an organization's HRM processes and practices. We also believe that the relationship between these three domains of research and literature are particularly worth exploring, since project-based organizations are occupied with a particularly demanding organizational integration activity and therefore tend to draw on resources from different sources, for example, line organizations, on a permanent and temporary basis. In such organizations, there is a close connection between work, employment, HRM, and integration capabilities, which is an observation that has generally been supported by the research and empirical observations presented in this book. This assertion leads to a call for a broader approach to HRM that centers on capabilities and context and the relationship between different kinds of capabilities.

We have argued that there is a need for research to more accurately address the contextualization matters of HRM. We focused on one part of the context – namely, the organizational structure – and especially pointed to the project-based organization as one significant context that calls for additional research. The project-based organization could be seen as an organizational innovation aimed at solving a series of intricate problems, including a better integration of knowledge across different areas of expertise, a more suitable organization for complex problem-solving, and an efficient use of human resources. For the individual worker, the project-based organization bears with it a series of difficulties, uncertainties, and strains. At the same time, a project-based organization – if designed and supported properly – may offer unique opportunities for individuals as well as companies. Undoubtedly, project-based organizations have become increasingly popular, and are, at present, a common context for HRM in many nations, industries, and businesses. This means that improvements of HRM in project-based organizations could mean a major difference for many people around the globe. Given our view that the capability to supply and develop human resources is a critical competitive weapon for the project-based organization, improving HRM in this type of organization would thus also ultimately lead to improved company performance.

In this final chapter, we summarize the major points and ideas presented in the book and seek to bring the various pieces together. We will primarily concentrate on how the four players – line managers, project managers, project workers, and HR specialists – in the HR quadriad work together. We thereby attempt to take a second look at the theoretical ideas about the collective nature of HRM, in association with the earlier mentioned points about the significance of context, configuration, and contingency. To that end, we discuss the investments and measures that companies decide upon to improve their use of the HR quadriad. We close the book with a discussion about the future challenges of project-based organizations and the demands that such challenges might put on the HR organization of the firm and the design of the HR quadriad.

Connecting to contextual HRM

Following the call for a more detailed and fine-grained treatise of various kinds of firms and organizational forms and their respective HRM challenges, this book focused on project-based organizations as an important case in point. Hence, we also wanted to explore some new ideas on how to manage human resources. The research contribution is, therefore, associated with the need for "small-scale, contextual studies of HRM" that recently have been brought forward in HRM research

(Boselie et al., 2009: 464). Nevertheless, in order to make it possible to study the context, in particular the structural context which is the prime focus here, we need to sort out the important situational factors or contingencies.

Besides the historical overview of HRM, we emphasized the significance of investigating innovations within the area to identify the major problems that companies currently experience concerning HRM. The examples of the new roles of line managers, the use of "prototypical project workers" such as those found in Workpool Engineering, and career and competence models for senior project managers are all ways to improve the current practice within the area of HRM (see Legge, 1995). In that respect, we intended to improve the understanding of the HR organization in a project-based organization. Two distinctions were particularly important here. First, there was the need to distinguish the concept of "HR organization" from the concept of "HR department". Second, there was the need to treat all actors involved in the HR organization as being engaged in the management of the relationship between employee/involvee and employer. These distinctions also made it possible to investigate the collective nature of HRM; to identify how these actors interact and work together, their respective roles and responsibilities; and how their roles and responsibilities should be designed to fit particular contingency factors pertinent in the organizational context. Looking at the context, the collective nature of HRM, and the importance of a particular set of contingency factors, the book has lent support to the following points:

- Project-based organizations represent one important organizational context which requires new approaches to HRM.
- HRM is increasingly distributive and collective and largely carried out in collaboration among several actors in the HR organization.
- HRM is not the sole responsibility of the HR department; other actors including line managers and project managers play important roles.
- The work setting is critical for the design of HRM. It entails the project participation and nature of project work, which in turn affects what type of HR support the individual project worker is in need of.
- Project workers have an increasingly important role to improve the effectiveness of HRM. Individuals develop skills that are critical for their communication with line managers, collaboration with project managers, and assistance to the HR department in developing their services. In that respect, the individual worker has an

important part in ensuring that the HRM system of the firm is accurately designed.

Connecting the pieces and patterns

Initially, we said that one of the core goals of the HR quadriad framework is to expand traditional views on the important relationships that exist in HRM and how firms can and should design their HR organization. A first step was to understand the driving parameters – the contingencies. In the suggested framework, one critical set of contingencies relates to the type of project work and project participation. The wish to better understand this set of contingencies would lead the designer of a firm's HR quadriad to raise questions about the kind of project-based work setting the organization is dealing with: What is the primary type of project work? What kind of project participation is primarily relied upon? And the answers to these questions would form the basis of the HR quadriad to be designed. In other words, although an HR organization is built to achieve economic efficiencies, to a great extent, its design process actually starts with taking into consideration the needs and work situation of the individual project worker.

In summarizing a few of the observations and findings of the previous chapters, we would like to point out a set of observations and conclusions pertaining to each of the roles in the HR quadriad. The general idea here is to summarize the developmental patterns observed in our case-study organizations and, at the same time, illustrate the complementarity operating among the roles in the HR quadriad.

Line managers. When employees perform an increasing part of their work in projects, a shift tends to occur in the role of the line managers. Project managers assume greater responsibilities for integration tasks, making it possible for line managers to spend more time on HRM. Our studies also demonstrate several attempts to create new kinds of line manager roles, including "competence coaches" with a greater focus on activities such as "project staffing," "competence mapping," and "career counseling." Our studies indicate, however, that the role of the line manager tends to depend largely on the type of work setting at hand: intra-functional work and fragmented participation have certain HRM challenges, which differ sharply from inter-functional work with focused participation. The latter normally also leads to greater responsibilities of the project manager in the daily HRM activities.

Project managers. As indicated, the role of the project manager is molded in a managerial tradition filled with action orientation, task focus, and progress plans. The focus of these tasks is quite different from conventional ideas about HRM and, as seen in our empirical illustrations, project managers typically do not associate their work with HRM. Instead, goals, results, and project deliveries stand at the fore. At the same time, we notice that the amount of HRM inherent in the role of the project manager depends on the nature of project work and project participation. In co-located projects where people are focused on one or two projects, the role of the project manager becomes more dominant as an important player for carrying out activities directly linked to HRM. In situations of intra-functional work, the role of the project manager is more indirect and tends to be more about taking part in activities initiated by the line managers, in giving input to performance reviews, in ensuring good working conditions, etc.

Project workers. Much research has stressed the increased responsibilities of the individual to stay "current" and "employable" (see, for instance, Barley and Kunda, 2004). As is evident in our fieldwork, individual project workers take on an increased responsibility for a variety of HRM processes and activities, which call for a closer analysis of the individual as an important player in the HR organization of the firm. We emphasized the role of a set of variables that seem to influence the challenges that the individual project workers face in their daily work. As pointed out earlier, the type of project work and participation are decisive factors in gaining an understanding of the challenges, problems, and hence, the support that project workers require to pursue their work and careers in project-based organizations.

HR specialists. The HR quadriad framework zeroes in on the need for a closer examination of the operational work setting and, from that perspective, to design appropriate HRM activities. Thereby, we pointed out the importance of separating the analysis of HRM in terms of strategic and operational matters; this, however, does not necessarily say anything about their importance. Operational matters, as seen in our illustrations, are essential for the strategic and important integrative capability on which most project-based organizations thrive. The HR quadriad further stresses the importance of the HR specialists to ensure that the interplay between the players in the HR quadriad is not only working but is continuously improving. In that respect, it is critical for HR specialists to understand not only the needs of the project worker as such, but also what roles line managers and project managers have in delivering the HRM practices of the firm.

As is evident from the aforementioned observations, a number of important developments affect the four roles in the HR quadriad. We demonstrate the transference of HRM to line managers and stress the increasingly important role that project managers have come to play in effecting HRM practices in project-based organizations. We also show the role of the individual in ensuring high-quality HRM and its concomitant implications for HR specialists. Figure 9.1 summarizes the general developmental patterns seen in our case studies. The figure thereby presents an overall picture of the ongoing developments and changes of HRM in the project-based organization.

The patterns depicted in Figure 9.1 generally indicate the linkages between the different parts of the HR quadriad. At the same time, these changes illustrate the importance of understanding and designing the HR quadriad in such a way that the roles support each other. A typical example would be the action-focused project manager who is aware of the importance of the line manager getting access to the information needed to be able to manage the flow of human resources; performance, involvement and communication; and ensure the development

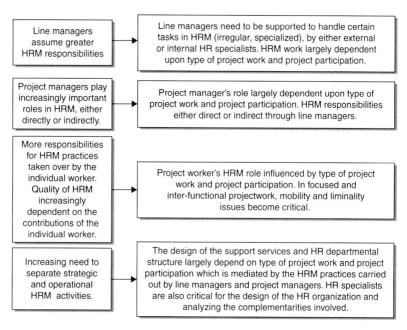

Figure 9.1   Underlying development patterns and relationships within the HR quadriad

of competences. Thus, the essence of HRM complementarities is taking into account changes in one area to initiate adjustments in other areas to gain overall improved effects.

Returning to the types of project-based work setting as either Type A or Type B, a few things could be discussed in light of the configuration of the HR quadriad. As indicated earlier, these two settings require quite different interplays between the actors in the HR quadriad. We argued that, in general, project-based work settings could be grouped into two primary types which constitute overall important aspects for the design of the HR quadriad. These work settings also have effects on the challenges that individual project workers face in their everyday work, and thus for carrying out their part of the HRM practice areas. To some extent, one might treat the Type A worker as one who needs to master several tasks at the same time, prioritize project assignments, and solve problems mostly with people who have similar professional and disciplinary backgrounds. The Type B worker is somewhat different since Type B work is focused on a single project in cooperation with people who are primarily from other professional backgrounds and disciplines. The challenge, of course, is to handle the continuous move from one project to another, to handle several different tasks but within the same project, and to communicate and collaborate with relative strangers.

In considering project managers, we might speak of two different kinds in relation to their HRM responsibilities. We argue that the indirect and direct alternatives are quite instrumental in this context. The indirect is commonly relied upon in project-based work settings resembling Type A, whereas the direct one is typically associated with Type B project-based work settings. The role of the line manager varies along similar lines. Here we have distilled two primary types depending on the work setting. In cases of Type A, the role of the line manager is to be more of a supervisor, responsible for direct assessment, typically involved in technological problem-solving and work conditions. In Type B settings, the role of the line manager transforms into that of a competence manager with the responsibilities of coordinating competence development and knowledge pools, working as a hub for assessment and performance reviews, and ensuring that the project worker has good prospects for new projects after having completed the current one. Finally, we move on to the HR specialists. In the chapter on HR specialists, we discussed two primary types of logics and department structures. To support organizations relying on project-based work similar to Type A, a task-based logic is favored which promotes the integration of activities with line managers and ensures that HR specialists understand the particular challenges associated with HRM in various line units. In these cases, we also see the use of "line-based HR structures." As for Type B settings, organizations tend to adopt the HR-based logic which promotes a focus on competence areas and relies, to a great extent, on a model where HR specialists work as "internal consultants." In these settings, we also tend to observe HR departments that follow the rationale of the "competence-based HR department".

In sum, we might then discern two rather different configurations for the HR quadriad depending on the type of project-based work setting. This generally also highlights the importance of creating a fit between the different actors and that alterations within one part of the quadriad might very well have either positive or negative consequences on the other parts. Figure 9.2 and 9.3 display the two ideal-typical configurations discussed here.

The analysis here points out the important factors influencing the design of the HR quadriad and the responsibilities for the various roles involved. It also gives further evidence to the relationship and complementarity among them. In addition, the analysis demonstrates not only the possibility of designing the HR quadriad in different ways depending on the type of project-based work setting, but also the distribution of responsibilities among the players in the quadriad. The latter indicates that the HR quadriad constitutes an important framework for the design of the configuration of the HR organization in project-based organizations and that the examination of one part of the quadriad needs to rest upon an understanding of the entire arrangement of the parts.

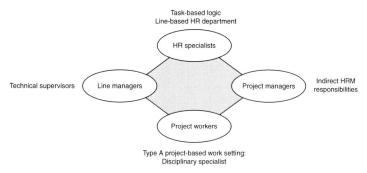

Figure 9.2   Complementarities in the HR quadriad: Type A

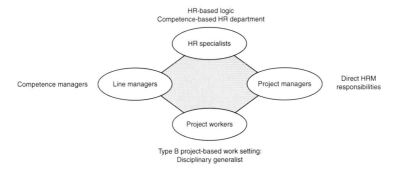

Figure 9.3   Complementarities in the HR quadriad: Type B

HRM practice areas and the HR quadriad

While comparing the various roles in the HR quadriad, we relied on a simple yet instructive categorization of HRM activities and processes, referred to as "HRM practice areas." The idea was to shed light on the broad spectrum of issues that are involved in the activities targeting the supply and development of human resources – key capabilities for the project-based organization. This categorization was applied to the analysis of line managers to identify their primary function with respect to each area. We also analyzed the roles of the project manager and the project worker based on this categorization to identify which areas are particularly relevant for the further analysis of the shared responsibilities among the actors in the HR quadriad. Finally, we used this categorization to distinguish the variation across contexts and how the focus and specific activities depend on the type of project-based work setting. This resulted in the summary comparison that was presented in the previous chapter on HR specialists in the HR quadriad. Bringing these insights together, the analysis generally highlights the collective nature of HRM in this organizational context. It also stresses the complementarity and configurational nature of HRM in these settings, which will be discussed further below. We repeat some of the primary observations in Table 9.1.

The table illustrates the broad array of activities that are critical to ensure the effective supply and development of human resources in the project-based organization. The following section presents how the various practice areas and particularly the roles within the HR quadriad are aligned and adopted to meet specific challenges with regard to the type of project-based work setting at hand.

Table 9.1 Actors in the HR quadriad: responsibilities and roles for HRM practice areas

	Line managers	Project managers	Project workers	HR specialists
Flows	Ensure the appropriate flow of human resources, selection, recruitment, and phase-out in collaboration with HR specialists. Project staffing and phase-out often in collaboration with project managers.	Project staffing often in collaboration with line managers, especially pronounced in inter-functional project work. Collaborate with line managers to manage upturns and downturns in resource needs in projects.	Know one's competence and qualities and build one's reputation. Be prepared for project assignments, reassuring a skilled entry when beginning project assignments (moving in). Skillful handover of assignments and information when leaving assignments (moving out). Plan future assignments to handle phase-out from projects.	Provide specialist support in recruitment and phase-out processes, by integrated collaboration with line managers or by service-on-demand. Provide support in human resource planning activities. Ensure an effective collaboration within the HR quadriad concerning assignments to, and shifts between, projects.
Performance	Facilitate knowledge-sharing within the line unit. Make sure that work conditions in the projects are appropriate.	Facilitate knowledge-sharing within the project. Detect and work to minimize problems in project work conditions. Give direct feedback to project workers on their performance.	Share knowledge with project team members and colleagues from the line to solve complex problems. Clarify expectations by role carving and redefinition. Search for feedback in assignments.	Provide specialist support in knowledge-sharing processes within line units and in projects. Ensure that work conditions in projects are continuously evaluated and improved. Provide HR competence concerning challenges with fragmented and focused project participation.

	Reassure reliable performance appraisals and reviews in collaboration with project managers.		Participate in performance appraisal and reviews together with line managers.	Ensure trustworthy performance appraisal and review processes.
Involvement	Involve project workers in the planning of future assignments. Promote project workers to projects they strive for. Support project workers in finding work-life balance.	Clarify assignments, roles and responsibilities, to make sure that project workers know their mandate and to improve project workers opportunities to influence their work and work conditions.	Get involved in decision-making processes. Actively influence work itself and work conditions. In some situations actively decide *not* to get involved, in order to cope with liminality.	Develop tools and processes for the effective involvement of project workers in the planning of careers and future assignments. Work to ensure that project workers get opportunities to influence their work conditions to minimize problems with stress and work-life balance.
Development	Match project assignments with development goals. Strive for a reasonable balance between short-term project needs, and long-term development needs.	Identify needs for competence development and competence shifts. Support project workers in their on-the-job training. Spread the word on positive experiences with project workers (support reputation).	Search and prepare oneself for new challenging assignments. Learn from experience. Network to build social capital, learn from others, and share knowledge with others.	Provide HR specialist support, integrated or by tools and processes, in matching project assignments with development plans. Provide tools and processes for competence mapping in projects as well as in the line.

From context to configuration

In terms of linkages with the research on HRM, we have aligned ourselves with some of the more recent organization-theory oriented approaches. The importance of organizational context has been discussed throughout the book, and we have discussed in what ways the project-based organization puts pressure on HRM. We have also made use of a broader view on HRM than what one often sees in current literature. That is, we pointed out the importance of four roles – how they interact and how changes in one area and role might have an impact on one or more of the other roles. This, then, also calls for addressing the HR organization of the firm in a novel way, not merely focusing on single, isolated practices as such. The notion of the HR quadriad is an attempt to trigger thinking in this direction. The theoretical idea and elaborations pursued in the book could be summarized with a set of "Cs," which links back to the initial presentation of the HR quadriad in Chapter 4.

Through these theoretical implications and concepts, we believe that we have offered not only a relevant framework for the analysis of project-based organizations but perhaps also made an important contribution to the HRM literature at large. In particular, we would argue that our studies have paved the way for a more nuanced approach to the "best-fit" studies and have demonstrated that there are a number of factors influencing the design of HRM systems, although some contingencies seem to be more important than others. Our framework also empirically documents the need to approach HRM as a collective phenomenon. It acknowledges that the ongoing devolvement, contracting, and emphasis on individual responsibilities generally accentuate the importance of approaching HRM as a shared and collective responsibility. Finally, the ideas of complementarity and configuration are not focusing on the practices as such. Instead, we opt for an organization-theory inspired interpretation in which the roles and responsibilities of the actors performing HRM activities are addressed. Accordingly, this turns attention to the fact that HRM and the capabilities to supply and develop human resources are enacted by an organization and by people who share and divide responsibilities among them; thus, to succeed with the building of capabilities the entire HR organization needs to perform well. In our opinion, this adds to the understanding of HRM in the sense that we are not only addressing different responsibilities but also the different roles of the players that carry out HRM activities. This follows from the observation that even if the HRM structure and

Table 9.2 Summary: the theoretical implications

Dimension of theoretical implication	Application
Context	The importance of project-based organizations as a particular context for HRM: The nature of the project-based organization as such, the need for integrative capabilities, problem-solving capabilities, and the like, trigger underlying changes of HRM within project-based organizations.
Collective	HRM is not an individual act or one unit's responsibility; it is a collective act of several players within the organization, including the individual. The collective nature of HRM is also accentuated by the paramount role of the project manager in arranging for problem-solving conditions within the project-based organization. In some projects, workers are co-located in such a manner that the project manager has direct and daily contact with them. This has important implications on HRM and highlights the need of the project to take part in the HRM practices within the firm.
Contingency	The importance of operational project-based work setting (project work and project participation): The distinction between project work that is either inter-functional or intra-functional, together with project participation as focused or fragmented, offers powerful explanations for the design of HRM in the project-based organization. The contingencies are then largely tied to the context mentioned earlier which influence the type of project work and participation needed to secure effective problem-solving situations within the firm.
Complementarity	Changes in one role might have implications for other roles. Changes in one role might require changes in other roles to realize system-wide efficiencies. This shows that both weaknesses and strengths of parts in the HR quadriad have implications for the other parts. It also shows the importance for the HR specialists to be responsive to those changes and how problems and weaknesses can be solved in quite a number of different ways.
Configuration	The design of the HR quadriad makes up the arrangement of the parts of the HR organization. The configuration of HRM centers on the fact that the HR quadriad involves a certain number of combinations and types. In the book, we have argued that type of project work and project participation are critical variables that can be combined in different ways leading, in turn, to particular and specific challenges within HRM.

its constituent functional domains and people are well-aligned, there is still the possibility that any modifications made in one area may also yield potentially negative effects on other areas in the HR organization of the firm.

Improving the HR quadriad: managerial implications

We now turn to the practical and managerial implications based on the ideas presented in the book. In this section we will address questions concerning: How can the people that hold roles in the HR quadriad do a better job? How can their collaboration be improved and adapted to fit the actual work setting in the organization? The intention here is to offer some alternative views on the theoretical implications of the research presented in the book. This section also presents some ideas on how to develop the functioning of the HR quadriad and how to improve its constituent parts.

As noted previously, the quadriad framework involves four primary roles. It covers the contingent nature and needs to be adapted to the particular requirements at hand. The first step for any organization that wants to improve its HR quadriad is thus, of course, to understand this broader framing of the HR organization. Is the operational work setting Type A, in which project work is intra-functional and project participation is fragmented? Or is it Type B, in which project work is inter-functional and project participation is focused? Or does the operational work setting combine these two dimensions in any other way? As we have seen in the previous chapters, these dimensions have a large influence on the roles and interplay between the actors in the HR quadriad.

We argue that the responsibilities of the actors in the HR quadriad are to a great extent collective and that there is a need to see the different actors relative to each other. As a consequence, this requires a broader understanding of the situation and interplay among the actors involved. Accordingly, designers of HR quadriads need to identify where the quadriad is weakest and raise questions such as: Do any of the four roles need to improve the quality of their actions, and, if so, how? Does the weakness, for example, have to do with the capacity and skills of the HR specialists? Or does it have to do with the willingness and interest of the project managers? These questions, however, are not sufficient to capture possible weaknesses and opportunities for improvement in the HR quadriad. Of equal importance is to look at the interaction between the actors in the quadriad. The study by Truss and Gill (2009) provides important insights in that it demonstrates that some weak elements within the HRM system can be identified relatively easily. Based on identification of these weak elements, it is then possible to identify the key problems in the relationships among the actors in the HR organization.

The four roles could be viewed as four primary areas where improvements could be made. These improvement efforts could focus on one of two dimensions. On the one hand, and as touched upon above, they could be directed toward the *acting* of the four roles and the players holding these positions. This involves simply clarifying the roles and their function in the HR quadriad. It may also comprise competence development efforts in terms of training programs designed for HRM in project-based work settings. For instance, line managers and project managers could be offered special training to understand their roles in HRM better, and increase their capabilities to handle their HRM responsibilities. The individual worker might need particular training and support to be prepared for the challenges that come with the ongoing flow in and out of new projects, new teams, and new assignments. HR specialists might also need customized training concerning the functioning of project-based organizations and work settings in general, and in particular, of the organization they work to support. Subsequently, they can develop certain areas of expertise that are very rare in the organization at large, although still critical to have available in-house.

On the other hand, the improvement efforts could also be directed toward the *interaction* among the actors involved. To some extent this might require a development of formal routines, processes, and tools for cooperation and communication. It might be equally important to clarify the centrality of this interplay for all parties involved, and create arenas for knowledge-sharing and informal collaboration. We would suggest that, for our studied firms, improving the HR quadriad is first and foremost a matter of improving the interaction between the involved actors, and second, initiating amendments and improvements in the four areas.

In what follows, we summarize the patterns of improvements that we have seen in our studies and offer examples of measures that strengthen the effectiveness of the HR quadriad. We build further on the four roles discussed earlier, and we will discuss improvement opportunities for each of these parts of the HR quadriad in relation to (1) the role itself – the acting - and (2) the collaboration and complementarities among the roles – the interaction with the other players in the HR quadriad. We begin with line managers, followed by project managers and project workers, and end with the improvement opportunities for HR specialists.

Line manager or competence manager: clarifying the role

Acting: As indicated, line managers generally tend to assume more responsibilities for activities related to flows, performance, involvement and development of human resources. Hence, there is a need for preparing and training line managers to assume this HR-oriented part of their role. As indicated in this book, the character of this HR orientation is, to a great extent, shaped by the project-based work setting. When project workers' activities are mostly cross-functional, the line managers' focus shifts from internal line-specific activities to the development and support of project workers' contributions to projects. Line managers need to adapt their acting to the temporary nature of projects by managing the project workers' ongoing transition between project assignments. This involves activities related to assignment to a project, relationship to and performance of the project worker during the assignment, assessment and evaluation after the project, planning of future project participation and finally, competence development according to individual and strategic goals.

More specifically, the acting of line managers could be substantially improved by a sound analysis of the type of project-based work settings in which they act out their roles. In Type A settings, the role would benefit from being clarified as primarily a 'line management' role, with dual responsibilities for line operations and HRM. Type A line managers are first and foremost experts on line-specific technology and competences. They manage project activities taking place in their unit, and they are important mentors and technological champions within the unit. They also have important HRM responsibilities in all four HRM areas, and these activities are, to a great extent, embedded in the line managers' work within the unit. In Type B settings on the other hand, we suggest this role to be clarified as primarily a 'competence management' role. The setting for this role is one in which project workers are, for most of the time, not located at the unit but in project teams. Type B competence managers are therefore not involved in managing the actual project activities: they are instead experts on the competences that the unit delivers to the projects. This role needs to be acknowledged as an HR-oriented role, in which the line manager is a champion for HRM at the operational level with particular knowledge about the challenges of inter-functional project work and focused project participation.

Accordingly, it is imperative to analyze the organization on an operational level to clarify whether the focus of this role is to manage project activities in the line organization or to manage competences for the project operations. Are they line managers of a unit of co-located project workers working in several parallel projects or competence managers of a network of project workers with a similar knowledge base, dispersed in co-located projects? Based on that, the role could be improved by, for example, adequate role descriptions, definition of relevant background, skills and personality of people holding the role, and training programs and support structures that are adapted to develop the HRM competences required for either line management or competence management roles.

Interacting: Our studies suggest that line managers and competence managers need to develop different patterns of interaction within the HR quadriad. Line managers have a close interaction with project workers concerning problem-solving issues as well as HRM issues, but they generally need to expand their interaction with project managers in HRM activities (Flows, Performance, Involvement, and Development). Moreover, they often express a wish for a more integrated collaboration with HR specialists to strengthen the HRM dimension of their management work. This is due to the difficulties of balancing the management of line activities and HRM activities. Competence managers, on the other hand, run the risk of being detached from the project workers with little control over their work situation. Here, there is a need to develop ways to closely interact with both project workers and project managers, even though the competence managers are physically separated from these two players during project assignments. This interaction is necessary so that the competence manager obtains input for the HRM process. For a competence manager, we suggest, the interaction with HR specialists might not need to be in the form of an integrated collaborator, but instead in the form of an HR service center for administrative support (see for example Ulrich and Brockbank, 2005).

Project managers: understanding the HRM dimension

Acting: The role of the project manager is undoubtedly critical for the two primary capabilities discussed in this book: the integrative capability and the capability to supply and develop human resources. To date, however, research on the role of the project manager has primarily been associated with the integrative capability. Without doubt, the role is challenging and there is some indication in previous research that it creates so much pressure that it is difficult for people to stay in the role of project manager for long, despite the fact that they are attracted to the idea of forming a temporary team and working under the pressure of a deadline with set targets (Ricciardi, 2000). This is particularly true in Type B settings, where the project manager leads a co-located team (often dynamic and constantly changing) for a limited period of time. One explanation could be that project managers are not trained to fulfill the role. According to Carbone and Gholston (2004), less than half of the organizations in their survey had any type of project management training program and only 41 percent of project managers felt their organizations prepared them for their role. Interestingly, from those project managers who had been trained, 73 percent felt the training prepared them for their role. Training could do a lot, and it should be the first, obvious step to improve the role of the project manager. However, one still has to realize that this is far from the only answer. Shenhar and Dvir (2007: 209) offer a quite drastic measure to improve the situation:

> Get the best people to lead projects. Avoid the temptation (and the norm) to put your best people in charge of operations. Remember that it is easier to manage operations than complex, uncertain projects. Future operations will be profitable only if the projects that created them were selected correctly and done well.

In addition, there is a need to understand better the particular human resource dynamics involved in projects and to develop skills and tools to analyze and measure the progress of projects in an HRM framework. The idea of HR Gates is one possibility; however, there are numerous other options, including team satisfaction surveys and climate reports.

Project managers have an important role to play in the context of leadership and management capacity in the project-based organization. Firms currently invest much of their money in certification, training, and network activities to improve leadership resources within this area. To some extent, these activities tend to focus on the formal and hard aspects of project management, including breakdown structures, planning techniques, and so on. This, paired with the general tendency of companies to promote their good engineers to become project managers could, of course, endanger the soft sides of project management. To put it frankly, projects could become planning and technology without people. What is needed are good role models, certification programs, and training programs that give priority to the human side of project management – not only the traditional concept of building a good team but also the concepts of understanding the HRM dimension of projects, the careers of people, the learning opportunities, and competence development. Accordingly, this would entail understanding that projects contain several connections to the overall practice areas, including Flows, Performance, Involvement, and Development.

Interacting: The studies in this book have highlighted the importance of viewing project managers as an important part of the HR organization. This is also one of the key areas about which we argue that there is generally room for improvement. The interaction with project members may not be the most problematic one, even though the HR dimension in this interaction often could be further developed. For example, to improve the flow of human resources, the project managers need to understand the critical issues for people in phases of entering new project assignments and how to best prepare for phase-out. In terms of performance evaluations, project managers typically have an important role in giving direct feedback to project workers. The interaction with line managers and competence managers concerning HR issues is one that has not received much attention either in management practice or in research. Nevertheless, our studies point to the importance of project managers collaborating with line managers to help them conduct appropriate performance appraisals, to discuss competence gaps and future needs, and to ensure appropriate working conditions. Another blind spot is the interaction between project managers and HR specialists. We would argue that Type B project managers, in particular, would benefit from developing interactions with HR specialists, especially to get input on how to handle the downsides with inter-functional and focused project participation.

As indicated earlier, for many complex projects, we see the application of principles resembling the shared leadership model. This is one way to strengthen the integrative leadership capacity within projects. It is also a potential solution to the HRM problems in project-based work settings. Yet, it requires that project managers collaborate so that the HRM dimension of the project is analyzed and handled and does not become a responsibility that falls through the cracks – with no member of the project management team taking on responsibility for this role.

Project workers: preparing for project work

Acting: Throughout the book, we have underlined the importance of the project-based work setting and the different types of project work and participation. We highlighted a set of similarities across work settings in project-based organizations and identified key differences with regard to what extent project work was inter-functional and to what extent participation was focused. In either case, we highlighted the continuous need to build new relationships and work together with new people. We also stressed the responsibilities for HRM that are expected of the individual worker, regardless of the type of project-based work setting. Of course, the free-agent route discussed earlier and the liminality issues are probably most apparent in situations of high mobility, which typically tends to be the case in inter-functional project work. The focus on the individual's responsibility for staying current is emphasized in all cases. It also highlights the importance of engineering skills as a tool that is increasingly used to sort out the liminality and cooperative difficulties. In that respect, a shrewd engineer is not the best one merely from a strictly technical point of view. As the case of Workpool Engineering confirmed, the skilled engineer is the one who can live with liminality, enter new problem-solving situations, communicate, and apply the relevant coping strategy depending on the situation at hand.

Interacting: Including the individual project worker in the HR quadriad also means making them an active part in the interaction instead of a passive receiver of HRM practices. This is an important stance, since it stresses the importance of developing the project workers' awareness of and responsibility for their interaction patterns with line managers, project managers, and HR specialists. We argue that these interactions can generally be improved, particularly in Type B settings in which project workers, to a higher degree, need to learn to live with liminality and mobility. We underline that these project workers will need interactions with their competence manager for primarily long-term HRM issues such as career planning, competence development, competence sharing, appraisal, and work-life issues. However, the interaction with project managers is also intensive, particularly concerning short-term HRM issues such as feedback, involvement during the project, and phase-out at the end of a project. Type B project workers might also need a more direct interaction with HR specialists with particular knowledge about managing liminality and mobility.

HR specialists: supporting the HR quadriad

Acting: A key goal of this book has been to show the value of addressing HR departments as one of the players in the HR organization of the firm. HR specialists typically have unique expertise in understanding HRM problems and opportunities and should of course be more involved in analyzing the HR quadriad on a day-to-day basis. As some of our illustrations point out, having HR specialists who understand the dynamics of project work and the nature of project-based organizations is a critical and increasingly important factor. Suitably designing the HR quadriad might in itself be a key aspect of improving the capability to ensure the continuous supply and development of human resources to participate in complex problem-solving processes. Correspondingly, HR specialists should have the primary responsibility as well as the skills to detect errors in the quadriad, to analyze patterns over time, and to observe differences across organizational units and projects. As indicated in the chapter on HR departments, the design of the HR department needs to be viewed in light of the rest of the players in the HR quadriad, which, in turn, are influenced by the type of project-based work setting. To reap the possibilities of complementarities is, therefore, the ultimate responsibility of the HR specialist and should be considered a critical skill that the designer of HR organizations should possess in project-based organizations. In that respect, the HR specialists also have a role to play when it comes to understanding the development opportunities for the other players, providing arenas for collaboration and experience sharing within the quadriad, monitoring environmental changes and opportunities, and learning from best practice in other industries and sectors.

Interacting: As indicated previously, the interaction between HR specialists on an operational level and the other players in the HR quadriad needs to be consistent with the type of project-based work setting and the resulting overall design of the HR quadriad. We have seen several examples of HR specialists struggling under structures that are not aligned with the requirements of the operational work setting and the key roles in it. One way of improving the interaction with the other players is to reinvent the organization of HR specialists at the operational level, basing it on the actual work setting and a good understanding of the work conditions of project workers. Another important improvement opportunity is to increase the HR specialists' competence in, and responsibilities for, supporting the interaction between the other players in the HR quadriad.

The future of HRM in project-based organizations

Doing research on HRM has certainly been a pleasure. Every day of field work and writing has felt enlightening and meaningful, in particular the actual work for and often together with managers and companies struggling to sort out the difficulties of HRM in project-based organizations. In our research, we have followed the general pleas for studying HRM in practice, getting engaged with managers, and making sense of the experience of people who work in project-based organizations. Thus, we build on a tradition within HRM that advocates in-depth case studies paired with comparative case-study research. Although the research presented in this book relied to a great extent on a comparative approach, in which we made use of findings from companies operating in diverse industries, we still had a particular focus on an organization heralded as an exemplar of a new organizational form. Even though we stressed that this is one important context, it is far from being the complete answer; there might be other contextual matters involved that equally must be addressed. Accordingly, the analysis presented here is limited in terms of the broader institutional, legal, and cultural frameworks that typically also play an important role in the design of HRM (Gooderham et al., 1999). This would of course be an important opening for further research, namely, to compare project-based organizations in different institutional settings and document the appropriate HRM solutions. Likewise, there might be other significant structural contexts and associated contingency factors. This illustrates the importance of broadening the general analysis of relevant contingency factors in the analysis of project-based firms to fully comprehend the variety of HRM challenges involved. For instance, in other project-based firms, location and client interaction might be critical factors, and the level of project uncertainty facing project workers would most probably also be important to understand what kind of support is called for (cf. De Meyer et al., 2002; Shenhar and Dvir, 2007). This is one important area where we believe that additional practice and research need to be developed and prepared.

Concerning the two sets of capabilities operating in the project-based organization that introduced the book, there is a need to ensure the ongoing development and cross-fertilization of these capabilities: the integrative capability of bringing knowledge, technologies, and solutions together, on the one hand, and, on the other hand, the supply and development of human resources. We believe that managing the HR quadriad in itself might constitute an important part in the capability of supplying and developing human resources. In addition, improving the understanding of the linkages between projects and the development of human resources would, of course, be a valuable and critical step to ensure the mutual exchange of the two sets of capabilities. Important questions include the following: What kind of projects lead to superior competence development? How should those projects best be organized to stimulate performance and learning? How should they best be staffed without reducing their probability for success? In times of increasing number of projects, particularly shorter, agile projects, these questions pose important challenges to management. In our mind the questions represent a second important area for future research as well as practice development in project-based organizations.

Since this book is about the management of human resources, the nature, quality, and location of human resources represent important matters. Linked to this are a number of important questions, including the appropriate balance between temporary and permanent staff, the collaboration and synergies among temporary and permanent staff, and the strategic risks involved. In addition, one of the fastest-growing lines of businesses are technical consultancies, which have an increasingly important role in organizing human resources on behalf of the type of companies investigated here. Technical consultancies are not only used to deal with numerical flexibility – the variability in demand – but also to make better use of knowledge processes, including knowledge sharing and knowledge transfer. Moving from project to project across organizational contexts can also be critical for the hiring firm, which benefits from people who have experienced and solved similar problems in other contexts and have absorbed knowledge in these situations – this spurs creativity in the focal problem-solving situation. The evolution of the organization of human resources in this perspective constitutes an important development opportunity for work relying on the HR quadriad framework. Thus, the question of who and where the human resources are in the project-based organization would be a third important area for future research and practice.

The role of the project manager has changed considerably in the past two decades. Shared leadership was singled out as one way of adding leadership and management capacity to complex projects. Such a measure would perhaps then also be important to the project manager assuming greater responsibilities for HRM. Other measures include changes to the formal role of the project manager: whether that role should have responsibilities for HRM; what those responsibilities are; how those responsibilities are taken; what training is needed; and what effects increased HRM responsibility might have on project performance, not only assessed as team satisfaction, but also against a number of criteria, including timely delivery and efficient and effective use of resources and money spent (Shenhar & Dvir, 2007). This then highlights a fourth important area; the continuing development of leadership capability and leadership models, such as the effects and possibilities of shared leadership models, and their resulting implications for the effectiveness and relevant practices of HRM.

As touched up on in the previous sections, the future of HRM in project-based organizations carries with it many opportunities for research and practice improvements. Summarizing some of them and ending the book on the "C" note relied upon earlier in this chapter, we think that the research needs to be directed toward the entire range of the theoretical dimensions of HRM mentioned earlier. The following list thus both summarizes some of the insights gained during our study and highlights some of the opportunities for future research and knowledge development.

Capabilities and HRM. Investigation of the relationship and dynamics between integrative capabilities and capabilities to ensure the continuous supply and development of human resources that can participate in complex problem-solving processes.

HRM in context. The book zeroed in on project-based organizations. Future research should continue to focus on the comparisons between different project-based organizations in different industries, sectors, and regions.

Collective HRM. As several studies have shown there are difficulties in handling the interplay between different actors in the HR organization. The collective nature of HRM presented here does not make things easier. To detail the responsibilities of the actors involved in the HR quadriad would be an important topic for future research.

HRM and contingencies. The studies presented here focused primarily on two chief contingency factors that constituted the project-based work settings. Other factors are, undoubtedly, important. Identifying these factors is important for both practice and research, and improving the understanding of the relationship between these factors would be an important next step.

HRM and complementarity. The relationship between HRM practices, HRM practice areas, and roles in the HR organization is critical to knowing what changes are needed to reap the full benefit of investments in HRM.

HRM and configuration. Future research should investigate further different aspects of the HR quadriad and analyze in-depth different solutions in terms of the interplay between the actors involved. A next step would be to detail the relevant performance measurements and analyze performance across different HR quadriads.

Appendix: Research Design and Methodology

The evidence: data and methodology

We have studied a number of R&D organizations and engineering-intensive firms during the past decade. The starting point for our empirical investigations was a series of studies of project processes and project management, typically in large complex development projects. This later emerged into a series of studies of the organization and management of project-based organizations, which are the prime focus of the work reported here. The focused studies began in 2003 with a comparative case study involving four companies which we here refer to with the code names: "Aerospace," "Automotive," "Pharma," and "Logistics." This work was published in a preliminary report in which we discussed four key challenges tied to HRM in project-based organizations. The study was important for several reasons. First, it broadly laid the foundation for our work on project-based organizations rather than focusing specifically on a particular kind of sector or industry. Second, it gave us a wide view of the complexity of the challenges of HRM in such organizations. Later, these ideas were further developed and published in a book: Perspektiv på HRM – nya organisationsformer, nya utmaningar (2005, *Eng: Perspectives on HRM – new forms of organization, new challenges*) and a number of more focused journal papers.

In the second step of our fieldwork, we explored in detail some of the observations made in our initial fieldwork. After the initial phase, we singled out a number of areas that required further scrutiny, including the role of the line manager, the variations of HR department across different types of project-based organizations, and the work situation of project workers (engineers, programmers, etc.). This book summarizes the main findings for practitioners, scholars, and students. It also presents an opportunity to make comparisons difficult to make in journal articles since these give limited space for expanding the text around, for example, empirical descriptions. We draw on a quite diverse set of cases involving companies and organizations from industries such as aerospace, automotive, pharmaceutical, packaging machinery, and telecommunications. Most of the companies have been studied in depth from a number of perspectives. Some of the companies have only participated in one of our substudies.

Table A1 presents the companies that have been involved in our studies and the type of research methodology and data that we have gathered. We have chosen to use code names for all the companies in this section. Some of the companies studied have requested that we not display their names, and, for clarity and readability, we have chosen not to mix code names with authentic names. In the chapters that include information only from companies that allowed us to use their names, their authentic names appear, and in chapters that include information from the code-name companies, all companies are referred to with code names (Fact Boxes excluded).

Contextual understanding through case studies

One of the underlying ideas with the empirical studies presented in this book was to contribute to the idea of "small-scale, contextual studies of HRM" (Boselie et al., 2009: 464). However, we also wanted to make comparisons across organizations to detect important differences and similarities. Generally, the studies presented in this book relied on good stories and constructs, drawing on the strength of individual examples and effective comparisons. In this respect, we followed conventional case-study research and multiple case-study logics (Eisenhardt, 1989). The initial phase encompassed the data gathering, interviews, secondary material, annual reports, and so on. The second phase focused on analyzing each individual case. The third phase focused on the cross-case analysis. Overall, we had the ambition to understand the company or the studied unit in detail: its history and its current practices. Although we relied on a limited number of interviews, we had access to the most knowledgeable people in the company who freely gave the details of their past and current practices. The companies also made it possible for us to return and check details, correct misunderstandings, and carry out follow-up interviews.

Besides this multiple case study, we also did a series of more focused studies to explore in further depth the different parts and players in the HR quadriad.

Line managers

This study centered on the change of the line-manager role in a number of different companies. The most intensive part of the work was a comparative case study of Tetra Pak and Saab. In total, we interviewed 20 senior managers and line managers in these firms and conducted an in-depth analysis of each firm. One of the studies was presented in Bredin and Söderlund (2007). Subsequently, we carried out a comparative analysis focusing on the solutions implemented in these firms and the roles and responsibilities of line managers. This comparison was presented in Bredin and Söderlund (2008). In addition to these case studies, we conducted studies in the following companies: Engine, Automotive, Pharma, and Logistics (code names). Some of these preliminary findings were already reported in a previous book (Söderlund and Bredin, 2005). The comparative study is also in part presented in a paper published in *Human Resource Management* (Söderlund and Bredin, 2006). The methodological idea underlying the study of line managers is decisively linked to perspectives and inferences that were evidently drawn from various information sources that we came across during our study, for example, interviews that we conducted, vignettes, and examples within contexts. We aimed to understand the organizational contexts, positioning the role of the line manager within the organizational structure, and analyzing the distribution of roles and responsibilities of HRM in the companies. The interviews followed a rather strict interview guide, although they typically turned into quite informal conversations about the line manager's everyday practices, responsibilities, and problems.

Table A1 An overview of the case-study companies

Company	Brief description and facts	Methodology and data
Aerospace	A large Swedish company with a long history of developing solutions for defense, aviation, and space. The company has approximately 13,000 employees. We studied one of the most R&D–intensive project-based units, which had approximately 900 people involved in their projects.	Case study of HRM challenges in project-based work settings. Study of changes in the HR organization, including data on HR specialists, project managers, and project workers. Focused study of line managers' role in HRM. Meetings with management team on line managers' role. Focused study on project management careers.
Automotive	Car manufacturer with, at the time of this study, more than 27,000 employees. The focus of our study was the R&D site with approximately 4,000 employees working in various development projects.	Case study of HRM challenges in project-based work settings. Study of changes in the HR organization, including data on HR specialists, project managers, and project workers. Focused study on project management careers.
Complex Machinery	A company within the packaging industry, which develops and produces processing, packaging, and distribution systems for foodstuff. The company employs more than 20,000 people worldwide. Our focus was a highly project-based unit with about 200 people working in its project operations.	Focused study on the new HR-oriented approach to line managers in project-based work settings. Included data on changes in the HR organization concerning HR specialists, project managers, and project workers.
Engine	A company within the aerospace sector. Our focus is on the R&D-intensive part, which employs approximately 3,000 people.	Case study with focus on line management in project-based work settings.

Logistics	A major state-owned logistics company with more than 30,000 employees. We studied one part of the company where IT, product, and organizational development were focus areas. Approximately 2,000 people worked in the different units that we covered in our research.	Case study of the projectification process and project management support systems. Study of HRM challenges in project-based work settings. Study of changes in the HR organization, including data on HR specialists, project managers, and project workers. Workshops on the structure of HR departments. Focused study on project management careers.
Medical Systems	A niche player within its industry, specializing in different kinds of medical systems and information security solutions. In total, there are 600 employees. Our study focused on one of the development units.	Case study of project management. Study of the HR departmental structure and the role of HR specialists.
Pharma	One of the leading players within the pharmaceutical industry. At the time of the study, the company employed about 64,000 people. Our study focused on a R&D site that employed 2,000 people. The company has a heavy emphasis on R&D and global development projects.	Case study of the change of HRM and project operations. Study of changes in the HR organization, including data on HR specialists, project managers, and project workers. Workshops on talent management and the future of project work. Study of project management careers.
Telecom	One of the leading Swedish players within the telecom industry. The company employs more than 70,000 people worldwide. Our focus was on the product development site that employed about 18,000 people. The company has a heavy focus on R&D and large projects.	Case study of the role of the HR department. Study of project leaderships. Study of project management careers.
Workpool Engineering	A major technical consultancy with approximately 800 engineers employed. Operating primarily in the aerospace and telecom industries.	Study of project manager careers. Workshops on talent management and the future of project work.

Project managers

Project managers have been part of our empirical work in several ways. Two parallel investigations have been carried out. First, we studied the change of the HR organization in the following firms, for which, as mentioned earlier, we will use code names: Pharma, Automotive, and Aerospace. Concurrently, we interviewed project managers about their view on human resource management and the role of the HR department. Some of the findings were presented in a paper published in *Human Resource Management* and a follow-up paper that appeared in *R&D Management* (Bredin and Söderlund, 2006; Söderlund and Bredin, 2006). Second, we have carried out a study of project managers with the aim of understanding their behavioral and organizational orientation. This study also revolved around the use of shared leadership in complex projects. To a large extent these investigations have been presented as in-depth portraits to contrast with the conventional broad-scale surveys that dominate the field. A number of master theses, written within our research program, have added to the number of interviews. In total, we have more than 30 studies of project managers in companies such as Scania, Volvo Aero, Saab, Posten IT, and Volvo Cars. The data presented in the book draw on several of these interviews. The portraits presented in Chapter 6 about project managers and HRM were primarily used to illustrate a few of the observations in previous research and the patterns we discerned concerning the difficulties of assuming HRM responsibilities. The voices and fact boxes are also taken from these studies.

Project workers

The major part of the data on project workers comes from an explorative study of engineers working in project-based settings. One may generally divide the study of engineers as either the study of contractors/engineers operating in the open market or the study of engineers working in traditional, permanent organizations. This former focus is common among scholars with an interest in exploring contractors, the new temporary workforce, and the difficulties and dilemmas of free agents (Barley and Kunda, 2006). Other studies explore engineer's working situations in hierarchies or at least more permanent organizational settings (such as Midler, 1995). The empirical data are from consultants/engineers that move from project to project in different parts of the organization, to different clients and different parts of clients' organizations. We interviewed a selection of high-skilled individuals to explore their working-life situation and how they deal with what we refer to as "liminality".

We followed the methodological ideas presented in earlier influential works on human resource management which touch upon aspects explored in our own work, such as Barley and Kunda's (2006) studies of technical contractors in the United States and Fenwick's (2007) investigations of network identities among change management consultants. Both Barley and Kunda and Fenwick base their research on in-depth interviews with experienced consultants. We adopted a similar approach to allow for comparative analyses. A primary goal of this empirical research was, however, to generate new insights, theoretical ideas, and analytical concepts.

We tried to develop methods to engage in innovative interviewing and the use of multi-level data. Such methods also require the researcher to use previously collected data and material as input for the interviews – in our case this was essentially a starting point for reflective and analytical discussions about a particular phenomenon observed in project-based organizations. Nevertheless, we believe that the interviews constitute a valid description of close studies of work, as called for by Barley and Kunda (2001)

> In other words, the insights derived from close studies of work in limited arenas alert researchers to patterns of variations and possible sources of comparison that are prerequisite for rigorous, grounded theorizing. As organization theory's intellectual history reveals, detailed comparative studies of work were crucial for successfully articulating a theory of bureaucratic organizing. (Barley and Kunda, 2001: 80)

The study was divided into three phases. In the first phase we interviewed managers and studied corporate material to get an overview of the context of the firm, its organization, and the various businesses and knowledge areas of the firm. In this phase, we also interviewed managers to get an idea of how the managers carry out their management roles and duties. Important here were activities linked to mobility and competence development. Several of the interviewed managers have long experience as consultants or are still working part time as consultants. In the second phase, we interviewed a number of engineers cum consultants. We selected 20 consultants with a broad variety of experience, both men and women, and with various types of engineering expertise. We were not, however, only focusing on the individual level. Because it was also important to gain an understanding of the organizational context, we made use of multilevel data. To acquire this data, we interviewed managers about the contexts for and general development of problem-solving and other activities within the firm of relevance to the management of human resources. In addition, we also carried out workshops and meetings to validate our observations.

The interviews were semistructured, entailing a set of open-ended questions. We followed an interview guide covering such topics as personal background, professional history and education, work role, assignments. We included a set of detailed questions about the engineers' current assignments. They were asked to talk about their typical project and their current assignment. The intention was to create a trustful conversation about their roles as consultants, perceived challenges and obstacles during projects, and their career and competence development. Our goal was to allow for open conversations about the engineers' working lives. We let them add comments on subjects that were not directly touched upon in our interview guide but which they considered important to their professional lives. Generally, the guide was used primarily as a checklist rather than as strict instruction. The interviews lasted between 1.5 and 2.5 hours and were recorded, transcribed, and analyzed. When quoting from the interviews we use code names (Manager I, Manager II, etc., and Project Worker A, B, etc.) since the engineer or manager might consider some of the information sensitive. In the third phase, we analyzed our data and carried out additional, complementary data gathering, such as telephone interviews and e-mail questions, to broaden our investigation and to correct any misunderstandings. The analysis focused on identifying a set of similarities and patterns across our dataset and a selection of differences among the interviewees.

Notes

3 Human Resource Management in Context

1. One important contributor to this research was Eric Flamholtz, who proposed a model for Human Resource Valuation in 1971 (Flamholtz, 1971), and published several additional papers on the topic during the 1970s.
2. This review of strategic human resource management is obviously far from complete. The purpose here is primarily to give a brief overview of the field and its main schools of thought. More comprehensive reviews can be found in for example, Lengnick-Hall *et al.* (2009), Martín-Alcázar, *et al.* (2005), Boxall and Purcell (2000), and Allen and Wright (2007).
3. Beer *et al.* (1984), Devanna, Fombrun and Tichy (1984), Hendry and Pettigrew (1992), Mohrman and Lawler (1997), Ulrich (1997), Brewster and Larsen (2000), Redman and Wilkinson (2001), McKenna and Beech (2002), Sisson and Storey (2003), Lengnick-Hall and Lengnick-Hall (2003), Boxall *et al.* (2007b).

5 Line Managers in the HR Quadriad

1. This chapter draws partly on findings reported elsewhere (Bredin and Söderlund, 2007, 2008; Bredin, 2008). The empirical illustrations presented in this chapter builds on two case studies in which we have interviewed senior and line managers, project managers and HR specialists. See Appendix for details about the studies. For a detailed presentation of the Tetra Pak case study, see Bredin (2006) and Bredin & Söderlund (2007). The case study of Saab is presented in more detail in Bredin (2008) and Bredin & Söderlund (2008).
2. This illustration comes from Saab AB, which should not be confused with the car manufacturer Saab Automobile AB. The two companies have a common history, but are since many years two separate companies with separate ownership structures.
3. Huemann, Turner, and Keegan have developed a model of the HR process in project-based organizations in which they depict these different steps (see for instance Huemann et al, 2004).

6 Project Managers and HRM

1. This chapter has benefitted from the work and assistance of a number of master students and research assistants. We are particularly grateful for the help from Ulf Mörk, Anders Ulander, Marie Rudolfsson and Anna Lindén. Some of the ideas discussed in the chapter were presented at the IRNOP 2002 Conference in Rotterdam. The work on shared and distributive leadership

draws upon ideas presented in Söderlund's (2005b) chapter on project leadership.

8   HR Specialists in Project-Based Organizations

1. The discussions and empirical material in the chapter draws on research reported elsewhere (Bredin and Söderlund, 2006, 2010, 2011).
2. These studies are reported in a comparative case-study analysis in Bredin and Söderlund (2006) and multi-case analyses in Bredin and Söderlund (2010) and Bredin and Söderlund (forthcoming, 2011). In the first paper, the focus was on changes in HR practices and in the roles of the players in the HR organization. The second paper analyzed the design and structure of HR departments, and the third one specifically addressed the HR quadriad framework.

References

Allen, M. R., & Wright, P. (2007). "Strategic management and HRM." In P. Boxall, J. Purcell, & P. Wright (Eds.), *The Oxford handbook of human resource management* (pp. 88–107). New York: Oxford University Press.

Allen, T. J. (1977). *Managing the flow of technology: technology transfer and the dissemination of technological information within the R&D organization.* Cambridge, MA: MIT Press.

Allen, T. J., & Katz, R. (1995). "The project-oriented engineer: a dilemma for human resource management." *R&D Management*, Vol. 25, No. 2: 129–40.

Alvesson, M. (1995). *Management of knowledge intensive companies.* Berlin/New York: de Gruyter.

Alvesson, M. (2001). "Knowledge work: ambiguity, image and identity." *Human Relations*, Vol. 54, No. 7: 863–86.

Archibald, R. D. (1992). *Managing high-technology programs and projects* (2nd edn.). New York: John Wiley & Sons.

Arthur, M. B., Claman, P. H., & DeFillippi, R. J. (1995). "Intelligent enterprise, intelligent careers." *Academy of Management Executive*, Vol. 9, No. 4: 7–22.

Arthur, M. B., DeFillippi, R. J., & Jones, C. (2001). "Project-based learning as the interplay of career and company non-financial capital." *Management Learning*, Vol. 32, No. 1: 99.

Arthur, M. B., & Parker, P. (2002). "Technology, community, and the practice of HRM." *Human Resource Planning*, Vol. 25, No. 4: 38–47.

Avots, I. (1969). "Why does project management fail?" *California Management Review*, Vol. 12, No. 1: 77–82.

Badaway, M. K. (1982). *Developing managerial skills in engineers and scientists.* New York: Van Nostrand Reinhold.

Barley, S. R., & Kunda, G. (2001). "Bringing work back in." *Organization Science*, Vol. 12, No. 1: 76–95.

Barley, S. R., & Kunda, G. (2006). "Contracting: a new form of professional practice." *Academy of Management Perspectives*, Vol. 20, No. 1: 45–66.

Barney, J. B. (1991). "Firm resources and sustained competitive advantage." *Journal of Management*, Vol. 17, No. 1: 99–120.

Barney, J. B., & Wright, P. M. (1998). "On becoming a strategic partner: the role of human resources in gaining competitive advantage." *Human Resource Management*, Vol. 37, No. 1: 31–46.

Bartlett, C. A., & Ghoshal, S. (2002). "Building competitive advantage through people." *MIT Sloan Management Review*, Vol. 43, No. 2: 34–41.

Beatty, R. W., & Schneier, C. E. (1997). "New HR roles to impact organizational performance: from 'partners' to 'players'." *Human Resource Management*, Vol. 36, No. 1: 29–37.

Beer, M. (1997). "The transformation of the human resource function: resolving the tension between a traditional administrative and a new strategic role." *Human Resource Management*, Vol. 36, No. 1: 49–56.

Beer, M., Spector, B., Lawrence, P. R., Mills, O. N., & Walton, R. E. (1984). *Managing human assets.* New York: Free Press.

Begin, J. P. (1993). "Identifying patterns in HRM systems: lessons from organizational theory." *Research in Personnel and Human Resource Management,* Supplement 3: 3–20.

Bell, D. (1999). *The coming of post-industrial society: a venture in social forecasting.* New York: Basic Books. (Original work published in 1973.)

Bennis, W. G. (1968). "Beyond bureaucracy." In W. G. Bennis & P. E. Slater (Eds.), *The temporary society* (pp. 53–76). New York: Harper & Row.

Bennis, W. G., & Slater, P. E. (1968). *The temporary society.* New York: Harper & Row.

Berggren, C. (2001). "Om projekt, projektledningsläran och andra perspektiv." In C. Berggren & L. Lindkvist (Eds.), *Projekt – Organisation för målorienterat lärande* (pp. 15–51). Lund, Sweden: Studentlitteratur.

Berglund, J. (2002). *De otillräckliga: en studie av personalspecialisternas kamp för erkännande och status.* Doctoral dissertation, Ekonomiska forskningsinstitutet (EFI), Handelshögskolan, Stockholm.

Boltanski, L., & Chiapello, E. (2005). *The new spirit of capitalism.* London: Verso.

Boselie, P., Brewster, C., & Paauwe, J. (2009). "In search of balance – managing the dualities of HRM: an overview of the issues." *Personnel Review,* Vol. 38, No. 5: 461–71.

Boxall, P. (1996). "The strategic HRM debate and the resource-based view of the firm." *Human Resource Management Journal,* Vol. 6, No. 3: 59–75.

Boxall, P., & Macky, K. (2009). "Research and theory on high-performance work systems: progressing the high-involvement stream." *Human Resource Management Journal,* Vol. 19, No. 1: 3–23.

Boxall, P., & Purcell, J. (2000). "Strategic human resource management: where have we come from and where should we be going?" *International Journal of Management Reviews,* Vol. 2, No. 2: 183–203.

Boxall, P., Purcell, J., & Wright, P. (2007a). "Human resource management: scope, analysis and significance." In P. Boxall, J. Purcell, & P. Wright (Eds.), *The Oxford handbook of human resource management* (pp. 1–18). New York: Oxford University Press.

Boxall, P., Purcell, J., & Wright, P. (Eds.). (2007b). *The Oxford handbook of human resource management.* New York: Oxford University Press.

Bredin, K. (2006). *Human resource management in project-based organisations: challenges and changes.* Licentiate's dissertation, Department of Management and Economics, Linköping University, Linköping.

Bredin, K. (2008). *Human resource management in project-based organisations – challenges, changes, and capabilities.* Doctoral thesis, Department of Management and Engineering, Linköping University, Linköping.

Bredin, K., & Söderlund, J. (2006). "HRM and project intensification in R&D-based companies: a study of Volvo Car Corporation and AstraZeneca." *R&D Management,* Vol. 36, No. 5: 467–85.

Bredin, K., & Söderlund, J. (2007). "Reconceptualising line management in project-based organisations: the case of competence coaches at Tetra Pak." *Personnel Review,* Vol. 36, No. 5: 815–33.

Bredin, K., & Söderlund, J. (2008). "Den nya linjechefsrollen: exempel på förändringen av personalarbete i projektintensiva företag." In T. Stjernberg, J. Söderlund, & E. Wikström (Eds.), *Projektliv – Villkor för uthållig projektverksamhet* (pp. 231–58). Lund, Sweden: Studentlitteratur.

Bredin, K., & Söderlund, J. (2010). "Fit for purpose? Designing HR organisations and HR departments in project-based organisations." *International Journal of Human Resources Management and Development*, Vol. 10, No. 4: 327–61.

Bredin, K., & Söderlund, J. (Forthcoming 2011). "The HR quadriad: a framework for the analysis of HRM in project-based organizations." *International Journal of Human Resource Management*.

Bresnen, M., Goussevskaia, A., & Swan, J. (2005). "Organizational routines, situated learning and processes of change in project-based organisations." *Project Management Journal*, Vol. 36, No. 3: 27–41.

Brewster, C., & Larsen, H. H. (Eds.). (2000). *Human resource management in Northern Europe: trends, dilemmas and strategy*. Oxford, UK: Blackwell.

Brockbank, W. (1999). "If HR were really strategically proactive: present and future directions in HR's contribution to competitive advantage." *Human Resource Management*, Vol. 38, No. 4: 337–52.

Brooks, F. P. (1995). *The mythical man-month*. Reading, MA: Addison-Wesley.

Brusoni, S. (2005). "The limits to specialization: problem solving and coordination in 'Modular Networks'." *Organization Studies*, Vol. 26, No. 12: 1885–907.

Brusoni, S., & Prencipe, A. (2001). "Managing knowledge in loosely coupled networks: exploring the links between product and knowledge dynamics." *Journal of Management Studies*, Vol. 38, No. 7: 1019–35.

Burns, T., & Stalker, G. M. (1961). *The management of innovation*. London: Tavistock.

Butler, A. G., Jr. (1973). "Project management: a study in organizational conflict." *Academy of Management Journal*, Vol. 16, No. 1: 84–101.

Carbone, T. A., & Gholston, S. (2004). "Project manager skill development: a survey of programs and practitioners." *Engineering Management Journal*, Vol. 16, No. 3: 10–16.

Castells, M. (1996). *The rise of the network society*. Oxford, UK: Blackwell.

Cheng, M.-I., Dainty, A. R. J., & Moore, D. R. (2005). "What makes a good project manager?" *Human Resource Management Journal*, Vol. 15, No. 1: 25–37.

Clark, I., & Colling, T. (2005). "The management of human resources in project management-led organizations." *Personnel Review*, Vol. 34, No. 2: 178–91.

Clark, K. B., & Fujimoto, T. (1991). *Product development performance: strategy, organization, and management in the world auto industry*. Cambridge, MA: Harvard Business School Press Books.

Clark, K. B., & Wheelwright, S. C. (1992). "Organizing and leading 'Heavyweight' development teams." *California Management Review*, Vol. 34, No. 3: 9–28.

Cunningham, I., & Hyman, J. (1999). "Devolving human resource responsibilities to the line." *Personnel Review*, Vol. 28, No. 1/2: 9–27.

Currie, G., & Procter, S. (2001). "Exploring the relationship between HR and middle managers." *Human Resource Management Journal*, Vol. 11, No. 3: 53–69.

Czarniawska, B., & Mazza, C. (2003). "Consulting as a liminal space." *Human Relations*, Vol. 56, No. 3: 267.

Dany, F., Guedri, Z., & Hatt, F. (2008). "New insights into the link between HRM integration and organizational performance: the moderating role of influence distribution between HRM specialists and line managers." *International Journal of Human Resource Management*, Vol. 19, No. 11: 2095–112.

Davies, A., & Brady, T. (2000). "Organisational capabilities and learning in complex product systems: towards repeatable solutions." *Research Policy*, Vol. 29, No. 7–8: 931–53.

Davies, A., & Hobday, M. (2005). *The business of projects: managing innovation in complex products and systems*. Cambridge, UK: Cambridge University Press.

DeFillippi, R. J., & Arthur, M. B. (1998). "Paradox in project-based enterprise: the case of film making." *California Management Review*, Vol. 40, No. 2: 125–40.

DeFillippi, R. J., Arthur, M. B., & Lindsay, V. (2006). *Knowledge at work: creative collaboration in the global economy*. Oxford, UK: Blackwell.

Delbecq, A., & Weiss, J. (1988). "The business culture of Silicon Valley: is it a model for the future?" In J. Weiss (Ed.), *Regional cultures, managerial behavior and entrepreneurship* (pp. 23–42). New York: Quorom Books

Delery, J. E., & Doty, D. H. (1996). "Modes of theorizing in strategic human resource management: tests of universalistic, contingency, and configurational performance predictions." *Academy of Management Journal*, Vol. 39, No. 4: 802.

De Meyer, A., Loch, C. H., & Pich, M. T. (2002). "Managing project uncertainty: from variation to chaos." *MIT Sloan Management Review*, Vol. 43, No. 2: 60–7.

Devanna, M. A., Fombrun, C., & Tichy, N. M. (1984). "A framework for strategic human resource management." In C. Fombrun, N. M. Tichy, & M. A. Devanna (Eds.), *Strategic human resource management* (pp. 33–55). New York: John Wiley & Sons.

Dovier, H. (2010). "AstraZeneca outsourcar för nästan 5 miljarder." *Personal & Ledarskap*, No. 2: 52–3.

Drucker, P. F. (1954). *The practice of management*. New York: Harper Brothers.

Dulewicz, V., & Higgs, M. (2003). "Leadership at the top: the need for emotional intelligence in organizations." *International Journal of Organizational Analysis*, Vol. 11, No. 3: 193–210.

Dunn, S. C. (2001). "Motivation by project and functional managers in matrix organizations." *Engineering Management Journal*, Vol. 13, No. 2: 3–9.

Dunne, E. J., Jr., Stahl, M. J., & Melhart, L. J., Jr. (1978). "Influence source of project and functional managers in matrix organizations." *Academy of Management Journal*, Vol. 21, No. 1: 135–40.

Eisenhardt, K. M. (1989): "Building theories from case study research". *Academy of Management Review*, Vol. 14, No. 4: 532–550.

Eisenhardt, K. M., & Tabrizi, B. N. (1995). "Accelerating adaptive processes: product innovation in the global computer industry." *Administrative Science Quarterly*, Vol. 40, No. 1: 84–110.

Ekstedt, E. (2002). "Contracts of work in a project-based economy." In K. Sahlin-Andersson & A. Söderholm (Eds.), *Beyond project management: new perspectives on the temporary – permanent dilemma* (pp. 59–80). Copenhagen, Denmark: Copenhagen Business School Press.

Ekstedt, E., Lundin, R. A., Söderholm, A., & Wirdenius, H. (1999). *Neo-industrial organising: renewal by action and knowledge formation in a project-intensive economy*. Malmö, Sweden: Liber Abstrakt.

Emery, F. E., & Trist, E. L. (1965). "The causal texture of organizational environments." *Human Relations*, Vol. 18: 21–32.

Engwall, M., Steinthórsson, R. S., & Söderholm, A. (2003). "Temporary organizing: a Viking approach to project management research." In B. Czarniawska & G. Sévon (Eds.), *Northern lights: organization theory in Scandinavia* (pp. 111–30). Malmö, Sweden: Liber and Copenhagen Business School Press.

Fenwick, T. (2007). "Knowledge workers in the in-between: network identities." *Journal of Organizational Change Management*, Vol. 20, No. 4: 509–24.

Flamholtz, E. (1971). "A model for human resource valuation: a stochastic process with service rewards." *Accounting Review*, Vol. 46, No. 2: 253–67.

Fombrun, C., Tichy, N. M., & Devanna, M. A. (Eds.). (1984). *Strategic human resource management*. New York: John Wiley & Sons.

Francis, H., & Keegan, A. (2006). "The changing face of HRM: in search for balance." *Human Resource Management Journal*, Vol. 16, No. 3: 231–49.

Gaddis, P. O. (1959). "The project manager." *Harvard Business Review*, Vol. 37, No. 3: 89–97.

Gällstedt, M. (2003). "Working conditions in projects: perceptions of stress and motivation among team members and project managers." *International Journal of Project Management*, Vol. 21, No. 6: 449–55.

Garrick, J., & Clegg, S. (2001). "Stressed-out knowledge workers in performative times: a postmodern take on project-based learning." *Management Learning*, Vol. 32, No. 1: 119–34.

Garsten, C. (1999). "Betwixt and between: temporary employees as liminal subjects in flexible organization." *Organization Studies*, Vol. 20, No. 4: 601–17.

Garsten, C. (2008). *Workplace vagabonds – career and community in changing worlds of work*. Basingstoke, UK: Palgrave Macmillan.

Gemmill, G., & Wilemon, D. L. (1970). "The power spectrum in project management." *Sloan Management Review*, Vol. 12, No. 1: 15–25.

Gersick, C. J. G. (1989). "Marking time: predictable transitions in task groups." *Academy of Management Journal*, Vol. 32, No. 2: 274–309.

Gersick, C. J. G. (1995). "Everything new under the gun: creativity and deadlines." In C. Ford & D. Gioia (Eds.), *Creative action in organizations* (pp. 142–8). Thousand Oaks, CA: Sage.

Gooderham, P. N., O. Nordhaug, & K. Ringdal (1999). "Institutional and rational determinants of organizational practices: Human Resource Management in European firms." *Administrative Science Quarterly*, Vol. 44, No. 3: 507–31.

Goodman, L. P., & Goodman, R. A. (1972). "Theater as a temporary system." *California Management Review*, Vol. 16, No. 2: 103–8.

Goodman, R. A. (1981). *Temporary systems: professional development, manpower utilization, task effectiveness, and innovation*. New York: Praeger.

Goodman, R. A., & Goodman, L. P. (1976). "Some management issues in temporary systems: a study of professional development and manpower – the theater case." *Administrative Science Quarterly*, Vol. 21, No. 3: 494–501.

Grabher, G. (2004). "Temporary architectures of learning: knowledge governance in project ecologies." *Organization Studies*, Vol. 25, No. 9: 1491–514.

Granovetter, M. (1995). *Getting a job: a study of contacts and careers*. Chicago, IL: Chicago University Press.

Guest, D. E. (1987). "Human resource management and industrial relations." *Journal of Management Studies*, Vol. 24, No. 5: 503.

Guest, D. E., & King, Z. (2004). "Power, innovation and problem-solving: the personnel managers' three steps to heaven?" *Journal of Management Studies*, Vol. 41, No. 3: 401–23.

Hedberg, B., Dahlgren, G., Hansson, B. & Olve, N.-G. *Virtual organizations and beyond: Discover imaginary systems.* Chichester: John Wiley & Sons Ltd.

Hällsten, F. (2000). "Decentraliserat personalansvar." In O. Bergström & M. Sandoff (Eds.), *Handla med människor: Perspektiv på Human Resource Management* (pp. 67–83). Lund: Academia Adacta.

Hällsten, F., & Tengblad, S. (Eds.). (2002). *Personalansvar och medarbetarskap.* Göteborg, Sweden: BAS.

Hammerton, J. C. (1970). "Management and motivation." *California Management Review*, Vol. 13, No. 2: 51–6.

Hedlund, G. (1994). "A model of knowledge management and the N-Form Corporation." *Strategic Management Journal*, Vol. 15 (Special Issue: Strategy: Search for New Paradigms): 73–90.

Heimer, C. A. (1984). "Organizational and individual control of career development in engineering project work." *Acta Sociologica*, Vol. 27, No. 4: 283–310.

Hendry, C., & Pettigrew, A. (1990). "Human resource management: an agenda for the 1990's." *International Journal of Human Resource Management*, Vol. 1, No. 1: 17–44.

Hendry, C., & Pettigrew, A. (1992). "Patterns of strategic change in the development of human resource management." *British Journal of Management*, Vol. 3, No. 3: 137–56.

Herzberg, F. (1966). *Work and the nature of man.* New York: World Publishing Company.

Hobday, M. (2000). "The project-based organisation: an ideal form for managing complex products and systems?" *Research Policy*, Vol. 29, No. 7/8: 871–94.

Hodgetts, R. M. (1969). "Leadership techniques in project organization." *Academy of Management Journal*, Vol. 11: 211–19.

Hodgson, D. (2002). "Disciplining the professional: the case of project management." *Journal of Management Studies*, Vol. 39, No. 6: 803–21.

Hodgson, D. (2004). "Project Work: the legacy of bureaucratic control in the post-bureaucratic organization." *Organization*, Vol. 11, No. 1: 81–100.

Hope-Hailey, V., Farndale, E., & Truss, C. (2005). "The HR department's role in organisational performance." *Human Resource Management Journal*, Vol. 15, No. 3: 49–66.

Hovmark, S., & Nordqvist, S. (1996). "Project organization: change in the work atmosphere for engineers." *International Journal of Industrial Ergonomics*, Vol. 17: 389–98.

Huemann, M. (2010). "Considering human resource management when developing a project-oriented company: case study of a telecommunication company." *International Journal of Project Management*, Vol. 28, No. 4: 361–9.

Huemann, M., Keegan, A., & Turner, J. R. (2007). "Human resource management in the project-oriented company: a review." *International Journal of Project Management*, Vol. 25, No. 3: 315–23.

Huemann, M., Turner, R., & Keegan, A. E. (2004). "Managing human resources in the project-oriented company." In P. W. G. Morris & J. K. Pinto (Eds.), *The Wiley guide to managing projects* (pp. 1061–86). Hoboken, NJ: John Wiley & Sons.

Huselid, M. A. (1995). "The impact of human resource management practices on turnover, productivity, and corporate financial performance." *The Academy of Management Journal*, Vol. 38, No. 3: 635–72.

Iansiti, M. (1998). *Technology integration*. Boston, MA: HBS Press.

Jackson, S. E., Schuler, R. S., & Werner, S. (2009). *Managing human resources* (10th edn.). Stanford, CT: South-Western Cengage Learning.

Jamrog, J. J., & Overholt, M. H. (2004). "Building a strategic HR function: continuing the evolution." *Human Resource Planning*, Vol. 27, No. 1: 51.

Jones, C., & DeFillippi, R. J. (1996). "Back to the future in film: combining industry and self-knowledge to meet the career challenges of the 21st century." *Academy of Management Executive*, Vol. 10, No. 4: 89–103.

Kamoche, K. (1996). "Strategic human resources management within a resource-capability view of the firm." *Journal of Management Studies*, Vol. 33, No. 2: 213–33.

Katz, R., & Allen, T. J. (1985). "Project performance and the locus of influence in the R&D matrix." *Academy of Management Journal*, Vol. 28, No. 1: 67–87.

Kaufman, B. E. (2007). "The development of HRM in historical and international perspective." In P. Boxall, J. Purcell, & P. Wright (Eds.), *The Oxford handbook of human resource management* (pp. 19–47). New York: Oxford University Press.

Keegan, A. E., & Den Hartog, D. N. (2004). "Transformational leadership in a project-based environment: a comparative study of the leadership styles of project managers and line managers." *International Journal of Project Management*, Vol. 22, No. 8: 609–17.

Keegan, A. E., Huemann, M., & Turner, J. R. (2010). "Beyond the line: exploring the HR responsibilities of line managers, project managers and the HR department in four project-oriented companies." Working paper. Amsterdam, Vienna, Limerick, Lille: Amsterdam Business School, Vienna University of Economics and Business Administration, Kemmy Business School, Lille School of Management.

Keegan, A. E., & Turner, J. R. (2003). "Managing human resources in the project-based organization." In J. R. Turner (Ed.), *People in project management* (pp. 1–12). Aldershot, UK: Gower Publishing Limited.

Keith, P. M. (1978). "Individual and organizational correlates of a temporary system." *Journal of Applied Behavioral Science*, Vol. 14, No. 2: 195–203.

Knight, K. (Ed.). (1977). *Matrix management: a cross-functional approach to organisation*. Westmead, Farnborough, Hants, UK: Gower Press, Teakfield.

Kunda, G., Barley, S. R., & Evans, J. (2002). "Why do contractors contract? The experience of highly skilled technical professionals in a contingent labor market." *Industrial & Labor Relations Review*, Vol. 55, No. 2: 234–61.

Lado, A. A., & Wilson, M. C. (1994). "Human resource systems and sustained competitive advantage: a competency-based perspective." *Academy of Management Review*, Vol. 19, No. 4: 699–727.

Larsen, H. H. (2002). "Oticon: unorthodox project-based management and careers in a 'Spaghetti Organization'." *Human Resource Planning*, Vol. 25, No. 4: 30–7.

Larsen, H. H., & Brewster, C. (2003). "Line management responsibility for HRM: what is happening in Europe?" *Employee Relations*, Vol. 25, No. 3: 228–44.

Laursen, K., & Mahnke, V. (2001). "Knowledge strategies, firm types, and complementarity in human-resource practices." *Journal of Management and Governance*, Vol. 5, No. 1: 1–27.

Lawler, E. E., III. (2005). "From human resource management to organizational effectiveness." *Human Resource Management*, Vol. 44, No. 2: 165–9.

Lawrence, P. R., & Lorsch, J. W. (1967). "New management job: the integrator." *Harvard Business Review* (November–December): 142–50.

Legge, K. (1995). *Human resource management: rhetorics and realities.* Basingstoke, UK: Palgrave Macmillan.

Legge, K. (2005). *Human resource management, rhetorics and realities.* (Anniversary edn.). New York: Palgrave Macmillan. (Original work published in 1995.)

Lengnick-Hall, M. L., & Lengnick-Hall, C. A. (2003). *Human resource management in the knowledge economy.* San Francisco, CA: Berret-Koehler Publishers.

Lengnick-Hall, M. L., Lengnick-Hall, C. A., Andrade, L. S., & Drake, B. (2009). "Strategic human resource management: the evolution of the field." *Human Resource Management Review*, Vol. 19, No. 2: 64–85.

Lindgren, M., & Packendorff, J. (2006). "What's new in new forms of organizing? On the construction of gender in project-based work." *Journal of Management Studies*, Vol. 43, No. 4: 841–66.

Lindgren, M., & Packendorff, J. (2009). "Project leadership revisited: towards distributed leadership perspectives in project research." *International Journal of Project Organisation and Management*, Vol. 1, No. 3: 285–308.

Lindgren, M., Packendorff, J., & Wåhlin, N. (2001). *Resa genom arbetslivet – Om människors organisationsbyten och identitetsskapande.* Lund, Sweden: Academia Adacta.

Lindkvist, L. (2004). "Governing project-based firms: promoting market-like processes within hierarchies." *Journal of Management and Governance*, Vol. 8: 3–25.

Lindkvist, L. (2005). "Knowledge communities and knowledge collectivities: a typology of knowledge work in groups." *Journal of Management Studies*, Vol. 42, No. 6: 1189–210.

Lindkvist, L., Söderlund, J., & Tell, F. (1998). "Managing product development projects: on the significance of fountains and deadlines." *Organization Studies*, Vol. 19, No. 6: 931–51.

Lundin, R. A., & Söderholm, A. (1995). "A theory of the temporary organization." *Scandinavian Journal of Management*, Vol. 11, No. 4: 437–55.

MacDuffie, J. P. (1995). "Human resource bundles and manufacturing performance: organizational logic and flexible production systems in the world auto industry." *Industrial Labor Relations Review*, Vol. 48, No. 2: 197–221.

March, J. G. (1991). "Exploration and exploitation in organizational learning." *Organization Science*, Vol. 2, No. 1: 71–87.

Martín-Alcázar, F., Romero-Fernández, P. M., & Sánchez-Gardey, G. (2005). "Strategic human resource management: integrating the universalistic, contingent, configurational and contextual perspectives." *International Journal of Human Resource Management*, Vol. 16, No. 5: 633–59.

McKenna, E., & Beech, N. (2002). *Human resource management: a concise analysis.* Harlow, UK: Pearson Education.

Melcher, A. J., & Kayser, T. A. (1970). "Leadership without formal authority: the project group." *California Management Review*, Vol. 13, No. 2: 57–64.

Meredith, J. R., & Mantel, S. J. (1995). *Project management: a managerial approach* (3rd edn.). New York: John Wiley & Sons.

Metcalfe, B. (1997). "Project management system design: a social and organisational analysis." *International Journal of Production Economics*, Vol. 52, No. 3: 305–16.

Meyerson, D., Weick, K. E., & Kramer, R. M. (1996). "Swift trust and temporary groups." In R. M. Kramer & T. R. Tyler (Eds.), *Trust in organizations* (pp. 166–95). Thousand Oaks, CA: Sage.

Midler, C. (1995). "'Projectification' of the firm: the Renault case." *Scandinavian Journal of Management*, Vol. 11, No. 4: 363–75.

Miles, R. E. (1965). "Human relations or human resources?" *Harvard Business Review*, Vol. 43, No. 4: 148–57.

Miller, R., & Lessard, D. (2001). "Understanding and managing risks in large engineering projects." *International Journal of Project Management*, Vol. 19, No. 8: 437–43.

Mintzberg, H. (1979). *The structuring of organizations: a synthesis of the research.* Englewood Cliffs, NJ: Prentice Hall.

Mintzberg, H. (1983). *Structure in fives.* Englewood Cliffs, NJ: Prentice Hall.

Mohrman, S. A., & Lawler, E. E., III. (1997). "Transforming the human resource function." *Human Resource Management*, Vol. 36, No. 1: 157–62.

Morley, E., & Silver, A. (1977). "A film director's approach to managing creativity." *Harvard Business Review* (March–April): 59–70.

Nordqvist, S., Hovmark, S., & Zika-Viktorsson, A. (2004). "Perceived time pressure and social processes in project teams." *International Journal of Project Management*, Vol. 22, No. 6: 463–8.

Paauwe, J. (2004). *HRM and performance: achieving long-term viability.* Oxford, UK: Oxford University Press.

Paauwe, J. (2009). "HRM and performance: achievements, methodological issues and prospects." *Journal of Management Studies*, Vol. 46, No. 1: 129–42.

Packendorff, J. (1995). "Inquiring into the temporary organization: new directions for project management research." *Scandinavian Journal of Management*, Vol. 11, No. 4: 319–33.

Packendorff, J. (2002). "The temporary society and its enemies: projects from an individual perspective." In K. Sahlin-Andersson & A. Söderholm (Eds.), *Beyond project management: new perspectives on the temporary – permanent dilemma* (pp. 39–58). Copenhagen, Denmark: Copenhagen Business School Press.

Penrose, E. (1959). *The theory of the growth of the firm.* London: Blackwell.

Perlow, L. A. (1999). "The time famine: toward a sociology of work time." *Administrative Science Quarterly*, Vol. 44, No. 1: 57–81.

Peters, T. H. (1992). *Liberation management: necessary disorganization for the nanosecond nineties.* Basingstoke, UK: Palgrave Macmillan.

Peters, T. H., & Waterman, R. (1982). *In search of excellence.* New York: Harper & Row.

Pfeffer, J. (1995). "Producing sustainable competitive advantage through the effective management of people." *Academy of Management Executive*, Vol. 9, No. 1: 55–72.

Pfeffer, J. (1998). *The human equation, building profits by putting people first.* Boston, MA: Harvard Business School Press.

Pfeffer, J. (2010). *Lay off the layoffs.* Retrieved February 5, 2010, from http://www.newsweek.com/2010/02/04/lay-off-the-layoffs.html

Pinto, J. K., & Slevin, D. P. (1987). "Critical factors in successful project implementation." *IEEE Transactions on Engineering Management*, Vol. 34, No. 1: 22–7.

Pitagorsky, G. (1998). "The project manager/functional manager partnership." *Project Management Journal*, Vol. 29, No. 4: 7.

Porter, M. E. (1985). *Competitive advantage*. New York: Free Press.

Prahalad, C. K., & Hamel, G. (1990). "The core competence of the corporation." *Harvard Business Review*, Vol. 68, No. 3: 79–91.

Prencipe, A., & Tell, F. (2001). "Inter-project learning: processes and outcomes of knowledge codification in project-based firms." *Research Policy*, Vol. 30, No. 9: 1373–394.

Redman, T., & Wilkinson, A. (2001). "In search of human resource management." In T. Redman & A. Wilkinson (Eds.), *Contemporary human resource management* (pp. 3–21). Harlow, UK: Pearson Education.

Reeser, C. (1969). "Some potential human problems of the project form of organization." *Academy of Management Journal*, Vol. 12, No. 4: 459–67.

Renwick, D. (2003). "Line manager involvement in HRM: an inside view." *Employee Relations*, Vol. 25, No. 3: 262–80.

Ricciardi, M. (2001). *Projektpsykologi: produktutveckling ur människans perspektiv*. Doctoral dissertation, Psykologiska institutionen, Göteborgs universitet.

Saxenian, A. (1996). "Beyond boundaries: open labor markets and learning in Silicon Valley." In M. B. Arthur & D. M. Rousseau (Eds.), *The boundaryless career: a new employment principle for a new organizational era* (pp. 23–39). New York: Oxford University Press.

Schuler, R. S., & Jackson, S. E. (1987). "Linking competitive strategies with human resource management practices." *Academy of Management Executive*, Vol. 1, No. 3: 207–219.

Sennett, R. (1998). *The corrosion of character*. New York: Norton.

Shenhar, A. J., & Dvir, D. (2007). *Reinventing project management: the Diamond approach to successful growth and innovation*. Boston, MA: Harvard Business School Press.

Sisson, K. (1993). "In search of HRM." *British Journal of Industrial Relations*, Vol. 31, No. 2: 1007–80.

Sisson, K. (2001). "Human resource management and the personnel function – a case of partial impact?" In J. Storey (Ed.), *Human resource management – a critical text* (pp. 78–95). Oxford, UK: Blackwell.

Sisson, K., & Storey, J. (2003). *The realities of human resource management*. Oxford, UK: Open University Press.

Söderlund, J. (2000). "Temporary organizing: consequences and control forms." In R. A. Lundin & Hartman (Eds.), *Projects as business constituents and guiding motives* (pp. 61–74). Boston, MA: Kluwer Academic Publishers.

Söderlund, J. (2005a). "Developing project competence: empirical regularities in competitive project operations." *International Journal of Innovation Management*, Vol. 9, No. 4: 451–80.

Söderlund, J. (2005b). *Projektledning och projektkompetens – Perspektiv på konkurrenskraft*. Malmö, Sweden: Liber.

Söderlund, J., & Bredin, K. (2005). *Perspektiv på HRM – nya organisationsformer, nya utmaningar*. Malmö, Sweden: Liber.

Söderlund, J., & Bredin, K. (2006). "HRM in project-intensive firms: changes and challenges." *Human Resource Management*, Vol. 45, No. 2: 249–65.

Stinchcombe, A. L. (1965). "Social structure and organizations." In J. G. March (Ed.), *The handbook of organizations* (pp. 142–69). Chicago, IL: Rand McNally.

Storey, J. (1992). *Developments in the management of human resources.* Oxford, UK: Blackwell.

Swart, J., & Kinnie, N. (2003). "Sharing knowledge in knowledge-intensive firms." *Human Resource Management Journal*, Vol. 13, No. 2: 60–75.

Sydow, J., Lindkvist, L., & DeFillippi, R. J. (2004). "Project-based organizations, embeddedness and repositories of knowledge: editorial." *Organization Studies*, Vol. 25, No. 9: 1475–89.

Teece, D. J. (2009). *Dynamic capabilities and strategic management.* Oxford, UK: Oxford University Press.

Tempest, S., & Starkey, K. (2004). "The effects of liminality on individual and organizational learning." *Organization Studies*, Vol. 25, No. 4: 507–27.

Tengblad, S. (2003). *Den myndige medarbetaren.* Malmö, Sweden: Liber.

Thompson, J. D. (1967). *Organization in action.* Chicago, IL: McGraw-Hill.

Thornhill, A., & Saunders, M. N. K. (1998). "What if line managers don't realise they're responsible for HR?" *Personnel Review*, Vol. 27, No. 6: 460–76.

Torrington, D., & Hall, L. (1996). "Chasing the rainbow: how seeking status through strategy misses the point for the personnel function." *Employee Relations*, Vol. 18, No. 6: 81–97.

Torrington, D., Hall, L., & Taylor, S. (2008). *Human resource management.* Harlow, UK: Pearson Education.

Truss, C., & Gill, J. (2009). "Managing the HR function: the role of social capital." *Personnel Review*, Vol. 38, No. 6: 674–95.

Truss, C., Gratton, L., Hope-Hailey, V., Stiles, P., & Zaleska, J. (2002). "Paying the piper: choice and constraint in changing HR functional roles." *Human Resource Management Journal*, Vol. 12, No. 2: 39–63.

Tuckman, B. W. (1965). "Developmental sequence in small groups." *Psychological Bulletin*, Vol. 63, No. 6: 384–99.

Turner, J. R. (1999). *The handbook of project-based management: improving the processes for achieving strategic objectives* (2nd edn.). London: McGraw-Hill.

Turner, J. R., & Cochrane, R. (1993). "The goals and methods matrix: coping with projects for which the goals and/or methods of achieving them are ill-defined." *International Journal of Project Management*, Vol. 11, No. 2: 93–102.

Turner, J. R., Huemann, M., & Keegan, A. (2008a). *Human resource management in the project-oriented organization.* Newtown Square, PA: Project Management Institute.

Turner, J. R., Huemann, M., & Keegan, A. (2008b). "Human resource management in the project-oriented organization: employee well-being and ethical treatment." *International Journal of Project Management*, Vol. 26, No. 5: 577–85.

Turner, J. R., & Müller, R. (2005). "The project manager's leadership style as a success factor on projects: a literature review." *Project Management Journal*, Vol. 36, No. 2: 49–61.

Turner, S. G., Utley, D. R., & Westbrook, J. D. (1998). "Project managers and functional managers: a case study of job satisfaction in a matrix organization." *Project Management Journal*, Vol. 29, No. 3: 11–19.

Ulrich, D. (1997). *Human resource champions – the next agenda for adding value and delivering results.* Boston, MA: Harvard Business School Press.

Ulrich, D. (1998). "A new mandate for Human Resources." *Harvard Business Review*, Vol. 76, No. 1: 124–34.

Ulrich, D., Allen, J., Brockbank, W., Younger, J., & Nyman, M. (2009). *HR Transformation: building human resources from the outside in*. New York: McGraw-Hill.

Ulrich, D., & Beatty, D. (2001). "From partners to players: extending the HR playing field." *Human Resource Management*, Vol. 40, No. 4: 293–307.

Ulrich, D., & Brockbank, W. (2005). *The HR value proposition*. Boston, MA: Harvard Business School Press.

Verona, G., & Ravasi, D. (2003). "Unbundling dynamic capabilities: an exploratory study of continuous product innovation." *Industrial and Corporate Change*, Vol. 12, No. 3: 577–606.

Weick, K. (1996). "Enactment and the boundaryless career." In M. B. Arthur & D. M. Rousseau (Eds.), *The boundaryless career: a new employment principle for a new organizational era* (pp. 40–57). New York: Oxford University Press.

Wernerfelt, B. (1984). "A resource-based view of the firm." *Strategic Management Journal*, Vol. 5, No. 2: 171–80.

Wheelwright, S. C., & Clark, K. D. (1992). *Revolutionizing product development quantum leaps in speed, efficiency and quality*. New York: Free Press.

Whitley, R. (2006). "Project-based firms: new organizational form or variations on a theme." *Industrial and Corporate Change*, Vol. 15, No. 1: 77–99.

Whittington, R., Pettigrew, A., Peck, S., Fenton, E., & Conyon, M. (1999). "Change and complementarities in the new competitive landscape: a European Panel Study, 1992–1996." *Organization Science*, Vol. 10, No. 5: 583–600.

Wilemon, D. L. (1973). "Managing conflict in temporary management systems." *Journal of Management Studies*, Vol. 10, No. 3: 282–96.

Wilemon, D. L., & Cicero, J. P. (1970). "The project manager – anomalies and ambiguities." *Academy of Management Journal*, Vol. 13, No. 3: 269–82.

Wilemon, D. L., & Gemmill, G. R. (1971). "Interpersonal power in temporary management systems." *Journal of Management Studies*, Vol. 8, No. 3: 315–28.

Woodward, J. (1958). *Industrial organization: theory and practice*. Oxford, UK: Oxford University Press.

Wright, P. M., Dunford, B. B., & Snell, S. A. (2001). "Human resources and the resource based view of the firm." *Journal of Management*, Vol. 27, No. 6: 701–21.

Wright, P. M., McMahan, G. C., & McWilliams, A. (1994). "Human resources and sustained competitive advantage: a resource-based perspective." *International Journal of Human Resource Management*, Vol. 5, No. 2: 301–26.

Yukl, G. A. (1994). *Leadership in organizations* (3rd edn.). Englewood Cliffs, NJ: Prentice Hall.

Zika-Viktorsson, A., Sundström, P., & Engwall, M. (2006). "Project overload: an exploratory study of work and management in multi-project settings." *International Journal of Project Management*, Vol. 24, No. 5: 385–94.

Author Index

Subject Index